Lecture Notes in Computer Science   14757

Founding Editors

Gerhard Goos
Juris Hartmanis

Editorial Board Members

The series Lecture Notes in Computer Science (LNCS), including its subseries Lecture Notes in Artificial Intelligence (LNAI) and Lecture Notes in Bioinformatics (LNBI), has established itself as a medium for the publication of new developments in computer science and information technology research, teaching, and education.

LNCS enjoys close cooperation with the computer science R & D community, the series counts many renowned academics among its volume editors and paper authors, and collaborates with prestigious societies. Its mission is to serve this international community by providing an invaluable service, mainly focused on the publication of conference and workshop proceedings and postproceedings. LNCS commenced publication in 1973.

Oussama Habachi · Gerard Chalhoub ·
Halima Elbiaze · Essaid Sabir
Editors

Ubiquitous Networking

9th International Symposium, UNet 2023
Clermont-Ferrand, France, November 1–3, 2023
Revised Selected Papers

Springer

Editors
Oussama Habachi (ID)
University of Clermont Auvergne
Clermont-Ferrand, France

Gerard Chalhoub (ID)
University of Clermont Auvergne
Clermont-Ferrand, France

Halima Elbiaze (ID)
University of Québec at Montréal
Montreal, QC, Canada

Essaid Sabir (ID)
TÉLUQ, University of Québec
Montreal, QC, Canada

ISSN 0302-9743 ISSN 1611-3349 (electronic)
Lecture Notes in Computer Science
ISBN 978-3-031-62487-2 ISBN 978-3-031-62488-9 (eBook)
https://doi.org/10.1007/978-3-031-62488-9

This Springer imprint is published by the registered company Springer Nature Switzerland AG
The registered company address is: Gewerbestrasse 11, 6330 Cham, Switzerland

If disposing of this product, please recycle the paper.

Preface

The International Symposium on Ubiquitous Networking (UNet) is an international scientific event that highlights new trends and findings in hot topics related to ubiquitous computing/networking. UNet 2023 was held in hybrid mode on November 1–3, in the fascinating city of Clermont-Ferrand, France.

Ubiquitous networks sustain development of numerous paradigms/technologies such as distributed ambient intelligence, Internet of Things, Tactile Internet, Internet of Skills, context-awareness, cloud computing, wearable devices, and future mobile networking (e.g., B5G and 6G). Various domains are then impacted by such a system, such as security and monitoring, energy efficiency and environment protection, e-health, precision agriculture, intelligent transportation, homecare (e.g., for elderly and disabled people), etc. Communication in such a system has to cope with many constraints (e.g., limited-capacity resources, energy depletion, strong fluctuations of traffic, real-time constraints, dynamic network topology, radio link breakage, interferences, etc.) and has to meet new application requirements. Ubiquitous systems bring many promising paradigms aiming to deliver significantly higher capacity to meet the huge growth of mobile data traffic and to accommodate efficiently dense and ultra-dense systems. A crucial challenge is that ubiquitous networks should be engineered to better support existing and emerging applications including broadband multimedia, machine-to-machine applications, Internet of Things, sensors, and RFID technologies. Many of these systems require stringent Quality of Service including better latency, reliability, and higher spectral and energy efficiency, but also some Quality of Experience and Quality of Context constraints.

The UNet conference series is a forum that brings together researchers and practitioners from academia and industry to discuss recent developments in pervasive and ubiquitous networks. This conference series provides a venue to exchange ideas, discuss solutions, debate identified challenges, and share experiences among researchers and professionals. UNet aims also to promote adoption of new methodologies and to provide the participants with advanced and innovative tools able to capture the fundamental dynamics of the underlying complex interactions (e.g., game theory, Mechanism Design theory, Learning theory, SDR platforms, etc.). Papers describing original research on both theoretical and practical aspects of pervasive computing and future mobile computing (e.g., 5G, 6G, AI-driven communications, IoT, TI, etc.) were invited for submission to UNet 2023.

Message from the General Chairs

On behalf of the organizing committee, it is our great pleasure to welcome you to the proceedings of the 9th International Conference on Ubiquitous Networking (UNet 2023), which was held in hybrid mode on November 1–3, 2023.

Technically sponsored by Springer Nature, and co-organized by LIMOS laboratory, University of Clermont Auvergne, France, LATECE Laboratory, NEST Research Group, STARACOM, and Université de Québec à Montréal, the 2023 UNet follows eight successful events held virtually, and in-person in Canada, France, Tunisia, and Morocco. Over the past editions, the reputation of UNet has rapidly grown and the conference has become one of the most respected venues in the field of ubiquitous networking and pervasive systems.

The conference would not have been possible without the enthusiastic and hard work of a few colleagues. We would like to express our appreciation to the Technical Program Chair, Essaid Sabir, for his valuable contribution in building the high-quality conference program. We also thank the track Chairs and all the organizing committee members. Such an event relies on the commitment and the contributions of many volunteers, and we would like to acknowledge the efforts of our TPC members for their invaluable help in the review process. We are also grateful to all the authors who contributed to the conference with their work.

Special thanks to our Keynote Speakers, the best in their respective fields, Emil Bjornson, Mehdi Bennis, Mohsen Guizani, and Mohamed Slim Alouini, for sharing their expert views on current hot research topics.

We hope that you enjoyed the rich program we built this year, that you made the most out of your participation, and that you will come back to UNet for many years to come!

November 2023

Oussama Habachi
Gerard Chalhoub
Halima Elbiaze

Message from the TPC Chair

It is with great pleasure that we welcome you to the proceedings of the 2023 International Conference on Ubiquitous Networking (UNet 2023), held in hybrid mode. You will find an interesting technical program of 5 technical tracks reporting on recent advances in ubiquitous communication technologies and networking, tactile internet and internet of things, mobile edge networking and fog-cloud computing, artificial intelligence-driven communications, and data engineering, cyber security and pervasive services.

UNet 2023 featured 4 keynote speeches delivered by world-class experts, shedding light on future 6G mobile standards, novel 6G enablers, global connectivity, AI-driven communications for 6G, Internet of everything, and smart cities. Moreover, an exciting tutorial covering the new trends of data-driven mean-field theory for ultra-dense networks and ubiquitous systems was also delivered.

In this edition, the UNet conference received 28 submitted manuscripts from 16 countries, out of which 14 papers were selected to be included in the final program with an acceptance rate of 50%. The selection of the program of UNet 2023 was possible in the first place thanks to the thorough review performed by our TPC committee members. Overall, the average quality of the submissions has respected the fairly high standards of the event. The selection process, we believe, has been conducted, in a rigorous and fair manner. More specifically, each paper has received at least 2 independent single-blind reviews made by TPC members, taking into consideration the quality of presentation, the technical soundness, the novelty, and the originality of the manuscripts. The evaluation scale for each aspect of the evaluation was set to range from 1 to 5.

Building this excellent program would not have been possible without the dedication and hard work of the different Chairs, the Keynote Speakers, the Tutorial Speakers, and all the Technical Program Committee members. We grasp the opportunity to acknowledge their valuable work, and sincerely thank them for their help in ensuring that UNet 2023 will be remembered as a high-quality event.

We hope that you enjoyed this edition's technical program, and we enjoyed e-meeting you during the conference.

November 2023   Essaid Sabir

Organization

General Chair

Oussama Habachi   University of Clermont Auvergne, France

Co-chairs

Gérard Chalhoub   University of Clermont Auvergne, France
Halima Elbiaze   University of Quebec at Montreal, Canada

TPC Chair

Essaid Sabir   University of Quebec at Montreal, Canada

Track Chairs

Vahid Meghdadi   Univ. of Limoges XLIM-SRI, France
Benoit Hilt   University of Haute Alsace, France
Gentian Jakllari   IRIT Toulouse, France
Elarbi Badidi   UAE University, UAE
Farrukh Aslam Khan   UAE University, UAE
Diala Naboulsi   ÉTS, University of Quebec, Canada
Vincent Barra   University of Clermont Auvergne, France
Hajar Hammouti   UM6P, Morocco
Slim Rekhis   Sup'Com, University of Carthage, Tunisia

Publicity Chairs

Antonio Jara   HOP Ubiquitous, Spain
Safaa Driouech   Orange Labs, France
Wissal Attaoui   Inwi Corporation, Morocco
Sujit Samanta Kumar   National Institute of Technology Raipur, India

Steering Committee

Mohamed-Slim Alouini	KAUST University, Saudi Arabia
Eitan Altman	Inria Sophia Antipolis, France
Francesco De Pellegrini	University of Avignon, France
Rachid El-Azouzi	University of Avignon, France
Halima Elbiaze	University of Quebec at Montreal, Canada
Mounir Ghogho	International University of Rabat, Morocco
Marwan Krunz	University of Arizona, USA
Essaid Sabir	University of Quebec at Montreal, Canada
Mohamed Sadik	ENSEM, Hassan II University of Casablanca, Morocco

Technical Program Committee

Abdelkrim Abdelli	USTHB, Algeria
Wessam Ajib	University of Quebec at Montreal, Canada
Brahim Alibouch	Ibn Zohr University, Morocco
Imran Shafique Ansari	University of Glasgow, UK
Elarbi Badidi	UAE University, UAE
Paolo Bellavista	University of Bologna, Italy
Asma Ben Letaifa	Sup'Com, Tunisia
Yann Ben Maissa	INPT, Morocco
Salah Benabdallah	University of Tunis, Tunisia
Mustapha Benjillali	INPT, Morocco
Yahya Benkaouz	Mohammed V University of Rabat, Morocco
Fatma Benkhelifa	Imperial College London, UK
Hassan Bennani	Mohammed V University of Rabat, Morocco
Olivier Brun	Laboratoire d'Analyse et d'Architecture des Systèmes, France
Stefano Chessa	Università di Pisa, Italy
Domenico Ciuonzo	University of Naples Federico II, Italy
Deepak Dasaratha Rao	Sysintel Inc, USA
Sabrina De Capitani di Vimercati	Università degli Studi di Milano, Italy
Yacine Djemaiel	University of Carthage, Tunisia
Elmahdi Driouch	Université du Québec à Montréal, Canada
Schahram Dustdar	Vienna University of Technology, Austria
Loubna Echabbi	INPT, Morocco
Hajar El Hammouti	KAUST, Saudi Arabia
Mohamed El Kamili	ÉST, Hassan II University of Casablanca, Morocco

Tom Pfeifer	IoT Consult Europe, Germany
Miodrag Potkonjak	UCLA, USA
Luis Quesada	Insight Centre for Data Analytics, Ireland
Khalid Rahhali	Mohamed V University of Rabat, Morocco
Mounir Rifi	ESTC, Hassan II University of Casablanca, Morocco
Domenico Rotondi	FINCONS SpA, Italy
Giuseppe Ruggeri	University of Reggio Calabria, Italy
Walid Saad	Virginia Tech, USA
Dhananjay Singh	Hankuk University of Foreign Studies, South Korea
Maha Sliti	University of Carthage, Tunisia
Razvan Stanica	INSA Lyon, France
Bruno Tuffin	Inria Rennes - Bretagne Atlantique, France
Om Vyas	Indian Institute of Information Technology, Allahabad, India
Wei Wei	Xi'an University of Technology, China
Konrad Wrona	NATO Communications and Information Agency, The Netherlands
Sherali Zeadally	University of Kentucky, USA
Ping Zhou	Apple Inc., USA

UNet 2023 Keynote Speakers

Intelligent Wireless Networking Using Pervasive AI

Mohsen Guizani

Abstract. The use of Artificial Intelligence (AI) has been growing rapidly in many applications. It is a great tool that can be used to reach the right decision for emerging applications. With this, it brings many challenges, such as energy fairness, security and efficiency. With the Internet of Things (IoT) transforming our society by connecting the world, anytime and anywhere, AI can be a great tool to achieve ultimate objectives. However, the use of AI in ubiquitous connections brings with it many challenges that range from providing efficient security to ubiquitous networks, for instance. On the other hand, adversarial AI can slow the adoption of these systems and in turn block such advances. These smart services rely on computation and communication resources. Furthermore, being able to provide adequate services using these complex systems presents enormous challenges. In this talk, we review the current efforts in using AI to mitigate some of these challenges. Then, we discuss applications on how to alert researchers to take care of adversarial AI. We showcase our research activities that will contribute to these efforts and advocate possible solutions using AI models. We provide ways to manage the available resources intelligently and efficiently to offer better living conditions and provide better services. Finally, we discuss some of our research results to support a variety of applications in smart environments.

Mohsen Guizani received the BS (with distinction), MS and PhD degrees in Electrical and Computer Engineering from Syracuse University, Syracuse, NY, USA in 1985, 1987 and 1990, respectively. He is currently a Professor of Machine Learning at the Mohamed Bin Zayed University of Artificial Intelligence (MBZUAI), Abu Dhabi, UAE. Previously, he worked in different institutions in the USA. His research interests include applied machine learning and artificial intelligence, smart city, Internet of Things (IoT), intelligent autonomous systems and cybersecurity. He became an IEEE Fellow in 2009 and was listed as a Clarivate Analytics Highly Cited Researcher in Computer Science in 2019, 2020, 2021 and 2022. Dr. Guizani has won several research awards including the 2015 IEEE Communications Society Best Survey Paper Award, the Best ComSoc Journal Paper Award in 2021 as well 5 Best Paper Awards from ICC and Globecom Conferences. He is the author of 11 books, more than 1000 publications and several US patents. He is also the recipient of the 2017 IEEE Communications Society Wireless Technical Committee (WTC) Recognition Award, the 2018 AdHoc Technical Committee Recognition Award and the 2019 IEEE Communications and Information Security Technical Recognition (CISTC) Award. He served as the Editor-in-Chief of IEEE Network and is currently serving on the Editorial Boards of many IEEE Transactions and Magazines. He was the Chair of the IEEE Communications Society Wireless Technical Committee and the Chair of the TAOS Technical Committee. He served as the IEEE Computer Society Distinguished Speaker and is currently the IEEE ComSoc Distinguished Lecturer.

VisionX: Semantic Communication Meets System2 ML

Mehdi Bennis

Abstract. This keynote talk will first provide a brief introduction to VisionX sitting at the intersection of machine learning and communication in terms of enablers and mathematical tools, while contrasting it with current efforts in the area. Then, recent results in semantics-native communication and learning communication protocols from data will be presented.

Mehdi Bennis is a full (tenured) Professor at the Centre for Wireless Communications, University of Oulu, Finland and head of the intelligent connectivity and networks/systems group (ICON). His main research interests are in radio resource management, game theory and distributed AI in 5G/6G networks. He has published more than 200 research papers in international conferences, journals and book chapters. He has been the recipient of several prestigious awards including the 2015 Fred W. Ellersick Prize from the IEEE Communications Society, the 2016 Best Tutorial Prize from the IEEE Communications Society, the 2017 EURASIP Best Paper Award for the Journal of Wireless Communications and Networks, the all-University of Oulu award for research and the 2019 IEEE ComSoc Radio Communications Committee Early Achievement Award, and was named a 2020–2021 Clarivate Highly Cited Researcher by the Web of Science. Dr. Bennis is an editor of IEEE TCOM and Specialty Chief Editor for Data Science for Communications in the Frontiers in Communications and Networks journal. Dr. Bennis is an IEEE Fellow.

Massive Spatial Multiplexing: When the Near-Field Becomes Far-Reaching

Emil Björnson

Abstract. Multi-antenna communication technology can, in theory, provide great bit rates between a transmitter and receiver through spatial multiplexing; that is, sending different spatial layers over different propagation paths. Unfortunately, traditional systems operate in the far field where there is often, at most, one strong propagation path. This might change in 6G. By increasing the carrier frequency, adding more antennas, and densifying the network infrastructure, we will enter a paradigm where communications mostly happen in the radiative near-field. In this keynote, we will revisit the fundamentals of multiple-input multiple-output (MIMO) communications and explore the new features that arise when operating in the near field. The relation between spatial modes, spherical wavefronts, and array geometries will be described and illustrated. Is massive spatial multiplexing the next untapped signal dimension that can sustain capacity growth in future networks?

Emil Björnson is a Professor of Wireless Communication at the KTH Royal Institute of Technology, Stockholm, Sweden. He is an IEEE Fellow, Digital Futures Fellow, and Wallenberg Academy Fellow. He has a podcast and YouTube channel called Wireless Future. His research focuses on multi-antenna communications and radio resource management, using methods from communication theory, signal processing, and machine learning. He has authored three textbooks and has published a large amount of simulation code.

He has received the 2018 and 2022 IEEE Marconi Prize Paper Awards in Wireless Communications, the 2019 EURASIP Early Career Award, the 2019 IEEE Communications Society Fred W. Ellersick Prize, the 2019 IEEE Signal Processing Magazine Best Column Award, the 2020 Pierre-Simon Laplace Early Career Technical Achievement Award, the 2020 CTTC Early Achievement Award, the 2021 IEEE ComSoc RCC Early Achievement Award, and the 2023 IEEE Communications Society Outstanding Paper Award. His work has also received six Best Paper Awards at conferences.

Towards Extreme Band Communications to Super-Connect the Connected and to Connect the Unconnected

Mohamed-Slim Alouini

Abstract. A rapid increase in the use of wireless services over the last few decades has led to the problem of radio-frequency (RF) spectrum exhaustion. More specifically, due to this RF spectrum scarcity, additional RF bandwidth allocation, as utilized in the recent past over "traditional bands", is no longer enough to fulfill the demand for more wireless applications and higher data rates. The talk goes first over the potential offered by extreme band communication (XB-Com) systems to relieve spectrum scarcity. Indeed, mm-wave, THz, and free space optics broadband wireless systems recently attracted research interest worldwide due to the progress in electronics and photonics technologies. By utilizing these extreme frequency bands and employing extremely large bandwidths, 6G target data rates over 100 Gbps could be achieved. The talk then summarizes (i) some of the challenges that need to be overcome before such kinds of systems can be deployed and (ii) some on-going activities in this area in order to achieve this goal.

Mohamed-Slim Alouini is a Distinguished Professor of Electrical and Computer Engineering at King Abdullah University of Science and Technology (KAUST), Thuwal, Makkah Province, Saudi Arabia. His research interests include the modeling, design, and performance analysis of wireless, satellite, and optical communication systems. He is a fellow of the Institute of Electrical and Electronics Engineers (IEEE) and OPTICA (formerly known as the Optical Society of America (OSA)).

Contents

Ubiquitous Communication Technologies and Networking

Artificial Intelligence-Driven Communications

A Comparative Analysis of Sentence Embedding Techniques and LSTM Models in Web Page Classification

Kerkri Abdelmounaim[1]($\boxtimes$)(iD), Mohamed Amine Madani[2], Rabhi Wiam[3],
Lamyae Belaouchi[3], and El Fahsi Oumayma[3]

[1] Laboratory of stochastic and deterministic modeling National School of Applied Sciences Mohammed Premier University Oujda, Oujda, Morocco
a.kerkri@ump.ac.ma
[2] Engineering Sciences Laboratory LSI National School of Applied Sciences Mohammed Premier University, Oujda, Morocco
[3] National School of Applied Sciences Mohammed Premier University, Oujda, Morocco

Abstract. Given the growing volume of online content, web page classification is crucial for ensuring accurate and efficient information retrieval. In this study, we explore several sentence embedding techniques, based on transfer learning models, in the context of a web page classification task. We further compare three of these sentence embedding techniques, with three other LSTM architectures: a vanilla LSTM model, bidirectional LSTM (BiLSTM) and LSTM with attention mechanism. The dataset we used contains roughly 11000 web pages that have been legally scraped from a well known news website. The comparison shows that BERT sentence embedding outperforms all models, including the LSTM hybrid model with attention mechanism.

Keywords: BERT · GloVe · USE. · LSTM · web page classification

1 Introduction

In natural language processing (NLP), sentence embedding is the process of representing a sentence or a piece of a text by a numerical vector, instead of representing each token separately. The extracted embeddings attempt to capture the semantics and the contextual dependencies in the text, in order to be used in machine learning models, for NLP tasks, such as text classification and named entity recognition. In this study, we compare three different sentence embedding techniques, specifically Bidirectional Encoder Representations from Transformers (BERT) [1], Global Vectors for Word Representation (GloVe) [2], and Universal Sentence Encoder (USE) [3], in the context of web page classification. The aforementioned models are transfer learning architectures, based on pre-trained models that we fine tuned. The comparison also includes three LSTM models,

O. Habachi et al. (Eds.): UNet 2023, LNCS 14757, pp. 3–16, 2024.
https://doi.org/10.1007/978-3-031-62488-9_1

one of which is a hybrid model that we created by adding an attention mechanism. Attention mechanism [4], is a deep neural network that mimics the human ability to give more attention to important parts of a text, it is considered one of the biggest breakthroughs in NLP models, as it demonstrated a substantial progress in all NLP tasks. Our selection of sentence embedding models is based on their ability to capture broader context than word embedding models. Given the sequential nature of text in web pages, we chose various LSTM architectures. The dataset, containing around 11,000 web pages with diverse topics and styles, calls for the use of models like BERT that have proven depth in text comprehension. The second section of this paper will briefly present the models used in the comparison, followed by a section about the scraping of the dataset as well as the classification pipeline description. The same section will also present the classification metrics of each model.

2   Review of the Models

2.1   BERT Sentence Embeddings

BERT is a pretrained model based on transformers, an architecture that introduced the notion of self attention mechanisms. BERT is available in two options: a base model that stacks 12 encoders of a transformer, and a large model that includes 24 encoders. The training of BERT was carried out on two different tasks: masked language modeling and next sentence prediction.

BERT Sentence Embedding, refers to using BERT's architecture to generate a single vector that represents the entire sentence, rather than individual tokens. Several studies have compared BERT's performance in text classification to other classical machine learning models, the comparison always has been in favor of the former [5]. To our knowledge, most of the studies have used BERT with single token embeddings, which motivated our choice for sentence embeddings.

2.2   Universal Sentence Encoder

One of the most powerful techniques in Sentence Embeddings currently is the Universal Sentence Encoder (USE) [3], which was developed by Google. The key feature of USE is its applicability to multi-task learning. This implies that the sentence embeddings we generate can be deployed for multiple tasks such as sentiment analysis, text classification, sentence similarity to name a few.

The USE is based on two encoder models:

– A transformer based architecture
– An architecture based on deep averaging networks (DAN) [6]

Both models take a word or a sentence as input and generate embeddings following these steps:

– The sentences are tokenized after converting them to lowercase.

- Based on the architecure type, the sentence is then converted to a 512 dimensional vector.
- The sentence embeddings are then fed into a neural network that is accustomed to the specific NLP task.

2.3   Global Vectors for Word Representation (GloVe)

GloVe, or Global Vectors for word representation [2], presents a probability based method for generating word embeddings, this model is built on a count-based system, leveraging global co-occurrence statistics, that is, the frequency of two words appearing together in a sentence.

The core intuition behind GloVe asserts that word co-occurrence provides the most significant statistical information available for the model to learn word representations. GloVe's loss function as stated in the original paper [2] is as follows:

$$J = \sum_{i,j=1}^{V} f(X_{ij})(w_i^T \tilde{w}_j + b_i + \tilde{b}_j - log(X_{ij}))^2 \tag{1}$$

where V is the size of the vocabulary, w_i is the word vector, $\tilde{w}_j$ are separate context word vectors and X_{ij} is the number of times the words i and j appear together.

2.4   Long Short Term Memory Networks

Before the revolution of transformers, LSTMs [7] were the state of the art model, in NLP applications. LSTM models have successfully overcome the deficiencies of traditional recurrent neural networks, particularly their inability to handle long-term dependencies due to the vanishing gradient problem. LSTMs unique architecture, which incorporates memory cells that retain state over long sequences, allows the network to learn from text sequences that are far apart in the corpus.

In this study, we used three variants of LSTMs:

A vanilla LSTM: This is the basic LSTM model without any modifications. Its architecture consists of an initial Embedding layer converting input integers into dense vectors. This is followed by an LSTM layer with 32 units. A Dropout layer with a rate equal to 0.5, is added to mitigate overfitting, and finally, a Dense layer outputs a probability distribution over classes using a softmax activation function.

Bi-directional LSTM (BiLSTM) [8]: This model contains an initial Embedding layer, identical to Model 1. It includes two LSTM layers, each with 32 units, where the first returns the full sequence for subsequent layer input. Two Dropout layers identical to Model 1 are added for overfitting prevention. Finally, a Dense layer, consistent with Model 1, concludes the architecture.

LSTM with Attention Mechanism: This hybrid model is built by adding an attention mechanism to the LSTM model. The attention mechanism allows the model to focus on different parts of the sequence for every output, weighting the importance of inputs differently.

3   Data Acquisition and Results

The study's implementation process started with data scraping and initial data processing, followed by the training of the aforementioned sentence embedding models for web page classification. Our primary focus is on three distinct categories: Sports, Africa, and Coronavirus.

3.1   Data Scraping

The data scraping phase involved two main aspects:

– Historical data scraping: this involved gathering past data that will serve in the training of our machine learning model.

– Recent data scraping: this involved gathering the most recent data from the news website for the purpose of performance testing of our models.

For scraping to be both legal and maintainable, it is essential to inspect the site's robots.txt file before initiating the scraping process. This file provides guidelines about the permissible activities on the site, which can help avoid legal issues and prevent wasted efforts on writing code for a site that might subsequently ban you for attempting content extraction via scraping. Compliance with these guidelines ensures the legality of the scraping operation and maintains the accessibility of the site for future interactions.

In this study, various technologies were employed: Python for coding scripts, Requests for simplified HTTP requests, Beautifulsoup (bs4) for parsing website HTML code and locating tags. We also used Selenium as a bot to automate clicking the'Show more' button for retrieving more web pages, and Pandas to create a database with category, title, and web page content columns, to be saved in a CSV file. A link to the repository that we created for the scraping is shared in the references [10].

3.2   Classification Pipelines

During this phase, we will present the NLP pipelines created using the models that we have previously presented. We utilized the open-source Spark NLP library, which provides an API for deep learning pipelines.

Post scraping the web site, we were able to assemble a dataset containing roughly 11000 web pages, labeled by their categories.

Pipeline 1: BERT Sentence Embeddings

In the first training pipeline (Fig. 1), we chose 2 different sentence embedding techniques that are all based on BERT:

– The first sentence embedding model is a large, case-sensitive version of the BERT model, designed for sentence-level tasks in English. This model maintains the distinction between uppercase and lowercase letters during processing, indicating that it was trained on data with original letter casing preserved.
– The second model is also a large scale version of the BERT model, specifically designed for sentence level tasks in English. This model is 'uncased,' meaning it treats all text as lowercase, regardless of the original letter casing in the training data.

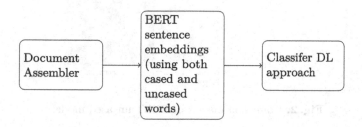

Fig. 1. The first learning pipeline based on BERT sentennce embeddings

Document Assembler prepares our dataset by converting web page content into a "document", a specialized data structure used by SparkNLP for storing textual content. This processed data is then used to generate sentence embeddings. These embeddings serve as input for the Classifier, known as the Deep Learning Approach (DL Approach), which employs a Deep Learning Network (DLN) for text classification tasks. Specifically, the classifier DL approach uses a softmax activation layer at the output stage to enable probabilistic classification across multiple categories.

The pipelines based on BERT sentence embeddings gave similar results on both cased and uncased words with an overall accuracy of 0.92 (Tables 1 and 2). However, there are a few differences to note. The pipeline using cased words slightly outperformed the uncased one in classifying web pages related to the categories: Africa and Coronavirus, as indicated by the higher F1-Score of 0.91 and 0.95 respectively, compared to 0.89 and 0.94 in the uncased pipeline. This suggests that the model might be capturing some information linked to casing, such as proper nouns, in these categories, which improves performance. For the detailed classification of the test set, we present the confusion matrices in Figs. 2 and 3.

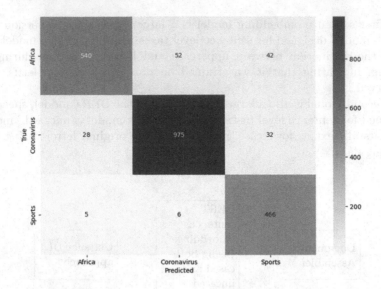

Fig. 2. Confusion matrix of BERT uncased model

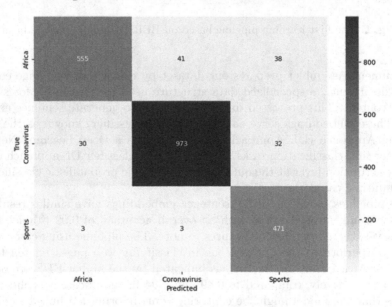

Fig. 3. Confusion matrix of BERT cased model

Table 1. Classification metrics of pipeline 1 with cased words

	Precision	Recall	F1-Score
Africa	0.94	0.88	0.91
Coronavirus	0.96	0.94	0.95
Sports	0.87	0.99	0.93
Overall Accuracy	0.92		

Table 2. Classification metrics for pipeline 1 with uncased words

	Precision	Recall	F1-Score
Africa	0.94	0.85	0.89
Coronavirus	0.94	0.94	0.94
Sports	0.86	0.98	0.92
Overall Accuracy	0.92		

As for the Sports category the accuracy is slightly lower: 0.87 compared to 0.86, resulting in a marginally lower F1-score: 0.93 compared to 0.92. This might be an indicator that the model is slightly better at finding relevant Sports pages when not taking casing into account.

Pipeline 2: Universal Sentence Encoder

In the second pipeline (Fig. 5), we generated sentence embeddings using the Universal Sentence Encoder. The Document Assembler and the classifier DL approach are used in the same way as pipeline 1.

In terms of individual categories, the highest F1-score of 0.92 was obtained in the Sports category (Table 3). This indicates that while the model is excellent at finding relevant Sports web pages (high recall), it also identifies a few irrelevant pages as Sports (slightly lower precision), this can be clearly noticed in the confusion matrix (Fig. 4).

Table 3. Classification metrics for USE pipeline

	Precision	Recall	F1-Score
Africa	0.89	0.79	0.84
Coronavirus	0.91	0.91	0.91
Sports	0.87	0.98	0.92
Accuracy	0.89		

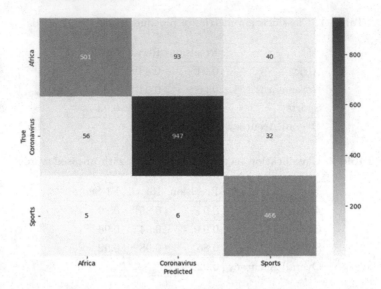

Fig. 4. Confusion matrix of the universal sentence encoder model

Table 3 presents the performance metrics of the Universal Sentence Encoder (USE) pipeline across the three categories. The overall accuracy of the model is 0.89. The confusion matrix, is presented in Fig. 4.

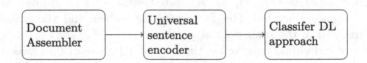

Fig. 5. The universal sentence encoder pipeline

Pipeline 3 : GloVe (Global Vector for Word Representation)

Since the GloVe implementation in Spark NLP library doesn't include the processing phase, we added it manually in the pipeline (Fig. 6). This processing includes tokenization, lemmatization and stop words removal. We extracted word embeddings using Glove, then we averaged the words within each sentence to get the final sentence embedding vector.

The classification metrics of this pipeline (Table 4) show that the overall accuracy of the model is 0.89. We see varying performance in each category, for example, the Coronavirus class has the highest precision and F1-Score of 0.92. On the other hand, the Sports class stands out with an impressive recall of 0.98,

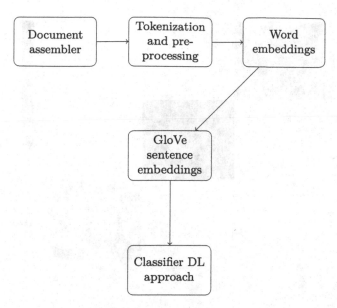

Fig. 6. Pipeline stages of GloVe sentence embeddings model

Table 4. Classification metrics of the GloVe pipeline

	Precision	Recall	F1-Score
Africa	0.90	0.80	0.85
Coronavirus	0.92	0.91	0.92
Sports	0.85	0.98	0.91
Accuracy	0.89		

indicating that the model is very successful in correctly identifying the positive Sports instances. The confusion matrix is presented in Fig. 7.

LSTM models

We used three variations of Long Short-Term Memory (LSTM) models for performance comparison: a Vanilla LSTM, a Bi-directional LSTM (BiLSTM), and an LSTM with attention mechanism. Similar to the previous pipelines, the three models' performance was evaluated through accuracy, F1 score, and recall.

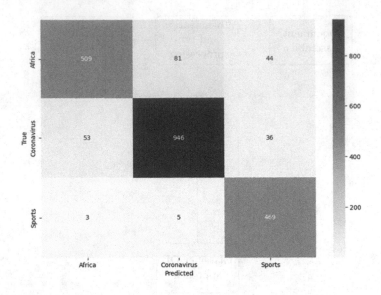

Fig. 7. Confusion matrix of the GloVe model

In the preprocessing phase of the three LSTM models, we limited the vocabulary to the 10,000 most common words and normalized sequence length to 500. Keras' Tokenizer transformed the text into integer sequences. The data was split into 80% training and 20% testing subsets, ensuring reproducibility with a fixed random state.

In the process of training, we used the categorical cross entropy loss function for multi-class classification, and the ADAM optimizer [9], which is a variant of stochastic gradient descent. Early stopping was adopted in order to prevent overfitting, which consists of halting training if the validation loss doesn't decrease after a given number of epochs. The models are trained for 10 epochs maximum, in batches of 32, with 20% of the training data set aside for validation.

The Vanilla LSTM displayed an accuracy of 0.8531 (Table 5), F1 score of 0.8509 and a recall of 0.8509. The model excels at classifying web pages related to Coronavirus but often misidentifies pages about Africa as Coronavirus related (Fig. 8). The BiLSTM exhibited marginally superior performance, with an accuracy of 0.854, an F1 score of 0.853, and a recall of 0.854. The slightly higher F1 score indicates a better balance between precision and recall as compared to the Vanilla LSTM. Compared to the previous LSTM model which had similar challenges, this BiLSTM model is proficient at categorizing web pages related to Coronavirus and Sports. However, it still misclassifies some Africa pages as Coronavirus (Fig. 9). It was the LSTM with attention mechanism that outperformed both the Vanilla LSTM and the BiLSTM. It delivered an accuracy of 0.8921, an F1 score of 0.8924, and a recall of 0.8921. These results point towards the effectiveness of the attention mechanism in enabling the LSTM to capture dependencies in different parts of the sequence, leading to a substantial enhancement in prediction accuracy. The LSTM model with attention mechanism accurately identifies Coronavirus web pages, reduces the confusion between Africa and Coronavirus, and is consistent in correctly classifying Sports content (Fig. 10).

Table 5. Classification metrics for Different LSTM Models

	Loss	Accuracy	F1-Score	Recall
Vanilla LSTM	0.4561	0.8531	0.8509	0.8531
BiLSTM	0.4926	0.8541	0.8532	0.8541
LSTM with Attention	0.3361	0.8921	0.8924	0.8921

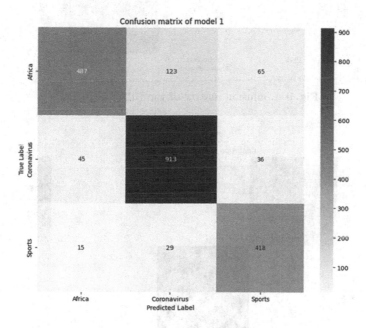

Fig. 8. Confusion matrix of the vanilla LSTM model

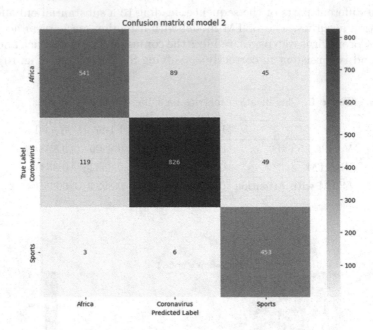

Fig. 9. Confusion matrix of the BiLSTM model

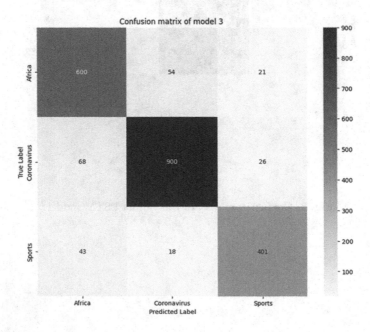

Fig. 10. Confusion matrix of the LSTM with attention mechanism model

4   Conclusion

This study presented a comparative analysis of different sentence embedding techniques and LSTM models, namely BERT (cased and uncased), Universal Sentence Encoder, GloVe, Vanilla LSTM, Bi-directional LSTM (BiLSTM), and LSTM with attention mechanism. The aim was to assess their performance in relation to a text classification task.

After the training and the assessment of the models, we found that BERT sentence embedding, with its two variations, cased and uncased, yielded the best performance. This is due to its transformer based architecture and its sophisticated treatment of the context. BERT's ability to understand the syntax and semantics at a deeper level than the other models appears to be a significant factor contributing to its superior performance.

The LSTM models, including the Vanilla LSTM, BiLSTM, and LSTM with attention mechanism, gave relatively good results, with the LSTM with attention mechanism notably outperforming the Vanilla LSTM and BiLSTM. The results clearly demonstrate the attention mechanism's ability to enhance the model's handling of long-term dependencies in text sequences. The GloVe and Universal Sentence Encoder, although not outperforming BERT, provided similar results to the LSTM with attention mechanism.

In conclusion, sentence embeddings can often be a more effective choice than word embeddings for certain tasks due to their ability to capture contextual information at a broader level. Future research can focus on combining the strengths of different sentence embedding techniques to further enhance text classification performance.

References

1. Devlin, J., Chang, M.-W., Lee, K., Toutanova, K.: BERT: pre-training of deep bidirectional transformers for language understanding (2018). arXiv preprint arXiv:1810.04805
2. Pennington, J., Socher, R., Manning, C.D.: GloVe: global vectors for word representation. In: Proceedings of the 2014 Conference on Empirical Methods in Natural Language Processing (EMNLP), pp. 1532–1543 (2014)
3. Cer, D., et al.: Universal sentence encoder (2018). arXiv preprint arXiv:1803.11175
4. Vaswani, A., et al.: Attention is all you need. In: Advances in Neural Information Processing Systems, vol. 30 (2017)
5. González-Carvajal, S., Garrido-Merchán, E.C.: Comparing BERT against traditional machine learning text classification (2020). arXiv preprint arXiv:2005.13012
6. Iyyer, M., Manjunatha, V., Boyd-Graber, J., Daumé, H.: Deep unordered composition rivals syntactic methods for text classification. In: Proceedings of the 53rd Annual Meeting of the Association for Computational Linguistics and the 7th International Joint Conference on Natural Language Processing, vol. 1(Long papers), pp. 1681–1691 (2015)
7. Hochreiter, S., Schmidhuber, J.: Long short-term memory. Neural Comput. 9(8), 1735–1780 (1997)

8. Graves, A., Fernández, S., Schmidhuber, J.: Bidirectional LSTM networks for improved phoneme classification and recognition. In: Duch, W., Kacprzyk, J., Oja, E., Zadrożny, S. (eds.) ICANN 2005. LNCS, vol. 3697, pp. 799–804. Springer, Heidelberg (2005). https://doi.org/10.1007/11550907_126
9. Kingma, D.P., Ba, J.: Adam: a method for stochastic optimization (2014). arXiv preprint arXiv:1412.6980
10. UMA-OO (2022). Aljazeera-Scraper. https://github.com/uma-oo/Aljazeera-Scraper

Federated Clouds: A New Metric for Measuring the Quality of Data Anonymization

Youssoupha Gaye[1]([✉])[iD], Maissa Mbaye[1][iD], Dame Diongue[1][iD],
Ousmane Dieng[2][iD], Emmanuel Adetiba[3,4], and Joke A. Badejo[3][iD]

[1] Laboratoire d'Analyse Numerique et Informatique/LANI, CEA-MITIC,
Gaston Berger University, 234 Saint-Louis, PB, Senegal
{gaye.youssoupha,maissa.mbaye,dame.diongue}@ugb.edu.sn

[2] Power-management and Real-Time Systems Lab, University of Pittsburgh,
Pittsburgh, PA 15260, USA
oud5@pitt.edu

[3] Covenant Applied Informatics and Communication African Center of Excellence,
Covenant University, Ota, Ogun State, Nigeria
{emmanuel.adetiba,joke.badejo}@covenantuniversity.edu.ng

[4] HRA, Institute for Systems Science, Durban University of Technology,
Durban 1334, South Africa

Abstract. Federated cloud has emerged as solution for cloud service providers to get scalability in serving the growing demand for cloud resources. In a federated cloud, a cloud member can provide service or request it from other cloud provider members in the federation. The federation enables its cloud provider members to be able to satisfy a service beyond the resources they owned by using the resources market in the federation. Data privacy is a major concern in federated clouds. As the privacy regulations and laws of the countries in the federation may vary, it is difficult to assess and confirm that they are in compliance. This makes protecting privacy even more challenging. Privacy management strategies primarily involve anonymization, cryptography, and data splitting. Anonymization is the traditional approach to preserving privacy, which aims at masking the link between the quasi-identifier and sensitive data. The most widely used anonymization techniques are k-anonymity, l-diversity and t-closeness. However, there is a lack of a formal metric to measure the quality of the anonymization process in terms of its ability to prevent re-identification. This paper examines the issue of assessing anonymization quality and introduces a new metric, $Mmaq$, for this purpose. It can be used to evaluate the anonymization of one or multiple attributes. The metric is a combination of the Shannon index, which measures diversity, and a stabilizer factor, which corrects the Shannon index for pathological cases. The initial results suggest that $Mmaq$ can be used to classify attributes as identifier, quasi-identifier, and anonymous. Furthermore, it can be employed as a Cloud Privacy Policy anonymization compliance checker.

Keywords: Data Anonymization Metric · Data Privacy · Federated Cloud Security · Federated Cloud · Cloud Computing

O. Habachi et al. (Eds.): UNet 2023, LNCS 14757, pp. 17–30, 2024.
https://doi.org/10.1007/978-3-031-62488-9_2

1   Introduction

Cloud computing offers Content Providers and Machine Learning Service Developers with highly accessible resources on the Internet. The next step in cloud computing is Federated Cloud Computing, which is designed to provide more efficient data access and sharing. This type of cloud computing is made up of resources from multiple clouds that are in different administrative domains. It is intended to address the increasing demand for computing and storage resources and to enable scalability for cloud providers to collaborate. In a federated cloud, members can both provide and request services such as computation, storage, and machine learning. This federation allows cloud providers to access resources beyond their own, enabling them to satisfy a service. Users of the federated cloud can be either simple users or other non-member clouds that require resources from the federation. Each cloud provider can offer data storage, machine learning, computation, and security services, while the federation provides access and authentication services, service discovery, negotiation, security, load balancing, and user interfaces (web, API, CLI). Federated cloud technology for medical applications can involve the sharing of personal and electronic medical records, diagnostic results, genomic data, and more. For example, Federated Genomics (FEDGEN) [2] is a federated cloud infrastructure in Nigeria for genomic data research on malaria and breast cancer in Africa. In a multi-national federated cloud, cloud providers' infrastructure can be located in different countries, and thus subject to different privacy laws and regulations. Providing federated cloud services presents three main privacy-related challenges: managing data authorizations, formalizing privacy protection legal rules, and developing privacy legal compliance verification services. There is a need to define a quantifiable metric to measure the quality of privacy protection measures in the federated cloud, particularly when transferring data between cloud members in different countries. Data anonymization is one approach used to ensure privacy, which involves modifying data [10] before sharing to prevent the identification of the data owner. However, anonymization should provide enough information to be useful while managing the risks of re-identification. The reconciliation of these two constraints leads to a risk of privacy-related attacks [16]. This paper proposes the use of the Shannon index and the stabilizer to assess the quality of anonymization of personal data in federated clouds. The Shannon index will be used to measure the diversity of the data, and the stabilizer factor will adjust the metric for any pathological cases of the Shannon index. The early results demonstrate that it is possible to classify attributes as identifier, quasi-identifier, and anonymous using $Mmaq$. This allows a Cloud Privacy Policy checker to use it to evaluate compliance in terms of anonymization. This paper is structured as follows. Section 2 provides the background and fundamental concepts of the research. Section 3 outlines the privacy protection strategies used in the federated cloud. Section 4 examines the proposed privacy protection approach and Sect. 5 summarizes the findings and potential future work.

2   Background

2.1   Federated Cloud Architecture and Services

A Federated Cloud is an aggregation of resources from different clouds that are in different administrative domains. These clouds provide services such as computation, storage, machine learning, and hosting that can be requested and managed at the federal level. Each cloud can provide services for other clouds in the federation and seek their resources for its customers. The architecture of federated clouds can be horizontal or vertical. In a horizontal federation, Provider-to-provider SLA (Service Level Agreement) enables collaboration between cloud providers in a peer-to-peer manner. In this architecture, each cloud must negotiate with other clouds to gain access to resources. The Vertical Federated Cloud architecture, on the other hand, includes a Federal/Federated Cloud Broker that manages internal and external interactions. This broker has interfaces with individual clouds via their local cloud brokers to discover and access resources and the user interface. All interactions in the federation are specified in a Federal Service Level Agreement (F-SLA). The F-SLA outlines interconnection rules and describes the responsibilities and authorized behavior of each member of the federation, as well as financial, administrative, or other sanctions in the event of non-compliance with the terms of the agreement. The F-SLA is managed by the federal broker, who is also responsible for negotiating with national brokers when federation users request data or resources. The Federal Broker hosts a variety of services (see Fig. 1):

- **Access Control**: This service provides Authentication and Access to members of the cloud federation;
- **Service Discovery**: This service will provide a map of the services and resources available within the federation;
- **Negotiation Service**: This service is for SLA establishment between clouds members for resources reservations, use and management;
- **Security service**: This service enforces the security policy at the federation level and prevents the propagation of security problems in the federation.
- **Load Balancing and Monitoring services**: Load balancing facilitates the allocation of tasks between cloud providers that are involved in a process. A monitoring service is used to collect data for the oversight of Federation resources.

Clients can access Federation clouds at the cloud level through an interface, such as a RESTful-API, Web application, or CLI, depending on the requested service platform. The Federal Cloud Broker is used to transparently obtain services. In recent years, the security and protection of privacy in the federated cloud has become a topic of increasing interest in the research community. Bernsmed et al. [4] identified four new security issues arising from the formation of federated cloud services: a longer chain of trust, limited auditability, the risk of malicious service components, and liability and legal issues. To address challenges related to security, interoperability, storage, processing, privacy, etc.,

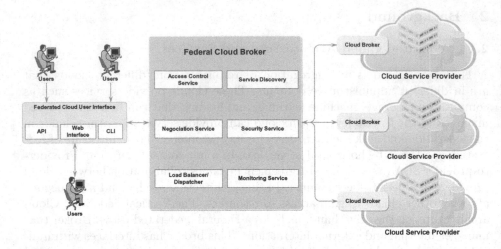

Fig. 1. Federated Cloud Vertical Architecture

several federated cloud architectures have been proposed in the literature. The RESERVOIR [13] project seeks to create an architecture to promote the adoption of open-federated cloud computing, address the scalability issues inherent in single-vendor cloud computing environments, and tackle the difficulties associated with interoperability between different cloud service providers. Additionally, the project aims to address the lack of integrated support for business service management in current cloud computing offerings. The ATMOSPHERE [6] project, a collaboration between Europe and Brazil, focuses on the development of a secure federated cloud platform to process sensitive data, particularly in the health field. The OPTIMIS [9] project proposes a specification and a toolkit for generating federated clouds, with security as one of the non-functional requirements that determine the final composition of a service. BioNimbuZ [14] is a federated cloud computing platform designed to meet the needs of bio-informatics applications, which often require high processing capacities and long run-times. This platform offers the ability to integrate and control multiple cloud infrastructure providers, each offering tailored bio-informatics tool chains as services.

2.2   Problem Statement

Federated clouds present a range of security issues, particularly in terms of privacy management. For instance, the services provided by the cloud federation often include storage and computational resources that are also used by other cloud services, such as Machine Learning. Storage services are widely used by data and content providers to enable low latency access and increased bandwidth. Machine Learning services may necessitate the transfer of data from one cloud data provider member to a geographically closer storage memory for improved efficiency. It is essential that sensitive or confidential information is kept safe in national domain clouds, in accordance with the data protection laws and regulations of the country. Most countries' laws state that sensitive and private data must not be stored outside their borders until the privacy and access confidentiality requirements have been fulfilled. Verifying and assessing compliance with privacy laws is a major issue in federated cloud research. This is due to discrepancies in legal data privacy policies and the need for anonymization, which can reduce the value of the data. Figure 2 shows a common federated cloud architecture with two cloud members in different jurisdictions. Cloud brokers in each country are responsible for coordinating activities at the federal level. They enable communication between the cloud members and the federation, allocating cloud resources to the federation members in accordance with Service Level Agreements (SLAs). Additionally, they check for compliance with local laws on security and privacy before transferring data to other clouds. However, data transfer between clouds in the federation presents several security challenges, such as managing data authorizations, formalizing privacy protection legal rules, and developing privacy legal compliance verification services.

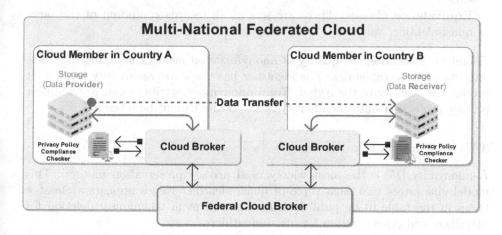

Fig. 2. Federated Cloud data transfer between cloud members in two countries

This paper presents an objective metric, $Mmaq$, to assess data privacy by evaluating the quality of data anonymization between clouds in the same nation or between two countries with different laws. The metric is based on the Shannon index to measure diversity and a stabilizer factor to address pathological cases. Initial results suggest that it can be used to classify attributes into identifiers, quasi-identifiers, and anonymizers, and thus could be employed by a privacy policy checker for automated evaluation.

3   Privacy Preserving Methods in Federated Cloud

Privacy protection in the federated cloud can be achieved through anonymization, cryptography, and data splitting [7]. Anonymization is a privacy-preserving technique that seeks to obscure the connection between quasi-identifiers and sensitive data. The most commonly used anonymization methods are k-anonymity, l-diversity, and t-closeness. In terms of data privacy, data columns can be divided into four categories based on their level of anonymization:

- **Identifier:** This is an attribute that uniquely identifies an individual (e.g. national identification number) and can be used as a key to distinguish each record;
- **Quasi-identifier:** This is a set of attributes that, combined with external data, can potentially identify the owner of the data (e.g. age, gender). Quasi-identifier attributes must be anonymized to avoid re-identification.
- **Sensitive attribute:** This represents information that if published can be prejudicial to the individual, such as health status, salary, religion, etc. This metric is subjective.
- **Anonymous attribute:** This is an attribute that make it difficult re-identification. If an attribute is totally anonymous no re-identification is possible.
- **Equivalence classes:** These are sets of all records composed of the same quasi-identifier values.

Therefore, measuring the quality of anonymization means classifying data sets into one of these categories. The identifier has the worst anonymity level, as it reveals the identity of the owner. Total anonymous attribute can provide best privacy protection since the identity of the owner cannot be retrieved.

3.1 K-Anonymity

K-anonymity [15] is the most widely used privacy preservation method. This model guarantees that each tuple of quasi-identifier values appears at least k times in the table to be published. It uses two main techniques: deletion for identifiers and generalization for quasi-identifiers.

Definition 1. *Let $T(A_1, ..., A_n)$ be a table, and QI_T, the quasi-identifiers associated with it. T satisfies k-anonymity if, for each quasi-identifier $QI \in QI_T$, each sequence of values in $T(QI)$ appears at least with k occurrences in $T(QI)$.*

Table 1 presents an example of a non-anonymized dataset of fictitious patient health information. It contains five attributes and nine records. To implement k-anonymity for a given value of k, two common techniques are used: deletion and generalization.

- **Suppression:** An attribute or part of an attribute is deleted and replaced by special characters such as the asterisk (*);
- **Generalization:** Here, the process of anonymization involves substituting the values of an attribute with a more general but still semantically appropriate value.

Table 1. Example of k-anonymity, where k=2 and QI={Age, Gender}

NIN	Name	Age	Gender	Disease
25580917	Khady	28	F	Hepatitis C
60608183	Fatou	51	F	Malaria
47833705	Cheikh	34	M	Syphilis
42662361	Nogaye	63	F	Measles
86276474	Serigne	40	M	VIH
60275595	Samba	30	M	Tuberculose
75392358	Abdou	42	M	Gonorrhoea
60258041	Bintou	25	F	Cholera
36001413	Ramata	64	F	Meningitis

Original data

NIN	Name	Age	Gender	Disease
25*	*	20-30	F, M	Hepatitis C
60*	*	20-30	F, M	Cholera
60*	*	20-30	F, M	Tuberculose
47*	*	35-45	F, M	Syphilis
86*	*	35-45	F, M	VIH
75*	*	35-45	F, M	Gonorrhoea
60*	*	50-65	F, M	Malaria
42*	*	50-65	F, M	Measles
36*	*	50-65	F, M	Meningitis

Anonymous data

Table 1 has been anonymized to a degree of three with respect to the attributes 'Age', and 'Gender'. Applying k-anonymity to a data set can create equivalence classes that do not provide enough variety for the values of the sensitive attribute, which can result in the disclosure of sensitive information. k-anonymized data can be exposed to attacks such as the Attribute Linking Attack, the Homogeneity Attack, and the Background Knowledge Attack [12].

L-diversity [12] and t-closeness [11] are extensions of the k-anonymity model that protect against attribute disclosure. An equivalence class respects the l-diversity constraint if it contains at least l "representative" values for a sensitive attribute. An equivalence class satisfies the constraint of t-closeness if the distance between the distribution of a sensitive attribute in that class and the distribution of the attribute in the complete table does not exceed a threshold.

3.2 Differential Privacy

Differential privacy, first introduced by [8], is a method of safeguarding individual records in a database by ensuring confidentiality.

Definition 2. *A randomized function k gives ϵ-differential privacy if for all data sets D_1 and D_2 differing on at most one element, and all $S \subset Range(K)$,*

$$Pr[K(D_1) \in S] \leq e^\epsilon * Pr[K(D_1) \in S] \tag{1}$$

where $Pr[K(D_1) \in S]$ means "the probability of observing S as a result of executing k on the database D_1".

This technique enables the extraction of useful information from databases that contain personal data of individuals while protecting the anonymity of their identities. This is usually accomplished by creating a system that adds random noise to the query results, making it impossible for an adversary to determine if a particular record is included in the database or not, regardless of any additional information they may have.

4   A New Metric to Measure Anonymization Quality

We introduce here our proposition, $Mmaq$ (Metric to Measure Anonymization Quality), which is a measure of anonymization quality. It is based on the Shannon index for measuring diversity and a factor that corrects it for pathological cases where Shannon cannot differentiate the state of the data.

4.1 $Mmaq$: Definition and Properties

The metric is used to measure the quality of anonymization of data for one or more attributes of a dataset.

Definition 3. *The Mmaq is defined as follows:*

$$Mmaq = \begin{cases} P & if\ H = 1 \\ (\frac{1}{1-H}) \times P\ otherwize. \end{cases} \tag{2}$$

Where H is the Shannon index and P is the correction factor.

When the $Mmaq = 1$, we have a **totally anonymous** attribute. If $Mmaq \longrightarrow 0$, then we have an **identifier**, whose metric value is $\frac{1}{N^N}$, where N is the number of lines. When $Mmaq \in]0, 1[$, the attribute is a **quasi-identifier**.

As S approaches N, the number of categories increases, leading to a decrease in anonymization quality as attributes become associated with an identifier.

4.2 Measuring Diversity of Data

The Shannon index [16], originally developed to measure the amount of information transmitted in communications, was later used in ecological research to quantify the diversity of a biological community. This index is a combination of two components: the number of species in the community (richness) and the relative frequency of these species (equitability). In this study, the index is used to measure the diversity of a column or a combination of columns in a dataset. The index H is calculated using the following formula:

$$H = -\sum_{n=1}^{s} p_i \log p_i \quad where\ p_i = \frac{n_i}{N}; \quad N = \sum_{i=1}^{s} n_i; \quad H_{max} = \log(S) \tag{3}$$

where p_i is the relative frequency of a category i in the attribute values and S is the number of categories, n_i is an absolute frequency of a Category, and N the total number of records. The maximum value of H is noted H_{max} and is reached when all categories are equally represented (same frequencies).

H increases as the number of categories increases ($S \longrightarrow N$) and the relative representation of each category becomes more balanced ($\forall i, j \in [1, S], p_i \approx p_j$). $H = 0$ when the column contains only one category (the same value in all rows). The higher H, the dataset is diversified. The maximum value of H_{max} will occur when all categories have the same frequency, in which case all p_i are equal ($\forall i, j \in [1, S], p_i = p_j$) and also when S = N.

To illustrate the properties of H, we used it in different synthesized datasets (like in Table 1) with seven attributes generally sensitive to privacy information: national identity number, surname, first name, gender, date of birth, place of

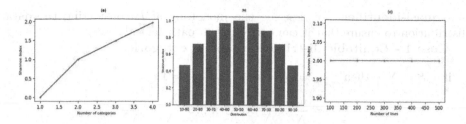

Fig. 3. Diversity index in relation to its variables

birth, disease, and hospital identifier. We worked mainly on an extract of 500 lines of data shows some of the attributes. The results are shown in Fig. 3.

In summary, for totally anonymized attributes $H = 0$. By increasing the number of categories, the anonymized attribute becomes a quasi-identifier, i.e. the number of categories tends towards the number of lines in the dataset, so the value of H increases. The column is an identifier when $S = N$ ($\forall\ i, j \in [1, N]$, $if\ i \neq j \Rightarrow val_i \neq val_j$). By applying generalization, to an attribute in a dataset attribute, the number of categories decreases, making the quasi-identifier tend towards a totally anonymous attribute.

Figure 3 shows that if the frequency for each category is $\frac{N}{S}$, then the value of H is the same for 100, 300, or 500 lines (Fig. 3c). When categories have the same absolute frequencies, the $H = H_{max} = log(S)$. On the other hand, if there is only one category, $H = H_{min} = 0$.

So, H can be used to recognize an identifier and a totally anonymous attribute. However, there is a pathological case : $H = H_{max}$, when $\forall i, j \in [1, S]$, $freq_i = freq_j$. It includes an identifier and an equally distributed attribute (Fig. 3b). So H gives the maximum for the worst and best cases. To correct this, we introduce another factor so the combination can be used to categorize attributes.

4.3   The Stabilizer Factor

The stabilized factor adjusts the value of H in order to distinguish Identifier and evenly distributed categories for a given attribute.

Definition 4. *Let p be the relative frequency that represents the probability that a value is in category $C(i)$. The stabilizer factor P is defined as follows:*

$$P = \prod_{i=1}^{s} p(x = C(i)) \quad where \quad p(x = C(i)) = \frac{n_i}{N} \quad and \quad \sum_{n=1}^{S} n_i = N \quad ; \quad (4)$$

Where x is a value in the column, C is the set of categories, $C(i)$ is the category number $i \in [1, S]$, n_i the absolute frequency of $C(i)$ so $S \leq N$.

When $P = 1$, we have a **totally anonymous** attribute. If $P \longrightarrow 0$, then we have an **identifier**, whose stabilizer value is $\frac{1}{N^N}$. When $P \in]0, 1[$, the attribute is a **quasi-identifier**. We describe the monotony of P considering the data distribution to ensure that it can correct H in pathological cases.

Case 1 - Equitable distribution among categories

– if $S = N$ then $n_1 = n_2 = n_3 = \ldots = n_S = 1$

$$P = \frac{n_1}{N} \times \frac{n_2}{N} \times \frac{n_3}{N} \times \ldots \times \frac{n_S}{N} = \frac{1}{N^N}$$

– if $S \in]1, N[$ then $n_1 = n_2 = n_3 = \ldots = n_S = a > 1$

$$P = \frac{n_1}{N} \times \frac{n_2}{N} \times \frac{n_3}{N} \times \ldots \times \frac{n_S}{N} = (\frac{a}{N})^S$$

Lemma 1. *Let D_1 and D_2 be two equitable distributions of the same attribute $C(i)$ with, respectively, S_1 and S_2 as a number of categories so that $S_1 < S_2$.*
$S_1, S_2, N \in \mathbb{N}^*$. $n_1 = n_2 = \ldots = n_{S_1} = a_1$; $m_1 = m_2 = \ldots = m_{S_2} = a_2$

$$\sum_{i=1}^{S_1} n_i = \sum_{i=1}^{S_2} m_i = N \; ; \; P_1 = \prod_{i=1}^{S_1} \frac{n_i}{N} = (\frac{a_1}{N})^{S_1} \; ; \; P_2 = \prod_{i=1}^{S_2} \frac{m_i}{N} = (\frac{a_2}{N})^{S_2}$$

$$S_1 < S_2 \Rightarrow P_1 > P_2 \tag{5}$$

Proof. Let $S_1, S_2, N \in \mathbb{N}^*$; $S_1 < S_2$

$$\frac{P_1}{P_2} = \frac{(\frac{a_1}{N})^{S_1}}{(\frac{a_2}{N})^{S_2}} \text{ however } N = a_1 S_1 = a_2 S_2, \text{then}$$

$$= \frac{(\frac{a_1}{a_1 S_1})^{S_1}}{(\frac{a_2}{a_2 S_2})^{S_2}} = \frac{(\frac{1}{S_1})^{S_1}}{(\frac{1}{S_2})^{S_2}} = \frac{S_2^{S_2}}{S_1^{S_1}} > 1$$

$$\frac{P_1}{P_2} > 1, \text{ then } P_1 > P_2$$

Conclusion: This mathematical proof demonstrates that when it comes to equitable distribution, the more categories there are, the lower the stabilizing factor's value becomes.

Case 2 - Non-equitable distribution among categories

This is the case when there are at least two categories that do not have the same frequency.

Lemma 2. *Let D_1 and D_2 be two non-equitable distributions of the same attribute $C(i)$ with, respectively, S_1 and S_2 as the number of categories, so that $S_1 < S_2$.*
$S_1, S_2, N \in \mathbb{N}^*$. $(n_{1,i})_{i=1}^{S_1}$ and $(n_{2,i})_{i=1}^{S_2}$ with $\begin{cases} n_{j,i} \in N^*; \; j \in \{1,2\}; \; i \in [1, S_j] \\ \sum_{i=1}^{S_j} n_{j,i} = N \end{cases}$

$$P_1 = \prod_{i=1}^{S_1} \frac{n_{1,i}}{N} \; ; \; P_2 = \prod_{i=1}^{S_2} \frac{n_{2,i}}{N}$$

$$S_1 < S_2 \Rightarrow P_1 > P_2 \tag{6}$$

Proof. The proof of lemma 2 is available on GitHub (https://urlz.fr/nnyU).

Conclusion: We have the same property.
Whether the distribution is fair or not, when $S_1 < S_2$ then $P_1 > P_2$.

4.4   Evaluation of *Mmaq*

Mmaq have been calculated for a synthetic data set with seven relevant attributes with sensitive information about privacy: National Identity Number (NIN), surname, first name, sex, date of birth, place of birth, disease, and hospital identifier. The dataset we used was composed of 200 lines of data. We use the values of *Mmaq* to classify attributes into relative identifiers, relative quasi-identifiers, and relative anonymous attributes. A relative identifier is associated with a specific database, while a global identifier is unique across the world and can be used to identify entities or individuals regardless of the database.

Table 2 shows the classification of the attributes in our dataset. Each row shows the name, category, metric value, and class of an attribute.

Table 2. Classifaction of attributes based on *Mmaq*

Name	Category	Mmaq	Class
NIN	200	8.758e-247	Identifier
FirstName	134	4.433e-171	Quasi-identifier
PlaceBirth	101	4.470e-157	Quasi-identifier
IdHospital	1	1.0	Anonymous
FirstName + Name	195	2.172e-228	Quasi-identifier
FirstName + Name + DateBirth	200	8.758e-247	Identifier

The number of categories is equivalent to the number of lines, and the *Mmaq* value is nearly zero, thus it is an identifier. For instance, the attribute 'NIN' has two hundred different values out of two hundred lines, so it is classified as an identifier. When the attribute is completely anonymous, the metric value is 1. This is the case for the 'IdHospital' attribute. The *Mmaq* decreases for the attributes 'PlaceBirth' and 'FirstName', which have 101 and 134 categories respectively, making them quasi-identifying attributes.

A drawback of our categorization technique is that it only permits us to perform local operations, meaning that the identifiers, quasi-identifiers, and anonymizers are specific to the dataset.

5   Related Works

Federate the clouds and you will also federate and scale the security problems. These latter are much more challenging in a federation of clouds due to two reasons: it inherits security issues from traditional clouds and new security problems will rise. In fact, even if the inherit security issues are well studied and most of them solved, they still remain challenging in a federation since a security issue is solved does not mean that it is implemented or properly implemented in a cloud provider of the federation. More importantly, some security problems are fundamentally a consequence of the federation of different clouds. These new issues are: longer chain of trust, limited auditability, the risk of malicious service components, liability and legal issues, and shared data privacy [4,18]. The most important and most challenging remain the privacy of shared user personal data.

Many approaches have been proposed to preserve user privacy when exchanging data in the context of clouds. However, traditional privacy management solutions cannot be applied as is in the context of cloud federation because - i) typical management of privacy and data-utility requirements must be extended to support multiple datasets and data owners [18]; ii) the lack of trust among cloud federation members on de-anonymization attacks protection [18]; iii) unclear user data privacy law to apply to what Cloud service due to the cross-border nature of federated Clouds [4]. Despite these limitations, promising methods are proposed to overcome the data privacy problem in a cloud federation.

Anonymization techniques are the key methods used to protect data privacy in clouds. Some well-known techniques such as k-anonymity [3,15], l-diversity [12], t-closeness [11], and differential privacy [8] are used for data anonymization in the federated cloud context. In addition to these well-known methods, specific solutions are proposed for a particular domain. For instance, to preserve privacy in a health data cloud, Abbasi and Mohammadi [1] proposed an anonymization approach that involves first removing the least frequent data that presents the greatest risk using a normal distribution and second, apply an improved k-anonymity through a k-means++ algorithm. Still in the medical domain, in a more scaled federated cloud - ATMOSPHERE, Blanquer et al. anonymize medical image data using in-memory and on-disk encryption in a secure environment following the following four steps: the deployment of the virtual infrastructure, the management of sensitive data through trusted execution environments, the distributed training of a classification model on GPUs attached to containers, and the production use of a trained classifier [5]. The most interesting aspect of their solution is that it reduces security risk even in untrusted cloud backends.

Even though anonymization is necessary to preserve privacy, after anonymization, the risk of re-identification is still a serious challenge and needs to be addressed. For this purpose, Taneja et al. [17] developed an approach to reduce the risk of identification on electronic medical data. They proposed a privacy model that combines k-anonymity, l-diversity, t-proximity, and δ-presence technique to identify the best values for the parameters to minimize risk and maximize the usefulness of the information.

Although these approaches focus on the anonymization of data while taking into account their usefulness and the risk of re-identification of already anonymized data. They give no information on the quality of the level of anonymization of research data. To our knowledge, this not previously been developed in the literature. Our solution makes it possible to assess or judge the quality of data anonymization. This proposal is detailed in the next section, and in the conclusion, a more in-depth comparison with related work is presented.

6   Conclusion and Future Works

In this paper, we proposed a metric to measure the quality of data anonymization in a federated cloud, which takes into account the diversity of data to classify it into one of three categories: identifiers, quasi-identifiers, and anonymous.

The results of our study validated the proposed metric for the federated cloud, allowing data owners or cloud administrators to determine whether the level of data anonymization meets the minimum level of privacy protection. Our method to measure the quality of anonymization of personal data in the context of federated clouds can also be applied to other platforms, such as Big Data.

As part of our future work, we plan to develop a system that uses fuzzy logic to determine how close quasi-identifiers are to anonymous identifiers or attributes. Additionally, we intend to create a tool to assess the level of anonymization of personal data and the risk of re-identification of an individual in a set of anonymized data in a federated cloud.

References

1. Abbasi, A., Mohammadi, B.: A clustering-based anonymization approach for privacy-preserving in the healthcare cloud. Concurrency Comput. Pract. Exper. **34**(1), e6487 (2022)
2. Adetiba, E., et al.: FEDGEN Testbed: a federated genomics private cloud infrastructure for precision medicine and artificial intelligence research. In: Misra, S., Oluranti, J., Damaševičius, R., Maskeliunas, R. (eds.) ICIIA 2021. CCIS, vol. 1547, pp. 78–91. Springer, Cham (2022). https://doi.org/10.1007/978-3-030-95630-1_6
3. Andrew, J., Karthikeyan, J., Jebastin, J.: Privacy preserving big data publication on cloud using Mondrian anonymization techniques and deep neural networks. In: 2019 5th International Conference on Advanced Computing & Communication Systems (ICACCS), pp. 722–727. IEEE (2019)
4. Bernsmed, K., et al.: Thunder in the clouds: security challenges and solutions for federated clouds. In: 4th IEEE International Conference on Cloud Computing Technology and Science Proceedings, pp. 113–120. IEEE (2012)
5. Blanquer, I., et al.: Federated and secure cloud services for building medical image classifiers on an intercontinental infrastructure. Futur. Gener. Comput. Syst. **110**, 119–134 (2020)
6. Brasileiro, F., Brito, A., Blanquer, I.: Atmosphere: Adaptive, trustworthy, manageable, orchestrated, secure, privacy-assuring, hybrid ecosystem for resilient cloud computing. In: 2018 48th Annual IEEE/IFIP International Conference on Dependable Systems and Networks Workshops (DSNW), pp. 51–52. IEEE (2018)

7. Domingo-Ferrer, J., et al.: Privacy-preserving cloud computing on sensitive data: a survey of methods, products and challenges. Comput. Commun. **140**, 38–60 (2019)
8. Dwork, C., Roth, A., et al.: The algorithmic foundations of differential privacy. Found. Trends® Theor. Comput. Sci. **9**(3–4), 211–407 (2014)
9. Ferrer, A.J., et al.: OPTIMIS: a holistic approach to cloud service provisioning. Future Gener. Comput. Syst. **28**(1), 66–77 (2012)
10. George, R.S., Sabitha, S.: Data anonymization and integrity checking in cloud computing. In: 2013 Fourth International Conference on Computing, Communications and Networking Technologies (ICCCNT), pp. 1–5. IEEE (2013)
11. Li, N., Li, T., Venkatasubramanian, S.: t-closeness: privacy beyond kanonymity and l-diversity. In: 2007 IEEE 23rd International Conference on Data Engineering, pp. 106–115. IEEE (2006)
12. Machanavajjhala, A., et al.: l-diversity: Privacy beyond k-anonymity. ACM Trans. Knowl. Disc. Data (TKDD) **1**(1), 3-es (2007)
13. Rochwerger, B., et al.: The reservoir model and architecture for open federated cloud computing. IBM J. Res. Dev. **53**(4), 4 (2009)
14. Rosa, M., et al.: Bionimbuz: a federated cloud platform for bioinformatics applications. In: 2016 IEEE International Conference on Bioinformatics and Biomedicine (BIBM), pp. 548–555. IEEE (2016)
15. Samarati, P., Sweeney, L.: Protecting privacy when disclosing information: k-anonymity and its enforcement through generalization and suppression (1998)
16. Silva, H., et al.: A re-identification risk-based anonymization framework for data analytics platforms. In: 2018 14th European Dependable Computing Conference (EDCC), pp. 101–106. IEEE (2018)
17. Taneja, H., Singh, A.K., et al.: Preserving privacy of patients based on re-identification risk. Procedia Comput. Sci. **70**, 448–454 (2015)
18. Yang, M., et al.: Differentially private data sharing in a cloud federation with blockchain. IEEE Cloud Comput. **5**(6), 69–79 (2018)

Smart City Development Through Collective Intelligence Based on Blockchain-IPFS-Data Analytics

Karidja Dominique Christelle Adje[1,2]([⊠]), Oussama Habachi[2], Asma Ben Letaifa[1], and Majed Haddad[3]

[1] Mediatron Research Lab, Sup'Com, University of Carthage, 77-1054 Tunis, Tunisia
{dominique.adje,asma.benletaifa}@supcom.tn
[2] LIMOS, University of Clermont Auvergne, 63000 Clermont-Ferrand, France
oussama.habachi@uca.fr
[3] LIA, Avignon University, 84029 Avignon, France
majed.haddad@univ-avignon.fr

Abstract. "Alone we go faster, together we go further". This popular quote characterizes exactly the vision on which our article focuses through our proposed collective intelligence system. It allows the different data holders of a country to share and store their large and structured data in a secure way thanks to the blockchain and the IPFS (Inter-Planetary File System). Then, such data are processed in a transparent and ethical way by a government entity. Indeed, to take advantage of all these data, we opt for a data integration approach based on ontology, which will enable to obtain rich and relevant information useful for the development of a smart city. In the literature, some works addressed the data sharing aspect based on blockchain and IPFS in specific domains, while others focused on the data analysis aspect. Our work differs in that it combines all these aspects and extends to several fields in order to achieve a common intelligence serving all dimensions of the smart city.

Keywords: Data Sharing · Blockchain · Smart Contract (SC) · IPFS · GDPR · Data Analytics

1 Introduction

When we talk about a city, we first refer to the buildings, infrastructure, environment. This indeed represents the physical space of a city [1]. However, a city also extends to systems, structures, networks, flows and processes [2] where each actor produces data during the execution of his tasks or activities. These actors are citizens, organizations or institutions like mobile network operators, restaurants, cinemas, hospitals, schools, etc. At the level of organizations, they generally store in their databases activity traces of the people for whom they are responsible. Ma et al. [1] gathered all these actors in the urban social space of a city. With the advent of the internet and smart phones, there are enough virtual activities, on social networks, on web pages. Ma et al. [1] gathered these activities in the cyber space of a city. If we aggregate and integrate the data from these three major components of the urban space mentioned, we will be able to define the city in order to identify its real needs and implement solutions to overcome its challenges. This will result in improving city functioning by making it smart, and thus increase the quality of life of the population: it is a smart city characterized by its sustainability, urbanization, smartness and quality of life [3–5]. However, different actors, especially the citizens, are reluctant to share their data. Indeed, they are not wrong since there are several malicious activities carried out with their data: privacy disclosure, data theft for resale, identity theft, etc. Thus, if we want to make data sharing effective, we must be able to reassure people and institutions about the security of their data and its ethical use. In this context, we propose our solution based on Blockchain, IPFS and data analytics, to enable secure data sharing and ethical treatment of these data with respect to the GDPR (General Data Protection Regulation). To enable efficient analysis of heterogeneous data collected from different sources, our approach integrates an ontology-based model. On the one hand, the combination of blockchain and IPFS as a secure data-sharing system between several actors is increasingly used in the literature, without however detailing the analysis aspect of such shared data. On the other hand, some research focused on data analysis using ontology-based data integration systems. In our case, our proposed model system combines a secure data sharing system and a data analysis system, to achieve a collective intelligence that develops the six smart city domains (smart mobility, smart living, smart people, smart economy, smart government, smart environment). Section II defines the important concepts in our work. Section III presents related work. Section IV details our model system. Section V presents a discussion, and we conclude with Section VI.

2 Definition of Key Concepts

2.1 Blockchain

Blockchain is a technology that enables a decentralized network and is recognized mainly for the immutability and trust it offers [6]. This allows it to ensure data integrity and traceability of actions carried out on this network. There are three types of blockchain.

Public blockchain: this type of blockchain is accessible to all, completely decentralized and works with a consensus mechanism. It is the most secure and transparent. But, given the accessibility to all, it can be confronted with a slowness caused by the validation process of the transactions. Indeed, each transaction requires a peer-to-peer verification before being approved [7]. Also, it is the most exposed to the storage problem that may be insufficient to satisfy a growing number of data [7].

Private blockchain: in this type of blockchain, only authorized users can participate and authorizations are controlled by an organization [8]. Thus, it has the advantage of being faster than the public blockchain since it includes fewer users in the validation process. However, it is less decentralized than the public blockchain. In addition, it is exposed to a security problem related to the centralized system, since there is still a regularization organization [9].

Consortium blockchain: this blockchain combines some characteristics of the other two. This makes it more scalable and faster than the public blockchain. But it is not accessible to everyone and is always controlled by an organization [9].

2.2 Smart Contract

A smart contract is a set of computer code lines stored on a blockchain. It is automatically executed according to the agreements made between the different network participants [10].

2.3 IPFS

Inter-Planetary File System (IPFS) is a peer-to-peer distributed file system allowing data sharing between its different nodes and large data storage [7]. It is based on a hash table that allows to know who uses the data and which data are used. Its particularity is that it uses content-based addressing [11], i.e., the data files are not all stored in one place, but are instead divided into several pieces and distributed to all nodes in the network. This ensures duplication of the files, preventing temporary or permanent loss of data.

2.4 Data Analytics

To really know a user and a city's daily life, it is necessary to know different profiles in terms of behavior, preferences and intentions, thanks to a careful analysis of the collected data. This analysis consists to discover correlations or patterns in these data, extract useful information and make predictions, thanks to data mining and ML (Machine Learning) techniques [12].

3 Related Work

An emerging architecture, enabling agility, intelligence, and automation and focused on data has been proposed [13]. However, the storage method used is the cloud. This means that the solution requires trust in cloud providers. While we precisely want to avoid trusting a third party for data storage, in order to increase data security and increase the trust of data holders. To improve diagnostic accuracy in healthcare systems, Hassan et al. [14] proposed using blockchain to enable secure sharing of reliable data, and then process such data through ML. However, they do not specify the technique for storing data and their architecture is limited to the healthcare domain. Al Asad et al. [15] proposed a blockchain-based healthcare data sharing approach to efficiently share data between several actors, such as the patients and the hospitals. They also focused on data interoperability, which involved using standards to facilitate data exchange between these stakeholders. However, in our case, data sharing only occurs between the data holders and the government entity, and we also address the collective analysis component. Bhattacharya et al. [16] are in the same context of blockchain-based data analytics, but they used a centralized server for storing EHR (electronic health record). The problem with a centralized server is that it is exposed to a single failure problem [17], which can lead to a temporary unavailability of services. Therefore, to address this problem, Makina et al. [17] proposed to use a consortium blockchain for data sharing between health actors and the user, and then an IPFS for decentralized data storage. However, the work deals with a specific case of the smart city which is the smart-health. Moreover, the data processing is only done at the level of edge devices such as a smart phone, while in our paper, we deal with all domains of the smart city with a collective data processing aspect. To secure access to IPFS and have a clear traceability of the actions taken, Nyaletey et al. [18] opted for a private blockchain, while Alizadeh et al. [7] used a public blockchain. However, in these two papers, the authors also did not address the collective data processing aspect. In the same vein, Hasan et al. [19] focused on the implementation of a secure data-sharing system based on blockchain and IPFS. Alamri et al. [20] adopted the same approach, but focused on the data exchange standards to be used to ensure data interoperability. However, they did not specify how these data are integrated and analyzed in order to obtain relevant information. The work of Vitor et al. [21] is part of our context of promoting data sharing. Indeed, the authors proposed an open data platform to aggregate environmental and mobility data, mainly from vehicular sensors, in order to make them available and usable by third parties. However, their work did not include prediction and used centralized data storage that sometimes faces the problem of scalability and single failure problem. Once data have been collected, an effective integration method is needed to facilitate analysis. In this context, Saha et al. [22] and Adel et al. [23] focused mainly on the data integration aspect by proposing an ontology-based approach.

Our Contribution
In our paper, we propose a collective intelligence system combining secure sharing and storage of massive data, analysis of these data and their applications in the smart city. It is described as follows:

- Data source: data are obtained via data holders, i.e., the citizens, environmental data collectors (traffic, climate, air, etc.) and organizations/institutions such as mobile network operators, restaurants, cinemas, hospitals, schools, etc. Thus, the data collected are heterogeneous.
- Sharing and storing data via public Blockchain-IPFS: we choose public blockchain because it offers more transparency and security than the other two types of blockchain. And our goal is to allow transparent and secure data sharing without intermediaries, to reassure people and institutions about the security of their data and its ethical use. The IPFS solves the problem of data overload that the blockchain can face, by storing all the real data files. Then, the metadata of these files related to the transactions are recorded in the blockchain (metadata is much smaller than the raw data [9]). Also, data is encrypted during sharing as well as storage, to enhance data security.
- Collective data analysis using data mining and ML techniques: to have good results, the data analyzed must be reliable and of good quality (complete and accurate data). Thus, blockchain allows to have reliable data while efficient data integration techniques allow to have more accurate information. In our case, we opt for a data integration approach based on ontology, as this enables the semantic representation and structuring of data relating to specific domains using concepts, relations, and axioms [22]. Once this treatment is done, particular events can be easily predicted thanks to ML techniques.
- Applications resulting from data analysis are applied in the city to make it smarter.

4 Our System Model

4.1 Description of the System Model (Fig. 1)

Data Storage by each Actor or Data Holder

Sensors Data. Environmental data such as climate, traffic, air, etc. are detected and provided via sensors.

Structured Data from Organizations/Institutions. These are structured data on people's daily activities. Examples: CDR (call detail record) data from mobile network operators; entertainment data from cinemas, restaurants, etc.; education and culture data from schools; demographic data (gender, workers, unemployed, children, youth etc.) that can be obtained from government institutions. In addition, we propose that a governmental institution be responsible for collecting and structuring the data from the social networks.

Citizen's Data. It concerns personal data (installed applications, pages visited on the Internet, GPS, etc.) of users from all the devices they use (smart phone, connected watch, laptop, etc.). The goal is to better understand the profiles of the inhabitants in terms of interests and preferences, since they may have different behaviors on each of their devices.

All these data obtained from the three sources mentioned are first pre-processed locally at each actor's level, before being shared. This pre-processing serves to anonymize the personal data and to structure them. Anonymization is to prevent people from being identified, in accordance with the rule on privacy protection established by the GDPR. Data structuring is to facilitate final data processing in the data analytics module.

Our Smart Contract Services. A smart contract is used to connect to services and call them through requests [7]. Thus, in our system model, our smart contract serves as a bridge between the blockchain and IPFS, executing our functionalities according to the agreement established between the different system actors. Thus, the services of our smart contract are as follows.

Each Data Holder or Actor has Access Only to the Data they have Shared. It is to protect the confidentiality of the actors' real data. Because it is well-known that, for example, given the existing competitiveness between organizations in the same field, they prefer their internal data to be confidential. This service will therefore allow actors to share their data with trust.

Data Storage. Data are storage in IPFS in an encrypted form. Since our ontology will contain precious information, it will also be stored in IPFS and accessed via the blockchain for greater security.

Data Processing is Done by the Data Analytics Module Managed by the Country's Government. In fact, it is a committee of experts and scientific researchers in data analytics, supervised by the government. It will be responsible for processing these data with efficient data mining and ML techniques. The aim is to extract valuable information from such reliable and integrated data, allowing useful services to be provided for smart city development. To be sure that the data are processed in a legal and ethical way, every action taken on these data will be recorded in the blockchain, in order to inform all actors. This service will increase the trust of the different actors, regarding the security of their data and its ethical use. Figure 2 shows the sequence diagram of the general operation of our system.

The major problem at this stage is the interoperability and integration of these heterogeneous data. Concerning data interoperability, to ensure effective data exchange, our system will need to be compatible with several data formats, such as CSV, JSON, XML, EHR standards. After recovering and decrypting the data in their original format, the next step is integration. To ensure the integration of heterogeneous data, we will first transform them into local ontologies, and then form a global ontology: it is a hybrid ontology approach. That approach is suitable for the semantic integration of different information from data sources, and it facilitates data source addition or deletion [24]. Once the global ontology is established, searching for relevant information becomes easier, making it possible to better understand the data and predict particular events using ML algorithms. Figure 3 shows this module.

Remove Access Rights. Data holders can reverse their decision at any time by removing access to their data.

4.2 Resulting Applications

This collective intelligence aims to improve each of the following smart city dimensions.

Smart Mobility. It will help the transport system, with route management and urbanization adapted to the mobility of all people (young, child, handicaped, etc.).

Smart Living. At the health level, for example, we will be able to have predictions of potential critical illnesses or pandemics; we will be able to know precisely the diseases to which the populations are most exposed, in order to take the appropriate precautions. In addition, thanks to the recommendations systems, the populations will be able to easily find exactly what they are looking for, thus improving their quality of life.

Smart Economy. There are activities recommendations that will be proposed to the populations, according to the interests and preferences resulting from the data analytics. Thus, organizations operating in these different areas of activity (leisure, tourism, catering, clothing, etc.) will be able to increase their customer base, thus generating incomes.

Smart Environment. This system will allow to know efficiently how the environment is managed, what are the challenges it faces and what are the consequences that will be generated.

Smart People. This system will allow to know the population needs in terms of education and skills, in order to make appropriate decisions.

Smart Government. The data analytics module managed by the government is an application of the smart government, since it will allow the government to easily know the society and its population, in order to better manage it by carrying out adapted actions.

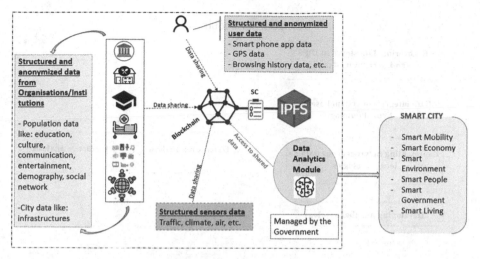

Fig. 1. Our system model.

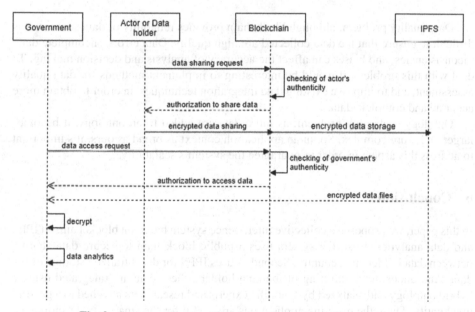

Fig. 2. Sequence diagram of the general operation of our system.

5   Discussion

Time execution problem: in this article, we have opted for the public blockchain. It offers greater transparency and security, which are essential features to motivate a city's stakeholders to share their data. However, as the network grows, this blockchain faces the problem of task execution time. Thus, a research direction to explore is to find a way to significantly reduce the execution time despite the size of the network.

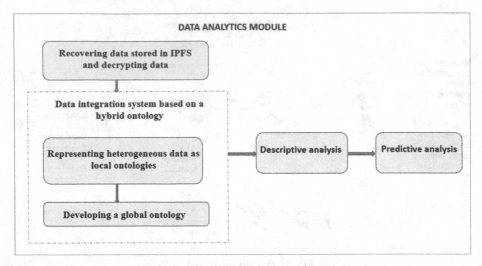

Fig. 3. Description of data analytics module.

Data quality problem: although blockchain provides reliability of data sources, it is difficult to ensure that the data collected are high quality. Data errors, incomplete data, inconsistencies, and biases can affect the accuracy of analysis and decision making. To deal with this problem, it would be interesting to implement methods for data quality assessment, and to improve existing data integration techniques, in order to obtain more accurate and complete data.

Ontology scalability problem: as more data are added to an ontology, it becomes larger and more complex. So, in an application context as broad as ours, it's important to address this aspect in order to guarantee the system's scalability.

6   Conclusion

In this paper, we proposed a collective intelligence system based on blockchain, an IPFS and data analytics. First, the system uses a public blockchain to secure data sharing between data holders in a country. Second, it uses IPFS for decentralized storage of big data. And under the monitoring of the data holders, these data are integrated using a hybrid ontology and analyzed by scientific experts and researchers attached to a government entity. Then, the resulting applications are useful for the smart city development. For our future work, we will focus on improving our system by addressing the challenges outlined in the previous section, and then we will implement it.

References

1. Ma, Y., Li, G., Xie, H., Zhang, H.: City Profile: using smart data to create digital urban spaces. ISPRS Ann. Photogram. Remote Sens. Spatial Inf. Sci., 75–82 (2018)
2. Batty, M.: The New Science of Cities. The MIT Press, London (2013)

3. Anthopoulos, L.: Understanding the smart city domain: a literature review. Public Adm. Inf. Technol. **8**, 9–21 (2015). https://doi.org/10.1007/978-3-319-03167-5_2
4. Silva, B.N., Khan, M., Han, K.: Towards sustainable smart cities: a review of trends, architectures, components, and open challenges in smart cities. Sustain. Cities Soc. **38**, 697–713 (2018)
5. Camero, A., Alba, E.: Smart city and information technology: a review. Cities **93**, 84–94 (2019)
6. Lemieux, V.L.: Blockchain and distributed ledgers as trusted record-keeping systems: An archival theoretic evaluation framework. In: Future Technologies Conference (FTC), pp. 1–11, Vancouver (2017)
7. Alizadeh, M., Anderson, K., Schelén, O.: Efficient decentralized data storage based on public blockchain and IPFS. In: 2020 IEEE Asia-Pacific Conference on Computer Science and Data Engineering (CSDE), IEEE, Gold Coast (2020)
8. McLean, S., Deane-Johns, S.: Demystifying blockchain and distributed ledger technology – hype or hero? Comput. Law Rev. Int. **17**(4), 97–102 (2016). https://doi.org/10.9785/cri-2016-0402
9. Islam, M.R., Rahman, M.M., Mahmud, M., Rahman, M.A., Mohamad, M.H.S., Embong, A.H.: A review on blockchain security issues and challenges. In: 2021 IEEE 12th Control and System Graduate Research Colloquium (ICSGRC), IEEE, Shah Alam (2021)
10. Cong, L.W., He, Z.: Blockchain disruption and smart contracts. Rev. Financ. Stud. **32**(5), 1754–1797 (2019)
11. Kumar, S., Bharti, A.K., Amin, R.: Decentralized secure storage of medical records using Blockchain and IPFS: a comparative analysis with future directions. Secur. Priv. **4**(5) (2021). https://doi.org/10.1002/spy2.162
12. Souza, J.T., Francisco, A.C., Piekarski, C.M., Prado, G.F.: Data mining and machine learning to promote smart cities: a systematic review from 2000 to 2018. Sustainability **11**(4), 1077 (2019)
13. Nguyen, D.C., et al.: Enabling AI in future wireless networks: a data life cycle perspective. IEEE Commun. Surv. Tutorials **23**(1), 553–595 (2021)
14. Hassan, M., Chen, J., Zhu, C., Zukaib, U.: Adoption of blockchain-based artificial intelligence in healthcare. In: 2022 5th International Conference on Artificial Intelligence and Big Data (ICAIBD), IEEE, Chengdu (2022)
15. Al Asad, N., Elahi, M.T., Al Hassan A., Yousuf, M.A.: Permission-based blockchain with proof of authority for secured healthcare data sharing. In: 2020 2nd International Conference on Advanced Information and Communication Technology (ICAICT), IEEE, Dhaka (2020)
16. Bhattacharya, P., Tanwar, S., Bodkhe, U., Tyagi, S., Kumar, N.: BinDaaS: blockchain-based deep-learning as-a-service in healthcare 4.0 applications. IEEE Trans. Network Sci. Eng. **8**(2), 1242–1255 (2021). https://doi.org/10.1109/TNSE.2019.2961932
17. Makina, H., Ben Letaifa, A., Rachedi, A.: Leveraging edge computing, blockchain and IPFS for addressing ehealth records challenges. In: 2022 15th International Conference on Security of Information and Networks (SIN), IEEE, Sousse (2022)
18. Nyaletey, E., Parizi, R.M., Zhang, Q., Choo, K.: BlockIPFS- Blockchain-enabled interplanetary file system for forensic and trusted data traceability. In: 2nd IEEE International Conference on Blockchain (Blockchain), IEEE, Atlanta (2019)
19. Hasan, H.R., Salah, K., Yaqoob, I., Jayaraman, R., Pesic, S., Omar, M.: Trustworthy IoT data streaming using blockchain and IPFS. IEEE Access **10**, 17707–17721 (2022)
20. Alamri, B., Javed, I.T., Margaria, T.: A GDPR-compliant framework for IoT-based personal health records using blockchain. In: 2021 11th IFIP International Conference on New Technologies, Mobility and Security (NTMS), IEEE, Paris (2021)

21. Vitor, G., Rito, P., Sargento, S.: Smart city data platform for real-time processing and data sharing. In: 2021 IEEE Symposium on Computers and Communications (ISCC), IEEE, Athens (2021)
22. Saha, S., Usman, Z., Jones, S., Kshirsagar, R., Li, W.: Towards a formal ontology to support interoperability across multiple product lifecycle domains. In: 2017 IEEE 11th International Conference on Semantic Computing (ICSC), IEEE, San Diego (2017)
23. Adel, E., Barakat, S., Elmogy, M.: Distributed electronic health records semantic interoperability based on a fuzzy ontology architecture. In: 2019 14th International Conference on Computer Engineering and Systems (ICCES), IEEE, Cairo (2019)
24. Alkhamisi, A.O., Saleh, M.: Ontology opportunities and challenges: discussions from semantic data integration perspectives. In: 2020 6th Conference on Data Science and Machine Learning Applications (CDMA), IEEE, Riyadh (2020)

Data Engineering, Cyber Security and Pervasive Services

Wearable IoT Sensor Combining Deep Learning for Enhanced Human Activity Recognition in Indoor and Outdoor Settings

Ala Mhalla[✉]🆔 and Jean-Marie Favreau🆔

Laboratoire LIMOS, CNRS UMR 6158, Université Clermont Auvergne,
63170 Aubière, France
ala.mhalla@uca.fr

Abstract. Human Activity Recognition (HAR) plays a pivotal role within a broader framework aimed at continuously monitoring human behaviors across various domains, including medical diagnosis, elderly care, rehabilitation, entertainment, and smart surveillance. This paper introduces an innovative HAR system that leverages the capabilities of wearable devices in conjunction with deep learning techniques. Its primary objective is to accurately identify physical activities performed by individuals in both indoor and outdoor environments.

The designed wearable sensor incorporates an Inertial Measurement Unit (IMU) and a Wi-Fi module, enabling data transmission to a cloud service and providing direct Internet connectivity. This sensor is integrated with a Convolutional Neural Network (CNN) architecture optimized for resource-efficient inference, making it suitable for deployment on cost-effective or embedded devices. Additionally, it enables real-time local activity prediction.

The system is custom-tailored for physical activity monitoring and achieves an impressive accuracy rate of 98,8% in distinguishing various activities.

Keywords: IoT · Second Human Activity Recognition (HAR) · Wearable device · Convolutional Neural Network (CNN)

1 Introduction

In recent years, wearable sensors have become increasingly important in both research and practical applications. The growing interest in these sensors is due to their versatility, made possible by their shrinking size and lower costs. They have a wide range of uses, such as monitoring sports and physical activities [15, 17], intelligent transportation system [14], and facilitating human-computer interaction [1]. This last point is especially crucial because the elderly population is growing, which presents significant challenges in both social terms [16].

Smart and wearable technologies have the potential to substantially enhance the quality of human life in an economically efficient manner while also diminishing the reliance on social and healthcare services. This is why active aging

O. Habachi et al. (Eds.): UNet 2023, LNCS 14757, pp. 43–53, 2024.
https://doi.org/10.1007/978-3-031-62488-9_4

scenarios, supported by these technologies [12], are gaining importance on a global scale, as evidenced by the numerous ongoing research initiatives and programs.

In this context, wearable sensors offer a wide range of possibilities, from basic panic button functionality to the continuous monitoring of the user's physiological parameters [5]. Among these applications, Human Activity Recognition (HAR) plays a significant role. It is widely recognized that an active lifestyle is fundamental to good health [11,15]. Therefore, it is possible to assess users' lifestyles by monitoring their physical activity levels, ultimately constructing a behavioral model. Such a model can be valuable for the early detection of anomalies that may be relevant to well-being.

Furthermore, to create a precise behavioral profile, it is essential to accurately identify the type of activity in which the user is engaged (e.g., walking, jogging, ascending/descending stairs). For example, a user may maintain regular movement, such as walking, but start avoiding more strenuous activities like stair climbing. This change in behavior could indicate increasing fatigue, which may suggest a potential decline in health conditions deserving further investigation.

Additional information can be gathered by incorporating the sensor into a more comprehensive IoT system [3]. Furthermore, concerning HAR algorithms, substantial progress has been made in automatically recognizing human activities. This is achieved by analyzing data from sources such as video cameras [7] or by integrating data from various types of sensors [8]. Deep learning has unlocked new possibilities for intelligent assistance in both indoor and outdoor environments, even in the presence of chronic patients [13].

It's crucial to emphasize that in the context of HAR, the device's ergonomics and user-friendliness are of paramount importance. The device should be worn 24/7 without causing any inconvenience to the user. For instance, although smartphones integrate all the necessary sensors and are used extensively throughout the day, they are not designed for continuous wear. Therefore, there's a need to develop devices and sensors that cater to these requirements.

Furthermore, it's essential to acknowledge that the quality of machine learning models heavily relies on the dataset used for training. A dataset that closely resembles real-world scenarios and is trained on specific users being monitored can ensure the highest level of activity recognition accuracy. Additionally, the ability to update the trained model is crucial for achieving optimal system performance, regardless of the number of users.

With the advancement of the Internet of Things (IoT) concept, it's now feasible to implement system architectures that connect the device directly to cloud services. This approach minimizes the number of devices involved in data acquisition and transmission, subsequently reducing costs, user burdens, and the level of technical expertise required [4,6].

In this paper, we introduce a HAR system that utilizes a wearable sensor and Deep Learning techniques. The system is designed to harness the capabilities of smart and wearable devices for recognizing physical activities in both indoor and outdoor environments.

In a broad overview, our architecture leverages the Arduino Nano chip and a neural network. The network is optimized to perform computationally intensive tasks, such as the training phase, on the cloud, while conducting real-time activity recognition on an embedded or low-cost local device. This design allows the system to predict activities in real time and transmit only the activity label instead of vast amounts of sensor data.

It's essential to note that our focus is on real-time activity recognition and long-term personalized activity monitoring among the patients. This monitoring aims to identify abnormal behaviors that may indicate health issues or emergent situations.

The structure of this paper is as follows: Sect. 2 provides an overview of related works, while Sect. 3 describes our proposed system, including details about the wearable device, the selection of neural network architecture. Section 4 presents the validation of the system through tests and subsequent discussions of the results. Finally, Sect. 5 concludes the article.

2   Related Works

Deep learning, a powerful computational technique, has gained significant attention in recent years due to its ability to automatically learn complex patterns from large and intricate datasets [15]. This approach has found numerous applications in various domains, and healthcare is no exception. The proliferation of sensor-equipped smartphones and wearable devices has revolutionized the way health data is collected and analyzed [10].

HAR is a critical component in various healthcare contexts, including monitoring patients, tracking physical activities, and identifying anomalies that could be indicative of health issues [11]. In essence, it involves recognizing and classifying different physical activities individuals engage in, such as walking, climbing stairs, or jogging.

A significant breakthrough in HAR came with the integration of wearable sensors and deep learning techniques. Traditional methods often relied on manually engineered features extracted from sensor data, which could be time-consuming and less accurate. In contrast, deep learning models, particularly Convolutional Neural Networks (CNNs) and Long Short-Term Memory (LSTM) networks, automatically learn discriminative features from raw sensor data, significantly improving accuracy and reducing the need for domain-specific knowledge [9, 15].

For example, in one study [20], researchers demonstrated that CNNs could capture local dependencies and scale-invariant features, enabling accurate recognition of variations within the same activity, resulting in an accuracy rate of 96.88%. These findings underscored the potential of deep learning in HAR, particularly when applied to mobile and wearable devices.

In practical applications, deep learning-powered HAR systems can be deployed on low-power wearable devices, making real-time activity recognition feasible without the need for additional hardware [18]. This approach has been implemented as Android apps and embedded algorithms, ensuring minimal computational requirements while delivering reliable results.

Furthermore, combining data from multiple body-worn inertial sensors and processing it using deep architectures, such as CNNs, can enhance the accuracy and robustness of HAR systems. These systems excel in handling intra-class variability (variations in how individuals perform the same activity) and inter-class similarity (similarities between activities like jogging and running).

In summary, the integration of wearable sensors with deep learning techniques has transformed the field of Human Activity Recognition, enabling accurate, real-time activity classification across various healthcare scenarios. These advancements have the potential to improve patient monitoring, enhance well-being management, and contribute to active aging initiatives while reducing the burden on healthcare and social services.

3   Proposed System

The system's structure is illustrated in Fig. 1. During the training phase, data collected by the wearable sensor are transmitted to the cloud. However, during daily use, this data can be processed either on the device itself or sent to another device for further analysis. For prototyping purposes, the data are processed offline and used to create datasets, which are essential for developing the neural network presented in this study.

Once the model is trained, we implement the personalized model within the device. The device then begins predicting activities in real-time during the inference phase. It sends activity labels to the cloud, enabling the synthesis of physical activities over various timeframes, such as an hour, a month, and so on.

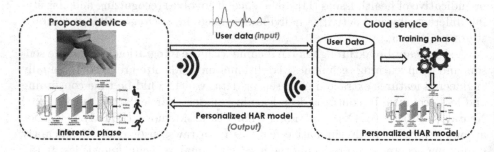

Fig. 1. The system architecture.

3.1   Hardware Platform

This section provides a detailed overview of the proposed wearable device called "EMob Device" on which we implemented our personalized DCNN model for testing and evaluating their performance in real-world scenarios.

The prototype of the wearable sensor (Fig. 2) is based on the Arduino Nano, which integrates an Inertial Measurement Unit (IMU) containing a 3D accelerometer, gyroscope, and magnetometer, along with a Wi-Fi module and an ATMega328P Microcontroller unit (MCU). The MCU of the Arduino Nano operates on an 8-bit architecture at a clock speed of 80 MHz and includes a network processor compliant with the IEEE 802.11b/g/n network protocol for radio communication.

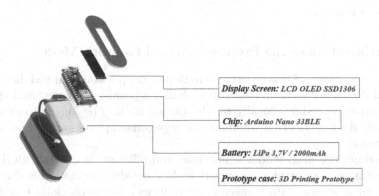

Display Screen: *LCD OLED SSD1306*

Chip: *Arduino Nano 33BLE*

Battery: *LiPo 3,7V / 2000mAh*

Prototype case: *3D Printing Prototype*

Fig. 2. The designed device consists of the following components, which have been integrated into a 3D model: Arduino Nano chip served as the fundamental hardware component for our embedded system, LCD display screen to facilitate visualization of predicted activities, 3.7V/2000mAh battery and prototype case manufactured by digital 3D printing.

In terms of ergonomics, a more compact board redesign is planned. The sensors' full-scale ranges are programmable, with acceleration sensing up to $\pm 8g$ and a magnetometer sensitivity of $\pm 4800 \mu T$, while the gyroscope operates within a full-scale range of $\pm 250°/\text{sec}$. All sensors have been configured to sample data at a rate of 50 Hz.

The wearable sensor connects directly to the Internet through the Wi-Fi module. Users simply need to press a button on the device, and a single LED pattern provides feedback. No technical expertise is required, making it user-friendly for installation.

Data is transmitted to the online cloud platform using the MQTT protocol with a Quality of Service (QoS) level of 2, ensuring reliable message delivery. The payload of the message is in JSON format, reporting the sensor's status.

Each wearable device has a unique ID, facilitating association with the cloud environment. This results in a truly "plug-and-play" experience. While the collected data on its own may not provide meaningful information, it requires interpretation to infer details about the user's actual activity, such as walking or sitting.

One approach could involve transmitting every sensor sample to the cloud for subsequent processing and interpretation. However, this means that the radio section, which is the most energy-intensive component of the sensor, is continuously active, thereby reducing battery life. To validate the entire approach, energy consumption of the sensor is considered.

To account for real-world usage scenarios, a low-capacity battery (Li-Ion 3.7V/2000mAh) was chosen, primarily due to ergonomic constraints related to size and weight. Human motion analysis often requires a high sampling rate of up to 50 samples per second. In addition to that, we incorporated an LCD display screen to provide users with a visual interface for viewing the predicted activities in real-time.

3.2   Architecture of the Proposed Neural Network Model

One of the objectives of this research is to deploy deep learning model directly on devices and personalize them based on each user's profile, while performing these personaliztion procedures locally on the device itself. The aim is to create an eco-friendly deep model that minimizes energy consumption and computational requirements.

By making the deep model lightweight and efficient, it can be run directly on devices such as smartphones, smartwatches, or edge devices. This eliminates the need for extensive data transfers and reduces reliance on cloud-based computations. This idea offers several advantages, including enhanced data privacy as user information remains on the device, reducing the need for external data transmission.

To achieve this, we propose a compact Deep Convolutional Neural Network (DCNN) that can be seamlessly integrated into mobile embedded devices, providing a satisfactory level of accuracy while ensuring minimal battery consumption.

In the first stage, we encode the multi-sensor time series data as a spatial grid consisting of values. Following this, the grid is segmented into a set of data sequences using a sliding window methodology. These data sequences are subsequently employed as input to the model for subsequent analysis and processing. The model architecture consists of two consecutive convolutional layers, one pooling layer, two fully connected layers, and a softmax layer used for predicting the probabilities of different physical activities. The architecture of the proposed DCNN network is depicted in Fig. 3.

4   Experimental Results

This section presents the various tests performed to evaluate the performance of our personalization model on several public HAR datasets.

4.1   Datasets

We have chosen two HAR datasets to evaluate our wearable device and personalized DCNN model. These datasets have been selected because they collectively

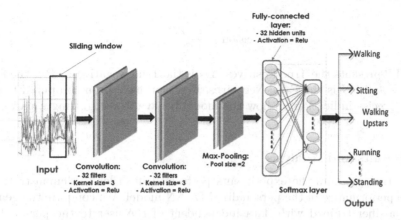

Fig. 3. Illustration of the proposed DCNN architecture used for a multi-sensor based human activity recognition problems.

encompass a broad spectrum of users, ranging in age from 23 to 65. The specific details are provided below.

The evaluation is performed on two datasets:

- **SHO dataset [19]:** This is one of the two datasets used for evaluation. SHO dataset contains labeled data of accelerometer, gyroscope and linear acceleration collected while subjects were performing 7 activities (walking, running, sitting, standing, jogging, biking, walking upstairs and walking downstairs).
- **UCI dataset [2]:** This is the second evaluation dataset, and it was collected with a group of 30 volunteers. Each subject performed six activities including walking, walking-upstairs, walking-downstairs, laying, sitting and standing.

4.2 Descriptions of Experiments

For each user in the evaluated dataset, we divided the data into 2/3 for personalization and 1/3 for the test. For each of the randomly formed holds ensure no overlap in user data. Further all classes (e.g. walking, running) in training also appear in testing.

We used a sliding window mechanism to segment the original raw sensor signal with a window width equal to 100 readings and with an overlap of 50%.

4.3 Evaluated Algorithms

Performance evaluation is done in terms of these parameters which are Accuracy, and Precision.

$$\text{Accuracy} = \frac{TP + TN}{TP + TN + FP + FN} \tag{1}$$

$$\text{Precision} = \frac{TP}{TP + FP} \tag{2}$$

where TP presents the True Positives, TN is the True Negatives, FP is the False Positives and FN is the False Negatives. Precision have been computed to give a more precise indication on how the model behave in recognizing a particular class.

4.4 Results and Analysis

This section presents the experiments performed in order to demonstrate the relative performance of the personalized DCNN model. We compare the generic HAR classifier trained with data independent of the user to the personalized HAR classifier trained with user-specific data.

Given each dataset and its annotation, we present the classification accuracy of the generic DCNN model, the personalized HAR one. Furthermore, the final line of both tables give the improvement between the generic HAR and the personalized one. The latter has a better accuracy than the generic model in all the performed experiments.

Table 1 shows that the personalized HAR classifier significantly outperforms the generic one. The median improvement is **187%** on all public datasets.

Table 1. Comparison of classification accuracy between a generic model and a personalized one

Approach/Dataset	SHO	UCI
Generic HAR	36%	32%
Personalized HAR	**98.8%**	**96%**
Improvement/generic	174%	200%

Table 1 demonstrates that the personalized HAR classifier that provides a superior performance than a generic one in several datasets.

A global accuracy of 98,8% has been reached. In Fig. 4, the confusion matrix related to the test-set in SHO datatset is shown. The confusion matrix indicates that there is no confusion between activity categories, illustrating the effectiveness of the DCNN model in distinguishing between activities.

4.5 Testing the Device in Various Real-World Scenarios:

Table 2 presents the different characteristics and computational cost of personalized HAR model in our embedded device tested in various real-world scenarios, including inference time, battery autonomy and storage size for model.

The resulting product offers a functional device for HAR applications in real-world conditions, which has the advantages of low cost, low power consumption, and high performance.

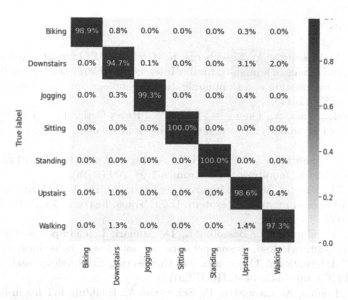

Fig. 4. Confusion matrix related to the test set of the SHO dataset in the case of using an accelerometer, a gyroscope, and a magnetometer.

Table 2. Description of running our personalized model on the proposed wearable device

Specification	Inference time (s)	Model Size (kB)	Battery autonomy (h)
Personalized model	1.6	80.3	12h in use, 24h in semi-standby

5   Conclusion and Future Work

This paper introduces an innovative IoT system for personalized person's activities in both indoor and outdoor environments. The system combines inertial sensors, Wi-Fi wearable sensors, and Deep Learning Techniques integrated in one device to provide information about various activities, aiming to detect abnormal behaviors. The approach can be expanded to systems requiring multiple wearable sensors to offer personalized insights.

The activity classification model can accurately classify data from various activities, achieving a high accuracy rate of 98.8% on the SHO dataset, even with a relatively small training dataset. This result demonstrates the ease of implementing various HAR systems tailored to different problem classes, such as different age groups.

However, the advantage of the proposed IoT device is energy efficiency achieved by processing and compressing data on the sensor itself before sending it to the cloud. Further battery savings may be possible in the future to extend the device's autonomy throughout the day.

Currently, one of our future works is to link the device with a web application to enable doctors to monitor their patients.

References

1. Ancans, A., Rozentals, A., Nesenbergs, K., Greitans, M.: Inertial sensors and muscle electrical signals in human-computer interaction. In 2017 6th International Conference on Information and Communication Technology and Accessibility (ICTA), pp. 1–6. IEEE (2017)
2. Anguita, D., Ghio, A., Oneto, L., Parra, X., Reyes-Ortiz, J.L.: A public domain dataset for human activity recognition using smartphones. In: Esann, vol. 3, p. 3 (2013)
3. Bassoli, M., Bianchi, V., De Munari, I.: A plug and play IoT Wi-Fi smart home system for human monitoring. Electronics 7(9), 200 (2018)
4. Bassoli, M., Bianchi, V., De Munari, I., Ciampolini, P.: An IoT approach for an AAL Wi-Fi-based monitoring system. IEEE Trans. Instrum. Meas. 66(12), 3200–3209 (2017)
5. Bianchi, V., Guerra, C., Bassoli, M., De Munari, I., Ciampolini, P.: The helicopter project: wireless sensor network for multi-user behavioral monitoring. In: 2017 International Conference on Engineering, Technology and Innovation (ICE/ITMC), pp. 1445–1454. IEEE (2017)
6. Bisio, I., Delfino, A., Lavagetto, F., Sciarrone, A.: Enabling IoT for in-home rehabilitation: accelerometer signals classification methods for activity and movement recognition. IEEE Internet Things J. 4(1), 135–146 (2016)
7. Cagnoni, S., Matrella, G., Mordonini, M., Sassi, F., Ascari, L.: Sensor fusion-oriented fall detection for assistive technologies applications. In: 2009 Ninth International Conference on Intelligent Systems Design and Applications, pp. 673–678. IEEE (2009)
8. Davis, K., et al.: Activity recognition based on inertial sensors for ambient assisted living. In: 2016 19th International Conference on Information Fusion (fusion), pp. 371–378. IEEE (2016)
9. Hammerla, N.Y., Halloran, S., Plötz, T.: Deep, convolutional, and recurrent models for human activity recognition using wearables. arXiv preprint arXiv:1604.08880 (2016)
10. Hassannejad, H., Matrella, G., Ciampolini, P., De Munari, I., Mordonini, M., Cagnoni, S.: Food image recognition using very deep convolutional networks. In: Proceedings of the 2nd International Workshop on Multimedia Assisted Dietary Management, pp. 41–49 (2016)
11. Kehler, D.S., et al.: A systematic review of the association between sedentary behaviors with frailty. Exper. Gerontol. 114, 1–12 (2018)
12. Malwade, S., et al.: Mobile and wearable technologies in healthcare for the ageing population. Comput. Methods Programs Biomed. 161, 233–237 (2018)
13. Mendes, D., Lopes, M., Parreira, P., Fonseca, C.: Deep learning and IoT to assist multi morbidity home based healthcare (2017)
14. Mhalla, A., Chateau, T., Gazzah, S., Amara, N.E.B.: An embedded computer-vision system for multi-object detection in traffic surveillance. IEEE Trans. Intell. Transp. Syst. 20(11), 4006–4018 (2018)
15. Mhalla, A., Favreau, J.-M.: Toward personalized human activity recognition model with auto-supervised learning framework. In: 2021 IEEE International Conference on Multimedia and Expo (ICME), pp. 1–6. IEEE (2021)
16. United Nations Department of Economic and Social Affairs. World population prospects: The 2017 revision — multimedia library (2017)

17. Qiu, H., Wang, X., Xie, F.: A survey on smart wearables in the application of fitness. In: 2017 IEEE 15th International Conference on Dependable, Autonomous and Secure Computing, 15th International Conference on Pervasive Intelligence and Computing, 3rd International Conference on Big Data Intelligence and Computing and Cyber Science and Technology Congress (DASC/PiCom/DataCom/CyberSciTech), pp. 303–307. IEEE (2017)
18. Ravi, D., Wong, C., Lo, B., Yang, G.-Z.: Deep learning for human activity recognition: a resource efficient implementation on low-power devices. In: 2016 IEEE 13th International Conference on Wearable and Implantable Body Sensor Networks (BSN), pp. 71–76. IEEE (2016)
19. Shoaib, M., Bosch, S., Incel, O.D., Scholten, H., Havinga, P.J.M.: Fusion of smartphone motion sensors for physical activity recognition. Sensors **14**(6), 10146–10176 (2014)
20. Zeng, M., et al.: Convolutional neural networks for human activity recognition using mobile sensors. In: 6th International Conference on Mobile Computing, Applications and Services, pp. 197–205. IEEE (2014)

On the Use of Autoencoders in Unsupervised Learning for Intrusion Detection Systems

Lea Astrid Kenmogne Mekemte and Gerard Chalhoub[✉]

University Clermont Auvergne, LIMOS-CNRS, Clermont-Ferrand, France
lea_astrid.kenmogne_mekemte@etu.uca.fr, gerard.chalhoub@uca.fr

Abstract. Cyber attacks are a major threat to countries, large organisations, and small businesses alike, with serious political, legal, and especially economic consequences. With these cyber attacks growing exponentially, we are faced with a major challenge which is to develop sophisticated and effective techniques to detect intrusions in the information systems of organisations in order to increase data and services protect. The majority of intrusion detection systems use signature-based approaches and supervised learning methods that depend on labelled training data. Generating this training data is usually a costly endeavour. In this study, we use autoencoders in unsupervised machine learning methods to improve intrusion detection system by performing binary traffic classification. The models were trained on four different types of autoencoders and with two datasets: CSE-CIC-IDS2018 and a dataset we generated with our home made scripts. The most relevant features for each dataset were selected to improve model generalisation, reduce complexity and improve performance. The performance of our models is evaluated in terms of accuracy and false positive rate. The error threshold of the used autoencoders is fixed with accordance to a specific objective. According to the obtained results, out of the four types of autoencoders we have studied, denoising autoencoder provides the best performance.

Keywords: Intrusion Detection Systems · Unsupervised learning · Autoencoders · Anomaly detection

1 Introduction and Background

Information security holds a paramount role in safeguarding the invaluable data of any institution. Organisations require robust security solutions that can efficiently shield their networks against malicious attacks and unauthorised usage. Despite the various strategies and technologies put in place to ensure the security of information systems, intrusion attacks still manage to go undetected. Intrusion detection systems play a crucial role in identifying intrusions and fortifying information systems against security breaches. In terms of intrusion detection, the most widely used and deployed methods are those based on signature-based

O. Habachi et al. (Eds.): UNet 2023, LNCS 14757, pp. 54–69, 2024.
https://doi.org/10.1007/978-3-031-62488-9_5

attack detection [1]. These systems can easily detect known attacks, as the signatures of these attacks are already stored in their databases. On the other hand, they are highly vulnerable to new attacks, for which the signatures have not yet been registered. It is therefore necessary to constantly update the database of attacks. Malicious actors can simply modify their attack sequences within malware and other types of attacks to avoid being detected. This main limitation has prompted a great deal of research into the use of machine learning techniques for network intrusion detection [2].

There are therefore two main network intrusion detection methods: misuse detection methods and anomaly detection methods [3]. Misuse detection methods identify abnormal behaviour by matching it against pre-defined patterns of events that describe known attacks, which we also call signature-based methods. Anomaly-based methods study normal behaviour traffic profiles and attempt to identify anomaly patterns of activities that deviate from the defined profiles. Signature-based methods generally have low false positive rates, they inevitably have high false negative rates (they fail to detect new attacks), because attack signatures are not available for new attacks. On the other hand, anomaly detection methods have low false positive rates because they can detect even new attacks, but they have greatly increased false negative rates because any previously unseen behaviour can be flagged as an attack even if it is benign.

Originally, intrusion detection systems can be classified based on data collection mechanisms [4]. We have, on one hand, host-based IDSs that detect intrusions based on different user activities and their behaviour on a given machine, and on the other hand, network-based IDSs that detect intrusions by observing various network activities. In this study, our focus covers both types of data collection mechanisms.

Figure 1 presents the general taxonomy of IDS mechanisms based on data collection methods and attack detection techniques.

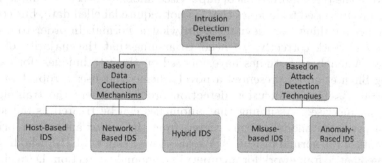

Fig. 1. IDS Classification based on Data Collection Mechanisms and Attack Detection Techniques. [5]

In this paper, we will focus on Machine Learning (ML) techniques for anomaly-based IDSs. We will build models based on unsupervised learning and autoencoders. We will test and evaluate those models on two different datasets: a publicly available dataset, and a home made dataset. The main contribution of the paper is benchmarking different autoencoders in a ML model by fixing the decision threshold of autoencoders according to an objective in terms of performance. The remainder of the paper is organised as follow. Section 2 presents a brief overview of ML techniques used in IDSs. In Sect. 3, we present our benchmarking methodology. In Sect. 4, we present the obtained results, and finally we conclude the paper is Sect. 5.

2   Machine Learning Techniques for Anomaly Detection

Many detection systems are developed based on ML techniques. Numerous approaches make use of supervised learning techniques. For instance, E. Tufan et al. [6] employed a supervised ML methodology for designing and developing an anomaly-based IDS. They trained models to study various intrusion attempts instead of training models for all attack types and they trained the model with various supervised learning algorithms, namely, Support Vector Machine, K-Nearest Neighbors, Naive Bayes, logistic regression, and Convolutional Neural Networks. D. P Gaikwad et al. [7] have set up an IDS using the Bagging Ensemble Method of Machine Learning. The REPTree base classifier is chosen to implement the IDS and they trained the model using different algorithms (Naive Bayes, random tree, C4.5/J48, and AdaBoost). In [8], they applied Naive Bayes algorithm to detect intrusions in a specific type of network (Software-Defined Network). The limitations of supervised techniques include (i) the inability to effectively detect new attacks for which it has not been trained, (ii) the need for labelled training data, which can be difficult to obtain especially for new attacks, and (iii) the poor ability to adapt in real time as relabelling data can be time-consuming.

To overcome these limitations of supervised anomaly-based techniques, other IDSs use unsupervised techniques that do not require labelled data, but consider as anomalies anything that deviates from what is normal. In order to do these techniques to work correctly, we need to assume that the majority of traffic is normal. A number of studies have focused on these techniques, for example Mei-Ling Shyu et al. [9] presented a novel scheme that uses a robust principal component classifier in intrusion detection problems where the training data may be unsupervised. Assuming that anomalies can be treated as outliers, an intrusion predictive model is constructed from the major and minor principal components of the normal instances. We also have Eskin et al. [10] who have proposed a geometric framework for unsupervised anomaly detection. Data elements are mapped to a feature space which is typically a vector space. Anomalies are detected by determining which points lie in sparse regions of the feature space. In [11], they applied five clustering algorithms (k-Means, improved k-Means, k-Medoids, Expectation-Maximization clustering and distance-based outlier detection) to train their models. They developed a Network Intrusion Detection System (NIDS) capable of identifying anomalies with unlabeled data by utilising unsupervised clustering algorithms. They assumed that clusters containing a substantial number of instances are indicative of normal behaviour, whereas those with relatively few instances are indicative of abnormal behaviour. However, one of the limitations of their approach is the absence of a defined method for establishing a threshold value to distinguish between what is considered normal and abnormal. The absence of an appropriate threshold may hinder the effectiveness of anomaly detection, as the determination of how many instances within a cluster should be classified as normal or abnormal is left to the discretion of the researcher. Furthermore, cluster analysis may struggle to effectively differentiate between normal and abnormal data, as its outcomes can be influenced by the initial configuration of clusters. We have a very recent work done by A. Adhikari et al. [12] in which they apply various supervised and unsupervised algorithms to detect intrusions. This is a host-based IDS that is trained on both supervised and unsupervised algorithms (K-Means and Gaussian Mixture). In [13], the Isolation Forest, an unsupervised machine learning algorithm, was trained using the KDD dataset. Its purpose was to identify anomalies and potential attacks within the data, with the evaluation based on the anomaly scores generated.

There are also works in the literature based on autoencoders. M. Sakurada et al. [14] conducted a study focusing on a technique that employs autoencoders for the purpose of anomaly detection. This approach hinges on the establishment of thresholds based on reconstruction errors. During the training phase, the autoencoder model is trained to recreate input data, which exclusively comprises normal data. In the testing phase, the model is exposed to test data, which it then uses to generate reconstructed test data. If the reconstruction error surpasses a specific threshold value chosen arbitrarily by the user, the data is classified as abnormal, and vice versa. This approach is built on the assumption that test data resembling the training data will undergo relatively accurate reconstruction, resulting in low reconstruction errors. Conversely, test data deviating significantly from the training data will exhibit higher reconstruction errors due to their divergence from the model's training data. We have also the Robust Autoencoder-Based Intrusion Detection System Model Against Adversarial Attacks (RAIDS) [15], in which the autoencoder reconstruction error is used as a prediction value in the classifier. Their work is based on two autoencoders and other ML classifiers. The first autoencoder learns from purely benign traffic and the second learns from purely malicious traffic. Each autoencoder can classify traffic according to a well-defined threshold. Results obtained from the autoencoders and the other classifier are fed back as input to the LightGBM classifier, which gives the final result as output. C. Hyunseung et al. [16] also developed an unsupervised learning approach for network intrusion detection system using autoencoders. Authors propose a heuristic approach to determine the reconstruction loss threshold based on the percentage of abnormal data present in the training data. Specifically, this method involves utilising the percentage of abnormal data within the training data, which subsequently becomes a threshold heuristic for truncating the percentage of the assumed normal distribution of reconstructed errors and classifying it as abnormal data. Mirsky et al. [17]

implemented an ensemble strategy that incorporated a range of autoencoder algorithms within the domain of Network Intrusion Detection Systems (NIDS), drawing inspiration from the methods introduced in [14]. This study made by Mirsky et al. holds significance as it applies the autoencoder-based anomaly detection methodology to the NIDS field.

In all these works that apply unsupervised learning for detection malicious traffic, it is imperative to set a specific threshold value for the autoencoders. The threshold for reconstruction loss plays a pivotal role as it serves as the criterion for distinguishing between normal and abnormal data. If the threshold is not appropriately configured, the performance of the unsupervised model cannot be assured. To overcome this limitation, the approach we propose in this paper allows us to calculate an optimal threshold according to the objective set. The choice is therefore made in a very specific and targeted way.

3   Methodology of Building the IDS Model

In order to train ML models, we need input data. For network intrusion detection, we need network traffic data. Some datasets are public, others are private. In this study, we will work with a publicly available dataset (CSE-CIC-IDS2018) and a home made dataset.

3.1   The Public Dataset: CSE-CIC-IDS2018

CSE-CIC-IDS2018[1] dataset is designed to support the development and evaluation of Machine Learning-based IDS solutions. It was created by the Canadian Institute for Cybersecurity (CIC) at the University of New Brunswick. It contains a large amount of network traffic data generated in a controlled and real-world environment, which contains different types of attacks and normal activities. This dataset is designed to represent real-world network traffic scenarios, making it valuable for training and testing intrusion detection models. It includes a combination of benign traffic and seven types of network attacks, namely, Brute-force, Heartbleed, Botnet, Denial of Service (DoS), Distributed Denial of Service (DDoS), Web attacks, and infiltration of the network from inside.

The specificity of this dataset is that it is formed from real traffic data, making it even more representative. Real traffic data is generated by real users and systems, making it more representative of the production environment. This means that ML models trained on such data are more likely to effectively detect real threats. In addition we have a diversity of scenarios. Real data can capture a variety of scenarios, including normal behaviour and real attacks. This allows models to train on a wider range of situations and generalise better to detect unknown attacks. Its main drawback is the fact that it is outdated. Network traffic today is much different than what it was back in 2018 when the dataset was captured.

---

[1] https://www.unb.ca/cic/datasets/ids-2018.html.

3.2   The Home-Made Dataset

The home-made dataset represents the dataset generated from traffic generator scripts that we developed. This approach allows us complete control over simulating desired attack scenarios, and enables us to target particular attacks to test the robustness of our detection system. On the other hand, the generated traffic is not very realistic as it is based on some predefined parameters. In this study, we are targeting denial-of-service attacks. The generated dataset contains a total of 225 473 samples, where 89,55% of samples represent benign traffic (201 920 samples) and 10,45% represent malicious traffic (23 553 samples).

3.3   Data Preprocessing

In this work, we use an unsupervised ML technique based on autoencoders to perform anomaly-based intrusion detection. Before training any ML model, it is necessary to perform data preprocessing to improve data quality and consistency for better model performance, by eliminating outliers, formalising features and managing missing data. Figure 2 shows the various stages of data preprocessing including data cleaning, data reduction, data imputation, data normalisation, and finally, data splitting.

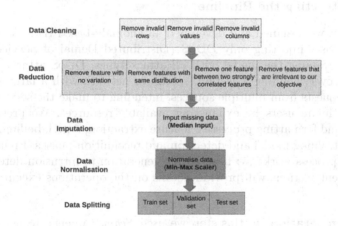

Fig. 2. Pipeline for data preprocessing.

- **Data Cleaning:** this step consists of removing invalid rows, invalid columns and invalid values. These are values that are erroneous and would negatively impact the learning process.
- **Data Reduction:** because IDSs deal with a large amount of data, one of the crucial tasks of IDSs is to keep the best quality of features that represent the whole data and remove the redundant and irrelevant features. It is therefore important to work on the relevant selection of the characteristics that would

best represent the model. This phase consists of making a selection of features to obtain a better generalisation of the model. We select features by removing features that do not vary as well for benign traffic as for abnormal traffic, features with the same distribution and features that do not give us relevant information to achieve our goal. We also studied the correlation between the features. For two highly correlated variables (correlation coefficient > 0.9), we keep only one variable.

- **Data Imputation:** it consists of completing a dataset by adding missing values. The aim is to fill in the missing values so that the dataset is complete and ready for model training.
- **Data Normalisation:** this step is crucial to scale the features of a dataset to a standard range which helps in improving the performance and convergence of our machine learning algorithms.
- **Data Splitting:** the dataset is divided into three sets: the training set, the validation set and the test set. The training set contains only benign data. The benign samples are divided between the three sets (80% for the training set, 10% for the validation set and 10% for the test set). Malicious samples are divided into two sets only (50% for the validation set and 50% for the test set).

3.4   Constructing the Pipeline

In this study, we designed and developed an anomaly-based IDS. We generated our own dataset injecting only DDoS (Distributed Denial of Service) attacks rather than training the model with all attack types. DDoS attacks consist of deliberately overwhelming a system, server, or network with a large number of malicious requests from multiple sources, intending to make the service unavailable to legitimate users by exhausting available resources. We present traffic generation and formatting processes, feature extraction, data labelling, data preprocessing, training model and detection and recognition phases. Figure 3 shows the general process workflow: from traffic generation to intrusion detection.

Subsequent sections will provide details on the operations executed at each step.

1. **Traffic generation:** in this step we used *Scapy* to generate normal traffic and DDoS attacks from the attacker to the victim. We generate normal traffic from multiple randomly selected IP addresses destined to our web server on the victim machine.
2. **Feature extraction:** once the traffic has been generated, we retrieve it from the victim machine in the form of a pcap file. To pass the data on to the ML module, the pcap file must first be transformed into a CSV file that can be understood by the module. We use a Python script to extract traffic characteristics from the pcap file and generate and calculate other characteristics from the data obtained from the pcap file.

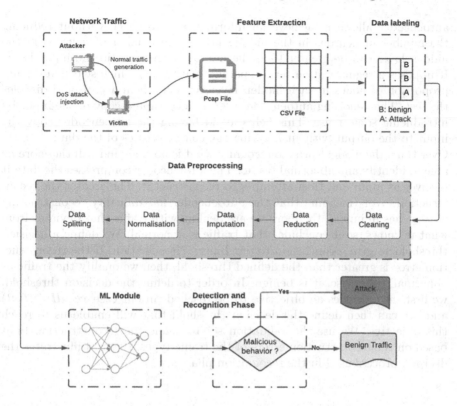

Fig. 3. Proposed workflow for the general process of ML model for IDS.

3. **Data labelling:** we assign a label to each sample in our file. Based on the IP addresses, we differentiate between the lines in the file that should be labelled "benign" and those that should be labelled "attack". When generating the traffic, we make sure to reserve a range of IP addresses that will only be used for attacks. This makes labelling simple: if the IP address (source or destination) is part of the range of addresses used for attacks, we label this line "attack", and if not, we label it "benign".

4. **Data preprocessing:** this is the data preparation phase as explained in Sect. 3.3.

5. **Detection and recognition phase:** the model is trained with a set of benign data on different types of autoencoders (undercomplete, stacked, sparse and denoising). The undercomplete autoencoder represents the basic autoencoder for which the dimensions of the hidden layers are smaller than those of the input layer. This limits the amount of information passing through the neural network and this means that the autoencoder captures only the most important features present in the data. The stacked autoencoder is characterised by the fact that it stacks several hidden layers; in a way, it is similar to the undercomplete autoencoder, but deeper. It creates more complex representations, which improves performance. The sparse

autoencoder allows to achieve an information bottleneck without reducing the number of neurons in the hidden layer. The number of neurons in the hidden layer can be greater than the number of neurons in the input layer. It imposes a regularisation term (sparsity constraint) which selects a certain proportion of nodes in each hidden layer to make them active, and disables the rest. The denoising autoencoder creates a corrupted copy of the input by introducing some noise. This helps avoid having the autoencoder copy the input to the output without knowing the characteristics of the data.

Over time, the model learns to recognise what is normal, and will therefore be able to identify any abnormal traffic. The autoencoder compresses the data it receives as input and then attempts to reconstruct it. The greater the reconstruction error (meaning that the autoencoder has difficulty reconstructing what it has in input), the more we are dealing with traffic that deviates from what it knows, so it concludes that traffic is abnormal. We define a decision threshold to give a conclusion to our binary classification. If the reconstruction error is greater than the defined threshold, then we qualify the traffic as abnormal, otherwise, it is benign. In order to define the decision threshold, we first set ourselves an objective to be reached (in our case *recall = 0.9*) and, we can then define the decision threshold that will enable us to reach this objective. We use the validation set to define the reconstruction limit based on the reconstruction errors of the traffic types. Figure 4 illustrates the decision process used in the recognition phase

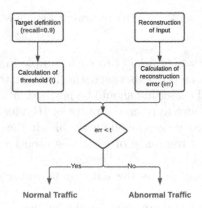

Fig. 4. Decision process.

4   Experimental Results

According to the taxonomy developed by H. Debar et al. [18], for an ideal IDS to be efficient, it must meet some minimum requirements. It must address the problem of properly detecting attacks and avoiding false positives and false negatives (accuracy), it must have a high rate to process audit events to allow real-time detection (performance), it should detect all attacks and not miss any intrusions (completeness), it must itself be resistant to attacks (fault tolerance), it must react as quickly as possible to prevent this from happening, and prevent attackers from compromising performance (timeliness) and it must be able to handle the worst case without loss of information (scalability) [19].

In this segment, we will provide the results generated by the models. The computer used during development was equipped with the following hardware and software specifications: an Intel Core i5-1155G7 CPU running at 2.5 GHz, 16 GB of RAM, and the Linux Ubuntu 18.04 operating system. Python scripts were created using different platforms, including Anaconda and Jupyter Notebook. We used the Tensorflow Python library to manipulate autoencoders, and the Sickit-Learn, Pandas and Numpy libraries to execute special functions for training our models.

To evaluate the performance of our models, we mainly use two metrics: F1-score and false positive rate. F1-score is the harmonic mean of precision and recall. Precision is the measure of how many of the predicted positive instances were actually correct, focusing on minimising false positives, whereas recall assesses how many of the actual positive instances were correctly identified by the model, emphasising the minimisation of false negatives. Together, they provide a trade-off between the accuracy of positive predictions and the ability to capture all positive cases. We choose to evaluate performance using F1-score rather than accuracy for two main reasons. Firstly, the classes in our dataset are unbalanced (there are many more samples in the "benign" class than in the "attack" class). In this case, accuracy can be misleading, as a model always predicting the majority class might still achieve high accuracy, but this does not mean that it is effective in identifying the minority class [20]. Secondly, the F1 score is generally more informative than the accuracy when we focus on the performance of the minority class (positive class). It puts more emphasis on the model's ability to correctly detect positive cases (attacks), which is crucial in intrusion detection.

The second metric is the false positive rate that measures the proportion of negative instances that are incorrectly classified as positive by the model.

We trained our model on the four types of autoencoders chosen for this work. For each type, we trained the model several times, varying the hyperparameters. The hyperparameters were varied empirically, taking into account the nature of each autoencoder type.

The hyperparameters presented in the results are mainly the number of epochs and the number of hidden layers. Increasing the number of epochs has the advantage of improving the reconstruction of input data, enabling the model to capture finer features and stabilising convergence through very good weight optimisation. However, this can lead to overlearning of noise, causing the model to learn or reproduce noise and details specific to the training data. In addition, an excessive number of epochs can lead to increased training time.

Increasing the number of hidden layers has the advantage that the model can capture richer, hierarchical representations of the data. But this can lead to overlearning in that our model, instead of reconstructing the data, will memorise and faithfully reproduce it. And this will lead to a considerable loss of performance on test data, as the model will have difficulty being generalised to new data. Also, an excessive number of epochs can lead to increased training time. It is therefore important for us to keep a close eye on model performance to find the right balance.

In order to achieve good performance, we introduce two callbacks during model training: EarlyStopping and ReduceLROnPlateau. To improve the efficiency and generalisation of the model by avoiding overlearning while optimising training time, we used EarlyStopping callback to mitigate this overlearning problem by monitoring the model's performance on a validation set during training and stopping training when performance starts to deteriorate, indicating that the model is starting to overlearn. To enable the model to converge faster and more reliably towards an optimal solution, we used the ReduceLROnPlateau callback, which automatically adjusts the learning rate during training to optimise the process of model convergence towards a minimum loss function. The results presented are those obtained with the test set using callbacks.

Table 1. Table summarising the best performances obtained on the different types of autoencoders on CSE-CICIIDS2018 Dataset.

Autoencoder	Epochs	Layers	Precision	Recall	F1-Score	FPR	FNR
Undercomplete	50	3	0.827	0.90	0.862	0.192	0.1000002
Stacked	45	7	0.838	0.899	0.867	0.185	0.10
Sparse	21	7	0.731	0.90	0.807	0.337	0.10
Denoising	34	7	0.852	0.90	0.875	0.159	0.10

The undercomplete autoencoder is trained on 50 epochs and 3 layers. It has no regularisation term, it was important for us to restrict the number of hidden layers as much as possible to avoid overfitting that's why it is trained on a single hidden layer. The second type of autoencoder on which we trained the model is the stacked autoencoder. The idea is to make the model a little deeper to improve performance. But, as the model is already too deep, the number of epochs must be limited and we are sure of the optimal number of epochs returned by the EarlyStopping callback.

Among the various model trainings we have done with the sparse autoencoder, the best performance is obtained with 21 epochs and 7 layers. This low number of epochs can be justified by the nature of the sparse autoencoder, which involves a regularisation term: the sparsity constraint. It favours the learning of essential features by encouraging selective activation of neurons in the hidden layer. With a small number of epochs, the learning process naturally favours the rapid identification of salient features enabling the model to efficiently capture essential information from the data.

The last models have been trained on the denoising autoencoder. With this autoencoder, as we introduce intentional noise into the input data, we force the model to learn more discriminating noise-resistant features. We found that increasing the number of epochs is like increasing the model's ability to learn more complex and abstract representations, and the model could very quickly focus on learning the noise rather than the significant features, leading to sub-optimal performance. Figure 5 shows the results obtained on the CSE-CICIDS2018 dataset.

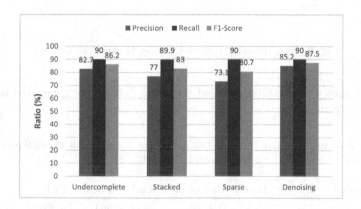

Fig. 5. Tests Results Comparison from CSE-CICIDS2018 dataset

Table 1 shows that the false-negative rate is virtually stable. The false-negative rate measures the proportion of positive instances that are incorrectly classified as negative by the model. In our case, it is the probability in which the authorised user is rejected by the system. This remarkable stability is due to the fact that this metric (FNR) is intimately linked to the recall that measures the system's ability to identify and raise alarms for all instances of actual intrusions. To calculate the threshold, we set recall at 0.9 as the target. We are interested in recall because we want the model to miss as few attacks as possible (reduce false negatives). The idea is that, of all the instances that are intrusions, the model should be able to predict a maximum number of these instances as being genuine intrusions. In view of the relatively stable false-negative rate, assessing the performance of our model comes down to evaluating it in relation to the false-positive rate. The lower the false positive rate, the better the model's performance. Figure 6 shows the variation in the false positive rate on the CSE-CICIDS2018 dataset.

The false positive rate is highest for the sparse autoencoder because it involves a regulariser (L1 regulariser). It favours the selection of important features by pushing certain coefficients toward zero. This can influence the way the model makes decisions and affect false positive rate.

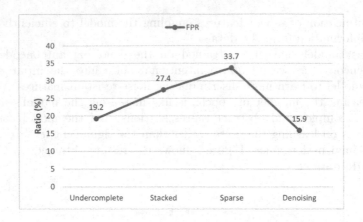

Fig. 6. False Positive Rate for CSE-CICIDS2018 dataset.

Table 2 shows the results obtained with the dataset we generated using our home-made traffic data.

Table 2. Table summarising the best performances obtained on the different types of autoencoders on our home-made generated dataset.

Autoencoder	Epochs	Layers	Precision	Recall	F1-Score	FPR	FNR
Undercomplete	15	3	0.9989	0.8992	0.964	0.00054	0.100782
Stacked	30	5	0.9991	0.8993	0.9466	0.000446	0.100612
Sparse	30	5	0.9992	0.8995	0.9467	0.000396	0.100442
Denoising	5	5	0.9994	0.8996	0.9469	0.000297	0.100357

The remarkable performance of the results obtained from our dataset can be justified by the fact that traffic data obtained is not very extensive; the model, therefore, does not have a large amount of data to learn from. The second reason is that traffic data are not very varied; we have only one type of attack (DDoS). In addition, traffic was generated in a very small network.

Figure 7 shows the best results obtained from our different training sessions on each of the autoencoder types for our dataset.

The high F1-Score indicates that our model works very well for its intended task. It may also indicate that our model is well adapted to the training data. It has succeeded in learning the important patterns present in our data and can generalise correctly on new data. Furthermore, it indicates that our model achieves a good balance between precision (ability to correctly predict positive examples) and recall (ability to capture the majority of positive examples). This means that our model minimises both false positives and false negatives.

Figure 8 shows the variation in the false positive rate on our home-made generated dataset.

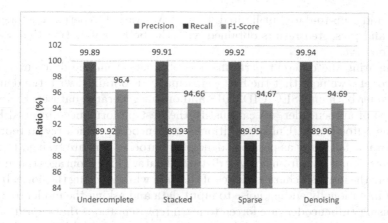

Fig. 7. Tests Results comparison using our home-made generated dataset.

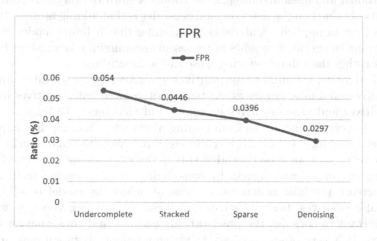

Fig. 8. False Positive Rate for our home-made generated dataset.

The false positive rate is higher for the undercomplete autoencoder than for other autoencoder types. This can be explained by the fact that the undercomplete autoencoder is a type of shallow autoencoder that may have a limited ability to extract discriminating features from the data. In addition, the architecture on which it is based (a single hidden layer) may have an impact on its efficiency in separating normal from abnormal examples in the learned latent space.

5   Conclusion and Discussion

In this paper, we presented how intrusion detection systems work and investigated the use of machine learning in this domain. We selected 4 autoencoders that we benchmarked in our unsupervised models using a complete but old dataset and a up-to-date but limited dataset. We varied hyperparameters of the models and presented results obtained with the best combination that we were able to observe.

Comparing the different performances obtained from the different types of autoencoders, we note that the best performance is obtained with the denoising autoencoder both on CSECICIDS2018 and on our generated dataset. Examining each type of autoencoder, we can justify the best performance obtained by the denoising autoencoder. Unlike traditional autoencoders, which try to reproduce input data as faithfully as possible, denoising autoencoders are trained to reconstruct noisy input data from noisy or disturbed data. This encourages the model to learn from the intrinsic characteristics of the data while ignoring the noise. In addition, by intentionally adding noise to input data and asking the model to denoise it, denoising autoencoders are forced to learn representations that capture underlying structures and patterns while ignoring random noise. This favours the creation of robust and meaningful representations. A third reason that could justify the results obtained on the denoising autoencoder is that adding noise to the data acts as a form of implicit regularisation, meaning that it limits model complexity by forcing the network weights to represent meaningful relationships between variables rather than simply storing noise in the input data.

An ideal model maximises true positives and true negatives while minimising false positives and false negatives. As true positives and true negatives increase, false positives and false negatives decrease, and vice versa. To limit false positives, i.e. to prevent the model from issuing alerts when nothing has happened, the model would have to become less and less sensitive to the characteristics that enable it to predict an attack. And if this is the case, the model runs the risk of passing up several real attacks by considering them as benign traffic, which would increase the false negatives. In general, when the model is adjusted to reduce false positives, false negatives will increase, and vice versa. It is therefore important to consider the practical implications and consequences of each in context. It is very often necessary to strike a balance between reducing false positives and false negatives, depending on safety priorities, available resources, and risk tolerance.

In our future work, we will work on creating a more realistic and up-to-date dataset to use with our learning models. The existing dataset is relatively old and our own dataset is very limited. Also, we will focus on including other types of malicious traffic in our own dataset and not only limit the attacks to Denial of Service attacks.

References

1. Díaz-Verdejo, J., Muñoz-Calle, J., Estepa Alonso, A., Estepa Alonso, R., Madinabeitia, G.: On the detection capabilities of signature-based intrusion detection systems in the context of web attacks. Appl. Sci. **12**, 852 (2022)
2. Pinto, A., Herrera, L.-C., Donoso, Y., Gutierrez, J.A.: Survey on intrusion detection systems based on machine learning techniques for the protection of critical infrastructure. Sensors **23**, 2415 (2023)

3. Khraisat, A., Gondal, I., Vamplew, P., et al.: Survey of intrusion detection systems: techniques, datasets and challenges. Cybersecur **2**, 20 (2019)
4. Lazarevic, A., Kumar, V., Srivastava, J.: Intrusion detection: a survey. Managing Cyber Threats (5), 19–78 (2005)
5. Singh, D., Singh, V.P.: Comparative study of various distributed intrusion detection systems for WLAN. Global J. Res. Eng. Electr. Electron **6**(12), 49–56 (2012)
6. Tufan, E., Tezcan, C., Acartürk, C.: Anomaly-based intrusion detection by machine learning: a case study on probing attacks to an institutional network. IEEE Access (9) (2021)
7. Gaikwad, D.P., Thool, R.: Intrusion detection system using bagging ensemble method of machine learning. In: IEEE International Conference on Computing Communication Control and Automation, pp. 291–295 (2015)
8. Jayasri, P., Atchaya, A., Sanfeeya, M., Ramprasath, J.: Intrusion detection system in software defined networks using machine learning approach. Int. J. Adv. Eng. Res. Sci. **8**(8), 99–110 (2021)
9. Mei-Ling, S., Shu-Ching, C., Kanoksri, S., LiWu, C.: A novel anomaly detection scheme based on principal component classifier. Miami University Coral Gables Fl Department of Electrical and Computer Engineering (2016)
10. E. Eskin, A. Arnold, M. Prerau, L. Portnoy, S. Stolfo: A Geometric Framework for Unsupervised Anomaly Detection Detecting Intrusions in Unlabeled Data. In: Applications of Data Mining in Computer Security. Advances in Information Security, vol. 2, issue 6, pp. 77–101 (2002). https://doi.org/10.1007/978-1-4615-0953-0_4
11. Syarif, I., Prugel-Bennett, A., Wills, G.: Unsupervised clustering approach for network anomaly detection. In: Benlamri, R. (ed.) NDT 2012. CCIS, vol. 293, pp. 135–145. Springer, Heidelberg (2012). https://doi.org/10.1007/978-3-642-30507-8_13
12. Adhikari, A., Krishna, B.: Machine learning technique for intrusion detection in the field of the intrusion detection system (2023)
13. Vikram, A., Mohana: Anomaly detection in network traffic using unsupervised machine learning approach. In: 5th International Conference on Communication and Electronics Systems (ICCES) on Proceedings, pp. 476–479. IEEE, Coimbatore (2020)
14. Sakurada, M., Yairi, T.: Anomaly detection using autoencoders with nonlinear dimensionality reduction. In: Proceedings of the MLSDA 2014 2nd Workshop on Machine Learning for Sensory Data Analysis (2014)
15. Sarıkaya, A., Günel Kılıç, B., Demirci, M.: RAIDS: robust autoencoder-based intrusion detection system model against adversarial attacks. Computers & Security (2023)
16. Hyunseung, C., Mintae, K., Gyubok, L., Wooju, K.: Unsupervised learning approach for network intrusion detection system using autoencoders. J. Supercomput. (2019)
17. Mirsky, Y., Doitshman, T., Elovici, Y., Shabtai, A.: An ensemble of autoencoders for online network intrusion detection. arXiv Preprint. arXiv:1802.09089 (2018)
18. Debar, H., Dacier, M., Wespi, A.: A revised taxonomy for intrusion-detection systems. Anales des Télécommun. **55**, 361–378 (2000)
19. Kruegel, C., Valeur, F., Vigna, G.: Intrusion Detection and Correlation - Challenges and Solutions. Springer, New York (2005). https://doi.org/10.1007/b101493
20. Berger, J.O.: Statistical Decision Theory and Bayesian Analysis. Springer, New York (2013). https://doi.org/10.1007/978-1-4757-4286-2

A New Strategy for Reducing Latency with Deep Learning in Fog Computing Environment

Birane Koundoul[1(✉)], Youssou Kassé[1], Fatoumata Baldé[1], and Bamba Gueye[2]

[1] Université Alioune Diop de Bambey, Bambey, Senegal
{birane.koundoul,youssou.kasse,fatoumata.balde}@uadb.edu.sn
[2] Université Cheikh Anta Diop, Dakar, Senegal
bamba.gueye@ucad.edu.sn

Abstract. The data generated by connected objects is becoming increasingly numerous and often cyclical. Fog computing (FC) has emerged as an attractive solution to bring data closer to the edge, meet requirements, and manage the growing demand for data. However, network congestion produced by connected devices increases latency and energy consumption. In addition, managing similar processes in fog nodes is difficult. Some processes evolve rapidly into complicated, heterogeneous, and dynamic structures. A reduction of latency, bandwidth, and energy consumption represents issues that can be addressed by neural networks. Indeed, Deep learning can offer fast, reliable processing times on huge quantities of data. Therefore, integrating deep learning in a fog environment would be interesting. Therefore, we proposed a new strategy that enables the selection of the best fog node within a given zone by leveraging a deep learning-based LSTM model (BRFC-LSTM) and metrics such as data size, bandwidth, and the number of layers in the node.

Keywords: IoT · deep learning · system efficiency · quality of service · fog computing

1 Introduction

In the digital world, data continues to increase while at the same time requiring minimal response time for certain applications. The Internet of Things is a paradigm of small interconnected devices such as sensors, smartphones, etc. Almost all users use these ubiquitous devices and their roles depend on the purpose and processed data type. Most of the data generated by connected objects requires efficient processing in terms of latency, confidentiality, low bandwidth, etc. which is a challenge for the cloud.

Fog computing has emerged to address these issues. The data stored and read in fog nodes are heterogeneous. According to [1], fog computing is a technology that provides users with scale (security, cognition, agility, latency, efficiency). However, connected objects cannot perform all the tasks, which is why they rely

O. Habachi et al. (Eds.): UNet 2023, LNCS 14757, pp. 70–84, 2024.
https://doi.org/10.1007/978-3-031-62488-9_6

on the cloud, with its virtually unlimited computing and processing power. This makes cloud and fog computing two complementary technologies.

However, fog computing encounters certain problems [2] that deep learning attempts to improve on FC applications to provide services such as security, resource management, accuracy, delay, energy reduction, cost, data processing, and traffic modeling. This was confirmed in [3]. According to [3], fog computing technology still suffers from performance and security issues. Most of these issues are already used and managed by deep learning (DL). DL can perform fast and reliable analyses of data to discover new information for predicting and even making important decisions. According to [2], integrating DL into CF enables more in-depth analyses and more intelligent responses.

DL, an Artificial Intelligence technology, is effective for analyzing huge multimedia data such as files, images, and videos. So using DL in FC improves the quality of service. The results obtained using DL pass through numerous layers for analysis of different characteristics. In addition, the size of incoming data is reduced as it passes from one layer to another. This integration of DL into FC reduces network traffic, latency, energy consumption, etc.

However, cloud computing is essential insofar as computationally-intensive tasks need to be redirected to this environment. Communication between fog computing and the cloud enables data to be switched [4]. Tasks that require high energy consumption should be run in the cloud.

Fog computing brings data closer to end users by placing it on network devices. It aims to overcome the previous issues faced by cloud computing. With the advent of connected objects, which continue to grow significantly [5] and have given rise to big data, things are getting complicated in the fog computing environment. For resource-constrained devices such as wireless networks, set-top boxes, switches, routers, base stations, and edge devices [6], the congestion produced by these devices delays latency, increases energy consumption, and results in high bandwidth utilization [7]. This creates problems in the system as depicted by [8,9].

In addition, the management of similar processes in fog nodes is difficult to manage in the fog environment because some processes evolve rapidly towards complicated, heterogeneous but also dynamic structures according to [10]. Consequently, integrating Deep Learning (DL) into the fog computing environment is an asset for improving applications and providing the services mentioned above. To get more in terms of service diversity and performance, fog nodes need to be improved [11].

With the use of deep learning, according to [11], the fog computing environment can benefit in many ways from DL, because it cannot solve the problems of cloud computing on its own. Applications are constantly growing and can open up new possibilities for 5G and artificial intelligence (AI) [12]. Most of these points are already used and managed by Deep Learning. Hence the integration of Deep Learning into our architecture [13] for improved quality of service.

The rest of the paper is structured as follows. Section 2 reviews the related work, whereas Sect. 3 describes our architecture integrating the LSTM model. Afterward, Sect. 4 illustrates the BRFC-LSTM module for data processing.

Section 5 presents the experimental parameters and the results obtained by making a comparison with the BRFC and DLEFN models [14]. Finally, Sect. 6 concludes the work and gives some perspective.

2   Related Work

Deep learning is one of the solutions for data prediction. With the plethora of data and its similarities, problems are beginning to appear in the fog environment. This has led scientists and researchers to work based on the available data to predict future results. Several methods have often been used, such as simple RNN (Recurrent Neural Network), CNN (Convolutional Neural Network), LSTM (Long-Short-Term-Memory), Bi-LSTM (Bidirectional Long-Short-Term-Memory), GRU (Gated Recurrent Unit), or even traditional methods like ANN (Artificial Neural Network).

In [2], the authors predicted that in the next five years, the number of connected objects could reach 50 billion. These objects produce an enormous amount of data, some of which are similar, posing a major problem for the fog computing environment. According to Shavan et al., deep learning offers highly accurate models while reducing response time, and requires a large amount of data. This is why, according to Shavan et al., the integration of DL into the fog environment has a positive impact, as it considerably increases computing performance. The limitations of fog computing can be managed by deep learning.

In [15], the authors developed a model for the detection of weapons in surveillance videos to alert the authorities to a possible crime. They integrated deep learning into a software-defined network (SDN) architecture to support delay-sensitive applications in a fog computing environment. The SDN is also explained in this paper to take into account the constraints of multimedia traffic. After simulation, results showed that "**YOLOv5n**" is better than "**YOLOv5-lite e**" and "**YOLOv5-lite s**". A reduction in bandwidth and system performance is noted. The mininet emulator was used to evaluate the model's performance. This revealed an improvement of up to 75%, 14.7%, and 32.5% in terms of respectively average throughput, average jitter, and quality of service.

According to [16], fog nodes have difficulty analyzing quickly all arriving data from their applications. This can take a long time and even impact system performance. The authors address the problems of managing mobile applications that are sensitive to latency, security, and confidentiality in a wide variety of scenarios such as communication between devices, smart homes, and transport management with connected vehicles. The author has used machine learning and deep learning to analyze big data.

In this respect, the authors have reviewed the advantages of fog computing in terms of the amount of data produced by connected devices, while at the same time highlighting the limitations of FC, which DL is ready to resolve [17]. Also in the same document, the authors explain that integrating DL into the FC environment enables much deeper analysis and provides smarter mission responses. In addition, the authors in [17] demonstrate several deep learning algorithms such as MPL (Linear Probability Model), CNN (Convolutional Neural Networks), and LSTM (Long Short Term Memory).

In [14], the authors proposed a model for entrusting fog nodes with a part of deep learning (DLEFN), which they applied to the agricultural domain. DLEFN decides on the best layer, taking into account computing capacity and available bandwidth. In [14], with DLEFN, they have proposed an algorithm that selects the fog node with a sufficient number of layers to handle the request.

However, the fog node does not have the required number of layers, it takes the available number of layers to reduce the number of expected layers. Indeed, it reduces the resource capacity for the incoming task. They measure the computing capacity and bandwidth required to process the incoming data to guarantee the quality of service for transferring the result to the cloud. Afterward, the algorithm returns the maximum number of layers that the fog node can execute within its resources. According to [14], the higher the number of layers assigned to fog nodes, the lower the volumes of data transmitted to the cloud via the network, potentially reducing network congestion and the computational load on the cloud.

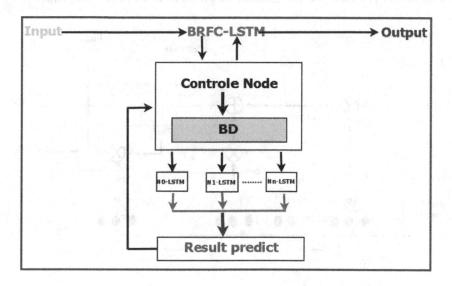

Fig. 1. Architecture of a zone by leveraging LSTM.

3   Architecture Integrating the BRFC-LSTM Module

This section describes a contribution that improves our former proposal [13]. Indeed, we considered a three-tier architecture composed of different layers such as IoT, fog computing, and cloud computing. At the fog computing level, we have a set of interconnected zones through a double-ring approach to facilitate data exchange between zones. Each zone has a controller node that communicates with the other nodes in the zone. Furthermore, the controller node holds some informations about each node, such as storage capacity, free memory space, processor capacity, RAM capacity, and the total number of available layers. In so doing, our algorithm can choose the most appropriate node.

With the integration of deep learning into the model, the controller node selects the best node based on the information it holds. The controller node is connected to the controller nodes of its neighbors. At the level of each node in the zone, we have integrated the LSTM model with a set of layers for data management as illustrated in Fig. 1. However, if a task arrives, the controller node checks which node has more available layers for request processing. Our algorithm extracts the task by retrieving certain characteristics to determine the best fog node to assign the task. Once the node has been selected, it processes the task and returns the result. The controller then updates the node processing the request.

In addition, node selection is not based on a single criterion, namely storage capacity. Our BRFC-LSTM algorithm is based on three parameters: bandwidth, storage capacity, and the number of layers in the node. The latter is very important in neural networks, as the number of layers reduces processing time.

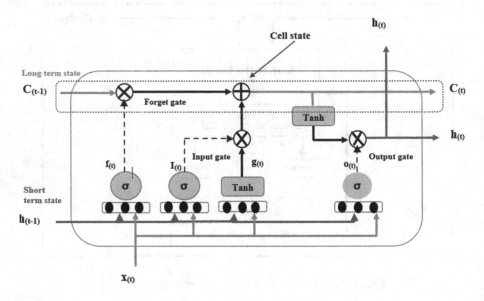

Fig. 2. The LSTM cell with its different doors.

4   Using the BRFC-LSTM with the LSTM Model

An LSTM (Long Short Term Memory) is a network composed of three gates called input, forget, and output as shown in Fig. 2. The input gate adds or updates new information in the network. The forget gate releases irrelevant information and finally, the exit gate transmits updated information. We have four recurrent layers with a set of units. The two short-term and long-term memories respectively represent information stored over a short and longer period.

Therefore, we have three inputs: observation data which enters the network $x_{(t)}$, the short-term memory $h_{(t-1)}$ and long-term memory $c_{(t-1)}$ which are the outputs of the previous iteration. These three inputs are managed by the three gates (inputs, forgetting, and output). Each input has an associated weight **w** which allows to trigger the activation function. Thanks to the bias $b_{(n)}$ with **n** equal to (**f, i, g and o**), a delay of the activation function is noted. Equations 1 to 4 give the result of the inputs associated with the weights plus the bias. For instance, Eqs. 5 to 6 give the result of the cell output.

Indeed, designed equations enable to manage the different gates and the information outputs. Equations 5 and 6 represent the outputs and, thanks to Eq. 5, we can keep the information much longer in the LSTM cell. This means that the information can be recovered over time.

$$f_{(t)} = \sigma(W_{xf}^T X_{(t)} + W_{hf}^T h_{(t-1)} + b_f) \tag{1}$$

$$i_{(t)} = \sigma(W_{xi}^T X_{(t)} + W_{hi}^T h_{(t-1)} + b_i) \tag{2}$$

$$g_{(t)} = \tanh(W_{xg}^T X_{(t)} + W_{hg}^T h_{(t-1)} + b_g) \tag{3}$$

$$o_{(t)} = \sigma(W_{xo}^T X_{(t)} + W_{ho}^T h_{(t-1)} + b_o) \tag{4}$$

$$c_{(t)} = f_{(t)} \otimes c_{(t-1)} + i_{(t)} \otimes g_{(t)} \tag{5}$$

$$y_{(t)} = h_{(t)} = o_{(t)} \otimes \tanh(c_{(t-1)}) \tag{6}$$

The six equations can be divided into three groups: the gate equations, the cell equations and the final output equation. Equations 1, 2 and 4 fall into the first category.

- Equation 1 is the forgetting gate equation which specifies the information to be removed from the cell state.
- Equation 2 is the input gate, which tells us what new information we are going to store in the state of the cell. This will depend on the value returned by the sigmoid function.
- Equation 4 depicts the output gate which is used to activate the final output of the lstm block at time **t**.

For the second category of equations, we have the cell state equations.

- Equation 3 represents the candidate for the state of the cell at time(t).
- Equation 5 represents the state of the cell (memory) at time t.

And finally the third category represents the final output, which will in turn be an input to the next layer. It is represented by Eq. 6.

4.1   Steps of the BRFC-LSTM Algorithm

BRFC-LSTM consists of choosing the best node at the zone level. The Fig. 3 describes the BRFC-LSTM algorithm for selecting the best fog node. Depending on the size of the task after extraction the controller node chooses the nodes capable of storing the task. In our architecture, we have a set of interconnected zones with fog nodes that are connected to the controller node. The controller receives all the requests and extracts the task to choose the best node. After feature extraction, our algorithm tries to find the most appropriate node for the request as shown in Figs. 4 and 5. However, if the controller node verifies that all the fog nodes in its zone cannot handle the request, the request is redirected to the neighboring zone. The redirection is based on the information held by the controller node. The controller node updates its tables once the request has been processed in the zone.

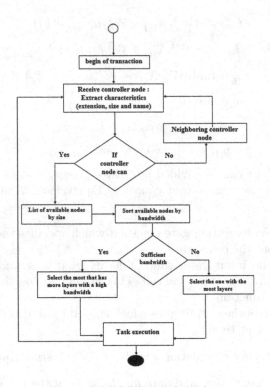

Fig. 3. BRFC-LSTM algorithm.

The sequence diagram, in Fig. 4, shows the interaction between the BRFC-LSTM module and the fog nodes. This provides a list of available nodes according to size. Based on the available list, a filter is made according to the number of layers. This is a very important criterion, since in neural networks, the size of the request decreases from one layer to another. According to [14], the higher the number of layers assigned to fog nodes, the lower the volumes of data transmitted to the cloud via the network, which potentially reduces network congestion and the computing load on the cloud.

Additionally, the sequence diagram illustrated in Fig. 5 shows the choice of the most appropriate node according to the number of layers about the threshold. The choice of parameters is based on empirical experiments. Three main steps summarise the choice of the best node:

- The first step is to select all the available nodes whose size is greater than the size of the request. This means that the zone receiving the request can process it. Based on the list obtained, the controller node checks the other two criteria. If the controller node cannot process the request, it is redirected to the most appropriate zone. Each zone is connected to two zones and holds information from neighboring controller nodes. This enables better redirection.
- The controller node then chooses the node with the most layers. This reduces processing time. The more layers a node has, the shorter the processing time. Priority is given to nodes with more layers than the threshold. Even if the nodes do not have more layers than the threshold, the task is still processed in the zone.
- Finally, depending on the list obtained, the nodes with more bandwidth are selected from the list. The higher the bandwidth, the lower the processing time.

5 Evaluation

In this section, we discuss the experimental parameters to obtain a result. The results obtained were compared with our BRFC model [13] and DLEFN model [14]. The BRFC model has a controller node in each zone to supervise the different nodes zone. This provides load balancing, but the placement time, execution time, and bandwidth are significant compared with the new proposal.

It is worth noticing that DLEFN algorithm does not have a global view of the system. As a result, part of a task may be handled by one node and the rest by another. In this paper, we have proposed a new architecture incorporating deep learning to improve request processing time.

Tables 1 and 2 show respectively the characteristics of a zone with all its parameters and the characteristics of a task, i.e. the resources required for a task. For our experiments, we chose the object sizes and the latency between fog nodes and between zones to represent the scenarios like [18]. Two scenarios were proposed in our case: a 5-zone scenario with 20 fog nodes within each zone; a second 10-zone scenario with 10 fog nodes within each zone. Each scenario contains 100 fog nodes. The choice of the duration of each service is between 0.1 and 4.2 ms [19]; a service time of each controller node is fixed at 0.2 s [20] and the simulation duration is 1000 s like in [21].

However, in one case, the data is randomly generated and tasks arrive following the exponential distribution. In another case, we assume that the arrival of tasks follows a Poisson distribution of mean rate λ and that each controller

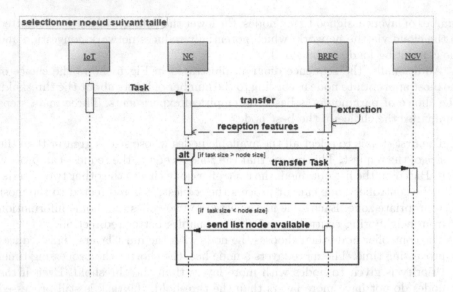

Fig. 4. Sequence diagram showing the selection of available nodes according to their sizes.

node processes tasks with a distributed exponential service time of mean rate μ. The system can be modeled as an **M/M/1/K** queue where **K** represents the capacity of the queue and in service. We have a single server (controller node) at each zone. The total number of jobs in the controller node does not exceed **K** (the queue capacity). **FIFO** (First In First Out) is applied to the tasks in the queue. This means that the first task in the queue is served and so on. It may not be the first to complete its execution. Each experiment is run 10 times to obtain stable results.

5.1 Experimental Parameters

5.2 Results

After simulation with the GridSim tool, we were able to obtain a better result compared with the BRFC models and the DLEFN model. We consider scenarios using 5 and 10 zones (sites). In our model, we generated data for five sites in our architecture with 100 nodes, i.e. 20 nodes per site. This corresponds to the first scenario. For the second scenario, we increased the number of sites and decreased the number of nodes at the zone level. The simulation was carried out on a DELL 1.8 GHz Intel Core i5 8th generation dual-core machine, 8 GB RAM, and 500GB SDD hard disk.

Figure 6 shows the average placement time of the random data. We used the RStudio tool with version 4.3.0 to generate the random data and the data following the exponential distribution.

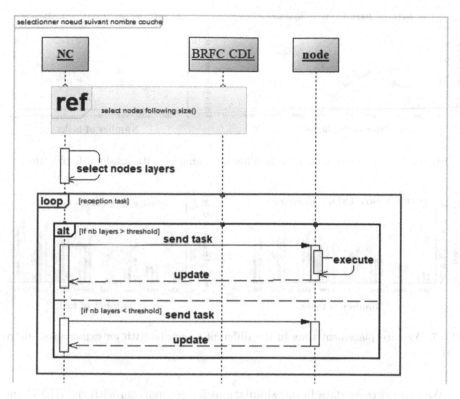

Fig. 5. Sequence diagram showing the selection of the best node according to the bandwidth and/or the number of layers.

Table 1. Characteristics of fog areas.

Parameters	Fog
Number of area	[5–10]
Number of nodes per are	[10–20]
Number of fog nodes in the system	100
Latency	50–100 ms between area
Number of tasks	24000
Bandwidth	500–2000 MB/S

Table 2. Characteristics of the task.

properties	Values
Storage capacity (MB)	[1–10]
Storage capacity (KB)	256
Bandwidth (MB/S)	[0,5–1]

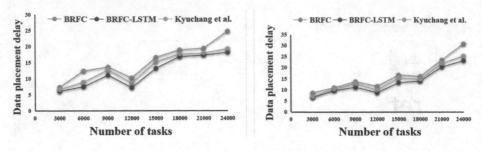

Fig. 6. Average placement time in different scenarios with random distribution.

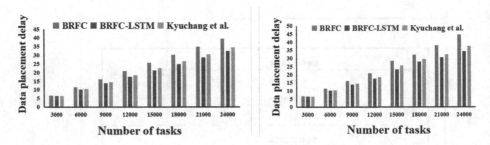

Fig. 7. Average placement time in the different scenarios with an exponential distribution.

We applied these data in our simulations for comparison with the BRFC and DFELN models. Figure 6-(a) represents the average data placement delay for 5 sites following a simulation time equal to 1000 s. In Fig. 6-(b), we used the same data for 10 sites. We note that our BRFC-LSTM proposal has a better data placement time than BRFC and the DLEFN proposal in [14]. We also note that the larger the number of sites, the longer the placement time. There is no great increase in terms of time, but a slight increase. In all cases, our proposal always offers a better data placement time.

In Fig. 7, we used the same scenarios (5 and 10 sites) to estimate the data placement time according to an exponential distribution with a Poisson distribution, with the same remark always depending on the number of sites. We observe that the placement time increases with the number of sites. We can see that the proposed model, BRFC-LSTM, has a better placement time even when increasing the number of zones.

The placement times of the DLEFN model and ours are not very different, as both methods use deep learning. The advantage of our model over DLEFN in [14] is that the controller node in our model selects the best node based on the information it holds and has a global view of the zone and information about neighboring controller nodes.

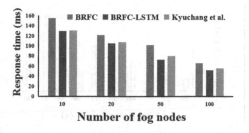
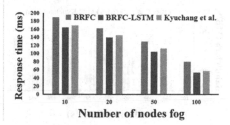

Fig. 8. Average response time for tasks in different scenarios depending on the number of fog nodes.

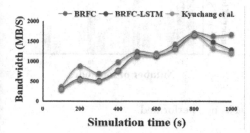
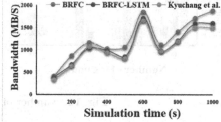

Fig. 9. Average bandwidth consumption in different scenarios with random distribution.

We also compared the average response time of the three models according to the number of fog nodes. We varied the number of fog nodes from 10 to 100 as shown in Fig. 8. In Fig. 8-(a), we tested with random data, and Fig. 8-(b) with data following an exponential distribution. The observation is the same: as the number of fog nodes increases, response time decreases and there is less loss of non-executed data, as shown in Fig. 11, where the number of lost tasks is represented. Our proposal greatly exceeds the BRFC model in terms of response time and bandwidth. This means that with the integration of deep learning in the fog environment, we have improved the response time, the placement delay, and also the bandwidth.

In Fig. 9, we have used the bandwidth parameter. We injected 24, 000 tasks at random, which arrive exponentially. Similarly, in Fig. 10, we have also used the same parameter, but the data follows an exponential distribution. The bandwidth consumed increases with the simulation time. But we observe that the bandwidth consumption of our proposal is somewhat similar to that of [14]. This is in contrast to the BRFC proposal where we note the absence of deep learning. The number of layers in a fog node is very important as it reduces the query size from layer to layer. Over a period of time, the DLEFN model of [14] has better bandwidth in the 5 and 10 scenarios. The difference is not huge.

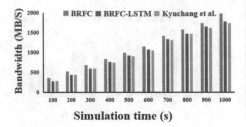
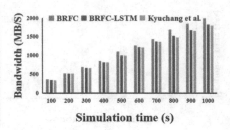

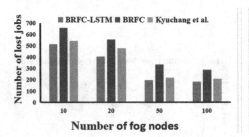
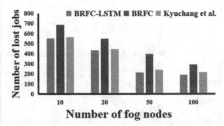

Fig. 10. Average bandwidth consumption in the different scenarios with an exponential distribution.

Fig. 11. Number of tasks not performed.

Packet losses were noted in the system. Depending on the number of fog nodes in the system, the number of lost packets decreases as shown in Fig. 11. The **M/M/1/K** queue model is applied in the system with **K** the number of tasks in the queue allowed. The system cancels new jobs if the queue capacity is exceeded. This leads to the loss of the task. According to the three models, our proposal has less packet loss whatever the number of fog nodes used in the simulation.

6   Discussions

In this paper, we used deep learning to improve the response time of requests. After simulation, we obtained a better response and placement time compared to the proposal of kyuchang et al.

However, our proposal has some limitations in terms of bandwidth compared to that of kyuchang et al. Our model consumes more bandwidth because a return to the controller node is made after each data placement to perform an update. The data sent and stored in the zone nodes. The information returned by the fog node storing the data is used to update its table. The information sent by the controller node and returned by the fog node consumes bandwidth compared to the Kychang model.

This allows the controller node to easily retrieve the information during future searches.

7   Conclusion

Deep learning is an artificial intelligence technology. Deep learning models tend to work with huge amounts of data. Integrating deep learning into the fog environment improves the quality of the system.

This article describes and evaluates, through simulations, three different algorithms for placing data in a fog environment. The results show that the BRFC-LSTM model consistently achieves the best performance in almost all the simulations carried out, both in terms of execution time and data placement delay. In terms of bandwidth consumption, the DLEFN model is better than our proposed model because the round-trip at the controller node consumes significant bandwidth.

Our BFRC-LSTM algorithm, after simulation, gave a better result than the BRFC and DLEFN models. With the proposed model, we obtained a data placement delay in both scenarios and a better response time compared to the two models compared. However, we observed an increase in latency as the number of zones increased. With 5 *zones, the response time is shorter than with* 10 zones. The same number of fog nodes is used for 5 and 10 zones.

In future work, we plan to develop a new module, integrating deep learning into the controller node to select a better fog node. This will allow the controller node to predict the best node. However, in terms of bandwidth, our proposal is somewhat similar to the DLEFN model. We have decided to make improvements to achieve a trade-off between response time and bandwidth. An improved model for low bandwidth consumption.

References

1. Margariti, S.V., Dimakopoulos, V.V., Tsoumanis, G.: Modeling and simulation tools for fog computing-a comprehensive survey from a cost perspective. Fut. Internet **12**(5), 5 (2020). https://doi.org/10.3390/fi12050089
2. Askar, S., Jameel, Z., Kareem, S.: Deep learning and fog computing: a review. Août 2021. https://doi.org/10.5281/zenodo.5222647.
3. Samann, F.E.F., Abdulazeez, A.M., Askar, S.: Fog computing based on machine learning: a review. Int. J. Interact. Mob. Technol. IJIM **15**(12), 12 (2021). https://doi.org/10.3991/ijim.v15i12.21313
4. Koundoul, B., Kasse, Y., Balde, F., Gueye, B.: Leveraging cloud inter-zone architecture for response time reduction. In: Faye, Y., Gueye, A., Gueye, B., Diongue, D., Nguer, E.H.M., Ba, M. (eds.) CNRIA 2021. LNCS, vol. 400, pp. 87–97. Springer, Cham (2021). https://doi.org/10.1007/978-3-030-90556-9-8
5. Hassan, S.F., Fareed, R.: Video streaming processing using fog computing. In: 2018 International Conference on Advanced Science and Engineering (ICOASE), pp. 140–144 (2018). https://doi.org/10.1109/ICOASE.2018.8548869.
6. Yi, S., Hao, Z., Qin, Z., Li, Q.: Fog computing: platform and applications. In: 2015 Third IEEE Workshop on Hot Topics in Web Systems and Technologies (HotWeb), pp. 73–78 (2015). https://doi.org/10.1109/HotWeb.2015.22.
7. Hashem, I.A.T., Yaqoob, I., Anuar, N.B., Mokhtar, S., Gani, A., Khan, S.U.: The rise of "big data" on cloud computing: review and open research issues. Inf. Syst. **47**, 98–115 (2015). https://doi.org/10.1016/j.is.2014.07.006

8. La, Q.D., Ngo, M.V., Dinh, T.Q., Quek, T.Q.S., Shin, H.: Enabling intelligence in fog computing to achieve energy and latency reduction. Digit. Commun. Netw. **5**(1), 3–9 (2019). https://doi.org/10.1016/j.dcan.2018.10.008

9. Hamad, Z.J., Askar, S.: Machine learning powered IoT for smart applications. Int. J. Sci. Bus. **5**(3), 92–100 (2021). https://doi.org/10.5281/zenodo.4497664

10. Abdulkareem, K.H., et al.: A review of fog computing and machine learning: concepts, applications, challenges, and open issues. IEEE Access **7**, 153123–153140 (2019). https://doi.org/10.1109/ACCESS.2019.2947542

11. Sharma, P.K., Chen, M.-Y., Park, J.H.: A software defined fog node based distributed blockchain cloud architecture for IoT. IEEE Access **6**, 115–124 (2018). https://doi.org/10.1109/ACCESS.2017.2757955

12. Li, L., Ota, K., Dong, M.: Deep learning for smart industry: efficient manufacture inspection system with fog computing. IEEE Trans. Ind. Inf. **14**(10), 4665–4673 (2018). https://doi.org/10.1109/TII.2018.2842821

13. Koundoul, B., Kasse, Y., Balde, F., Gueye, B.: A dual ring architecture using controllers for better load balancing in a fog computing environment. In: Mambo, A.D., Gueye, A., Bassioni, G. (eds.) InterSol 2022. LNCS, vol. 449, pp. 144–154. Springer, Cham (2022). https://doi.org/10.1007/978-3-031-23116-2-11

14. Lee, K., Silva, B., Han, K.: Deep learning entrusted to fog nodes (DLEFN) based smart agriculture. Appl. Sci. **10**, 1544 (2020). https://doi.org/10.3390/app10041544

15. Fathy, C., Saleh, S.N.: Integrating deep learning-based IoT and fog computing with software-defined networking for detecting weapons in video surveillance systems. Sensors **22**(14), 5075 (2022). https://doi.org/10.3390/s22145075

16. Csr, P.: Fog computing, deep learning and big data analytics-research directions (2019). https://doi.org/10.1007/978-981-13-3209-8

17. Ahmed, K.D., Askar, S.: Deep learning models for cyber security in IoT networks: a review. Int. J. Sci. Bus. **5**(3), 61–70 (2021)

18. Confais, B., Lebre, A., Parrein, B.: Performance analysis of object store systems in a fog and edge computing infrastructure. In: Hameurlain, A., Küng, J., Wagner, R., Akbarinia, R., Pacitti, E. (eds.) Transactions on Large-Scale Data- and Knowledge-Centered Systems XXXIII. Lecture Notes in Computer Science, pp. 40–79. Springer, Heidelberg (2017). https://doi.org/10.1007/978-3-662-55696-2-2.

19. Xu, X., et al.: Dynamic resource allocation for load balancing in fog environment. Wirel. Commun. Mob. Comput. **2018**, e6421607 (2018). https://doi.org/10.1155/2018/6421607

20. Balde, F., Elbiaze, H., Gueye, B.: GreenPOD: leveraging queuing networks for reducing energy consumption in data centers. In: 2018 21st Conference on Innovation in Clouds, Internet and Networks and Workshops (ICIN), pp. 1–8 (2018). https://doi.org/10.1109/ICIN.2018.8401602.

21. Gueye B., Leduc, G.: Resolving the noxious effect of churn on internet coordinate systems. In: Spyropoulos, T., Hummel, K.A. (eds.) Self-Organizing Systems. Lecture Notes in Computer Science, pp. 162–173. Springer, Heidelberg (2009). https://doi.org/10.1007/978-3-642-10865-5-14.

Data Balancing Process to Strengthen a Malaria Control Prediction System in Senegal

Kodzo Parkoo[1]($\boxtimes$), Bamba Gueye[2], Cheikh Sarr[1], and Ibrahima Dia[3]

[1] Université Iba Der Thiam, Thies, Senegal
kmawuessenam.parkoo@univ-thies.sn
[2] Université Cheikh Anta Diop, Dakar, Senegal
[3] Institut Pasteur de Dakar, Dakar, Senegal

Abstract. Malaria is a public health problem in Senegal. Despite the implementation of prevention and treatment programs, the prevalence rate remains high, although there has been a noticeable decrease over the years.

To further strengthen our efforts in the fight against malaria, we have previously developed a prediction system aimed at assessing the presence or absence of Anopheles larvae in specific sites. This system, is a crucial component of our anti-larval control (ALC) strategy, which involves gathering physico-chemical parameters from the site and using them to predict the likelihood of larvae presence. Given that, our prediction system relies on these physico-chemical parameters, ensuring the reliability and quality of the data is paramount. In our previous study, although we had access to reliable and high-quality data, we encountered an issue with data imbalance. To validate the accuracy of our prediction system, it is essential to address this data imbalance.

Keywords: SMOTE algorithm · balanced data · data prediction · malaria

1 Introduction

In 2021, the World Health Organization (WHO) reported an estimated 247 million cases of malaria worldwide, resulting in 619,000 deaths [1]. Africa accounted for about 95% of all malaria cases and 96% of the associated deaths [2]. Particularly in Senegal, there were 536,850 reported cases and 399 deaths in 2021. These numbers represented an increase compared to the year 2020 with the 445,313 confirmed cases and 373 deaths reported in 2020 [3]. Thus, despite the diligent efforts made through the national malaria control program, malaria is still present in Senegal.

One unique particularity of malaria control in Senegal is its focus on combating the adult stage of the Anopheles. An essential strategy involves area-specific interventions targeting the larval development phase, known as Larval Control (LAL). To enhance LAL efforts, previous work has aimed to develop a predictive model to determine the presence or absence of larvae. The prediction process relies on physico-chemical parameters from Anopheles breeding sites [4].

O. Habachi et al. (Eds.): UNet 2023, LNCS 14757, pp. 85–95, 2024.
https://doi.org/10.1007/978-3-031-62488-9_7

However, it should be noted, that the quality of predictions from the previous model is questionable due to the confusion matrix of the latter. Indeed, the results from the confusion matrix of the prediction model yield four results: True Positive (TP), True Negative (TN), False Positive (FP) and False Negative (FN), with respectively TP corresponding to the presence of larvae and TN to the absence of larvae. An analysis made on the results of the confusion matrix shows that the value of TN is equal to zero (0). This value revealed an imbalance in the data source used to set up the prediction model [4]. There are various potential solutions to address the data source imbalance. One option is to create a new database, which would involve gathering and processing new data. However, this approach needs substantial costs. In order to maintain the reliability of the results of the prediction model, it is therefore necessary to balance the existing data and re-test the model. The efficiency of this prediction model will be a benefit in the LAL.

The remaining sections of this document are organized as follows. Section 2 deals with the motivations for choosing the SMOTE algorithm. Afterwards, Sect. 3 discusses the different tools, methods used, and implementations made in this research. Section 4 presents the outcomes and findings from the implementation and comprehensive discussion of the results. Finally, Sect. 5 depicts the conclusion presents some perspectives and challenges.

2 Various SMOTE Algorithms

Faced with the need to balance data in order to improve prediction, the use of SMOTE seems appropriate. SMOTE (Synthetic Minority Oversampling Technique) appears to be a well-suited approach for oversampling minority observations [5]. As data imbalance is a frequent problem in classification and affects the performance of machine learning models, a suitable solution should be proposed.

In the field of medicine, data analysis methods have proved extremely useful in healthcare for early diagnosis to provide better medical treatment and thus minimize the mortality rate in cases such as breast cancer, diabetes, coronary heart disease, kidney disorders, and more. However, a survey of existing models reveals shortcomings in data processing analysis and also in learning classification algorithms. This is due to the imbalance in the data, leading to unbalanced results. To address these challenges and ensure the reliability of predictions, the SMOTE algorithm, more precisely Distance-based SMOTE (D-SMOTE) and Bi-phasic SMOTE (BP-SMOTE) coupled with learning algorithms, have enabled Sowjanya A. M. et al. to propose hybrid sampling techniques that enhance prediction accuracy in unbalanced health data [6].

The existence of several variants of SMOTE allows for its adaptation to various types of data or problems. These variants include: classical SMOTE, proposed by Chawla et al. [5] as an alternative to random cloning of minority data, which can lead to overlearning.

SMOTE-NC (Nominal Continuous), which is an extension of SMOTE for mixed data, i.e., data containing both numerical and categorical variables. It was introduced by Chawla et al. [7] as an improvement on classical SMOTE, which cannot handle categorical variables without encoding them in numerical form, giving rise to errors. Therefore, Borderline-SMOTE [8], focuses on minority observations located at the border between classes since they are more difficult to classify.

Furthermore, ADASYN (Adaptive Synthetic Sampling).[9], adapts the number of synthetic data to be generated according to the degree of nesting between classes whereas SVMSMOTE considers an SVM (Support Vector Machine) to figure out the most relevant minority observations to oversample.

On the other hand Safe-Level-SMOTE [10] defines a safety level for each minority observation, based on the number of neighbors in the same class, and favors observations with a high safety level. In contrast, Cluster-SMOTE, groups minority observations into clusters, and generates synthetic data within each cluster. In addition to adapting to different types of data, these different variants also pave the way for new SMOTE-based methods.

The ASN-SMOTE, as proposed by Yi et al. [11], represents a novel approach to oversampling unbalanced data. It is based on the classical SMOTE but improving the neighbor's selection and synthetic data generation. Its aim is to reduce noise and improve data quality for the minority class. The main idea is to use the majority class to perceive the decision frontier, and adoptively select qualified neighbors for each minority observation. This reduces noise and improves data quality for the minority class [11].

Regarding its advantages, the SMOTE algorithm provides several key benefits. It improves the performance of classification models despite the presence of imbalances. In addition, it prevents overtraining and preserves information. SMOTE generates synthetic samples by combining characteristics of neighbors and reduces classification bias that can occur when the model is strongly biased towards the majority class. These advantages bring SMOTE a highly suitable algorithm for addressing imbalances in preparation for predictive modeling.

3 Materials and Methods

3.1 Experimental Settings

The implementation of the SMOTE algorithm was carried out using Python. To do this we deployed a virtual machine, Windows 7, with 4 GB of RAM, 60 GB of storage and 4 Intel processors at 2.10 GHz. On this machine, we installed Anaconda 3, with different applications: Jupyter Lab and Jupyter Notebook.

The main steps of the data processing were: import of libraries, import of the initial database (unbalanced), removal of non-determinant columns, exploratory analysis for descriptive statistics of the data, implementation of the SMOTE algorithm, and verification of the balancing of the data.

3.2 Data Examination for Balancing

The data under consideration stems from measurements conducted in October 2020 within the Toubacouta district and its surroundings due to the sympatric presence of An. *Arabiensis*, An. *Gambiae* and An. *Coluzzii* species and the observation of contrasting hybridization rates between the latter two. In order to collect these physicochemical parameters, an inspection was made at each site, the larvae were collected using either the «dipping» or «pipetting» method, depending on the size of the sites, and were subsequently placed in labeled jars denoting the site number.

For each site, a comprehensive record was made of the presence or absence of Culicidae other than Anopheles, as well as observations regarding vegetation, turbidity, and sunlight. Following this, precise measurements of nests dimensions (length, width, depth) were taken with a decameter, alongside the assessment of additional factors such as their status, turbidity, sunlight exposure, and the presence of vegetation or other mosquito larvae.

Subsequently, the following parameters were then measured with a portable field tester (SD Card Real time Datalogger): temperature, amount of dissolved oxygen, salt content and pH. The larvae were then sorted in the laboratory and stored in tubes containing 70° ethanol. The dataset encompasses a representation of the physicochemical characteristics and the presence or absence of larvae.

Table 1. Presentation of the data collected

PH	Temp	Conductivity	Saltiness	Dissolved oxygen	Turbidity	Sunshine	Vegetation	Status
7,45	32,5	43,9	0	11	0	0	0	1
7,68	34,1	227	0	8,7	1	0	1	0
7,26	30,2	52,6	0	20,2	1	0	0	1

In Table 1, only the physico-chemical characteristics and the presence of larvae are of interest. Furthermore, our final data source will retain only the latter [4]. The main reason for the imbalance in the data comes from the fact that out of 4700 record lines are composed mostly by the presence of larvae.

3.3 Imbalance Concept and Balancing Algorithm

Unbalanced data is a common situation when dealing with real data. We can evoke the imbalance when we have observations distributed in two (02) classes and the frequencies of these two (02) classes are not in a ratio of 50% each. However, in real data, the notion of imbalance is evoked if the ratio is between 10% and 90%, i.e. if the imbalance exceeds 10% for the minority class.[12].

In case of data imbalance, the need to rebalance the data goes through two (02) methods: subsampling and oversampling.

Subsampling consists of removing part of the majority class in order to give more importance to minority individuals. Oversampling consists in increasing the number of minority individuals so that they have more importance in the modeling. These two (02) balancing methods implemented thanks to the SMOTE algorithm on which we have previously exposed. In our particular case, an oversampling will be performed on the minority class characterized by the absence of larvae at the status level. This allows to densify the population of minority individuals in a more homogeneous way [5].

3.4 SMOTE Implementation

The data that require balancing were collected in October 2020 by a team from the Pasteur Institute of Dakar in Toubacouta, Senegal. These initial data include information on the deposit, the physico-chemical characteristics of the deposit and the presence or not of larvae. For our prediction, we focused on the physico-chemical characteristics and the presence or absence of larvae. It is worth noticing that fixed chemical parameters and a couple of physical parameters will be kept as well as the presence or absence of larvae.

Table 2. Retained physico-chemical parameters.

pH	Temperature	Conductivity	Salinity	Dissolved Oxygen	Turbidity	Status
7.45	32.5	43.9	0	11	0	1
7.68	34.1	227	0	8.7	1	0
7.26	30.2	52.6	0	20.2	1	1
6.87	32.7	25.5	0	5.2	1	1
7.70	33.6	68.9	0	23.6	1	1

The Table 2 informs about the physico-chemical parameters retained in our prediction.

Table 3. Database description

	pH	Temperature	Conductivity	Salinity	Dissolved Oxygen	Turbidity	Status
count	4794.0	4794.0	4794.0	4794.0	4794.0	4794.0	4794.0
mean	7.387	31.3489	208.6042	0.0080	21.4931	0.531915	0.9148
std	0.9886	2.732198	271.673	0.0192	8.421062	0.49932	0.2790
min	3.630	25.00	15.80	0.0	5.20	0.0	0.0
25%	6.980	29.80	58.10	0.0	15.7	0.0	1.0
50%	7.360	32.10	112.70	0.0	21.10	1.0	1.0
75%	7.790	33.60	255.0	0.010	26.80	1.0	1.0
max	9.90	34.30	1520.0	0.10	35.70	1.0	1.0

In Table 3, we can notice that our database consists of 4794 occurrences, with an average value of approximately 0.914894 for the «Status» column. Notably, this column represents the presence and absence, denoted by 0 and 1, respectively. The average value of 0.9148 for this column is indicative of the extent of the data imbalance.

Table 4 illustrates valuable insights into the extent of the data imbalance. Specifically, we observe that there are 4386 occurrences indicating the presence of larvae compared to

Table 4. Status options count

Status value	Count
1	4386
0	408

only 408 for the absence of larvae. To correct this imbalance, we resort to oversampling, thanks to the SMOTE algorithm. The objective of the execution of the SMOTE algorithm is to achieve parity between the occurrences of the minority class and the majority class.

3.5 Verifying Data Balance

The execution of the oversampling with the SMOTE algorithm on our data provided us with a result. In order to know whether the balancing was successful, we performed a descriptive analysis of our data source.

Table 5. Database description after SMOTE

	pH	Temperature	Conductivity	Salinity	Dissolved Oxygen	Turbidity	Status
count	8772	8772.0	8772.0	8772.00	8772.0	8772.0	8772.0
mean	7.442376	31.484302	199.656920	0.006651	20.517004	0.516986	0.500
std	0.749027	2.661693	219.109651	0.015416	9.630774	0.499740	0.500029
min	3.63	25.000	15.800	0.000	5.200	0.000	0.000
25%	7.27	29.800	58.100	0.000	10.500	0.000	0.000
50%	7.36	32.100	120.500	0.000	21.100	1.000	0.500
75%	7.79	34.000	255.000	0.010	26.800	1.000	1.000
max	9.90	34.300	1520.000	0.100	35.700	1.000	1.000

As shown in Table 5, the average related to the distribution of the status (regrouping the presence or absence of larvae, represented by 0 and 1 is 0.5.

Our main objective is to confirm the reliability of the prediction system implemented in [4]. Indeed, it is mandatory to recalibrate the confusion matrix using the balanced data source.

3.6 Confusion Matrix

The confusion matrix, often referred to as a contingency table, serves as a vital tool for assessing the performance of a classification model. In its basic form, it compares the actual data for a target variable with the predictions made by the model [13].

After splitting our balanced database by SMOTE into two for training and prediction, we implement the logistic regression algorithm to the data.

The confusion matrix result in Table 6 indicates the reliability level of our possible prediction tests.

Table 6. Confusion matrix result

Result	Count
True Positive (TP)	1181
True Negative (TN)	1100
False Positive (FP)	1094
False Negative (FN)	1011

3.7 ROC Curve

The ROC (Receiver Operating Characteristic) curve is a graphical tool used in the context of classification problems. It allows us to evaluate the performance of different classification models. Its use also includes the AUC (Area Under the Curve), which helps to compare different models [14].

In our specific case, we have access to the results of the confusion matrices for our data before and after applying the SMOTE algorithm for balancing. Table 6 shows the results obtained after applying SMOTE, while Table 7 presents the results before SMOTE was applied.

Table 7. Confusion matrix result without SMOTE [4]

Result	Count
True Positive (TP)	2193
True Negative (TN)	0
False Positive (FP)	204
False Negative (FN)	0

To construct the ROC curve, we need to determine the True Positive Rate (TPR) and the False Positive Rate (FPR). The respective mathematical representations are as follows: $\text{TPR} = \text{TP}/(\text{TP} + \text{FN})$ and $\text{FPR} = \text{FP}/(\text{TN} + \text{FP})$ [14]. After evaluating our model, we obtain the classification thresholds as detailed in Table 8.

Table 8. Threshold's classification

Class. Thresh	0.1	0.2	0.2	0.3	0.4	0.5	0.6	0.7	0.8
t_v_posi	0.01	0.11	0.13	0.02	0.03	0.04	0.05	0.06	0.8
t_f_posi	0.01	0.03	0.08	0.015	0.25	0.42	0.65	0.08	0.95
t_v_posi_smote	0.05	0.18	0.42	0.63	0.76	0.87	0.92	0.96	0.99
t_f_posi_smote	0.01	0.03	0.08	0.15	0.25	0.42	0.65	0.8	0.95

4 Results and Discussion

4.1 Balanced Data

The results presented in table 5 indicate an average value between the presence and the non-presence at 0.5. This leads to an equality of distribution on the presence and non-presence of larvae. This enables to correct the imbalance that was posed on all our collected data, Table 9.

Table 9. Status options count after balancing

Status value	Count
1	4386
0	4386

4.2 Reliability of the Prediction System

The reliability of the prediction system implemented in [4] is based on the data balance on one hand and on the confusion matrix on the other. The interpretation of this matrix is based on True Positive (TP) and Positive False (PF). TP presents the accuracy and PF the recall on the accuracy of the predictions. Thus, with a high accuracy and a high recall we can assume that our data are well managed by the model.

4.3 Representation of the ROC Curve

The result of the verification of our classification thresholds grouped in Table 8 gives the curve illustrated in Fig. 1.

By observation of Fig. 1, we distinguish the curves representing data from our initial database and those for the database balanced using SMOTE. The point (0,0) represents the threshold where everything is classified as negative, i.e., no false positives (FPR = 0) and no true positives (TPR = 0). The point (1,1) represents the threshold where everything is classified as positive, i.e., no true negative (FPR = 1) and no false negative (TPR = 1). We can see that the ROC curve in red, representing data balanced by SMOTE, evolves gradually for TPR values tending towards 1. In our particular case our TPR is 0.95, expressing better logistic regression performance on the balanced database.

4.4 Discussions

The implementation of a reliable prediction system requires measures to ensure its sustainability and accuracy. The system set up in [4] faced reliability issues, particularly in its tendency to predict situations of larval presence. The root of the problem was the imbalance in the training data used for the model, it was therefore imperative to have a balanced data source in order to retest the prediction system. The first option to have a

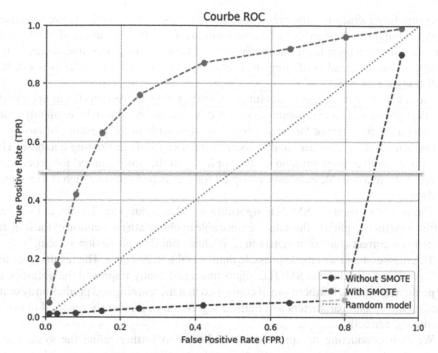

Fig. 1. ROC curve

new source of data, was to make a new collection of on the field by taking this time, the care to collect on zones of which was sure of the absence of the larvae.

This processing enables to have a database with a near balance on the presence or non-presence of larvae. This first option could not be implemented, because of various constraints associated with scientific fieldwork. A second option was therefore proposed, to balance the existing data. To achieve this, we employed the SMOTE algorithm, utilizing oversampling techniques. This approach promotes building a new database, which in turn facilitates the retesting of our prediction system.

Based on the results obtained from the ROC curve, we can confidently conclude that the use of the SMOTE algorithm to balance our data enhanced the prediction system's quality and reliability. At this stage, we can affirm the system's dependability for predictive purposes.

5 Conclusion

The establishment of a reliable and balanced database for collecting physico-chemical parameters from Anopheles breeding sites and determining the presence or not of Anopheles larvae, proved to be a complex task.

The database we have created, used for prediction, is the result of collecting physico-chemical parameters directly on the deposits. These data have a major particularity justifying their use: all parameters are correlated by the presence or absence of larvae.

This point being crucial in the prediction, this database was suitable. However, based on its exploitation, the confusion matrix resulting from the execution of the logistic regression shows a significant imbalance in the database. This led to inaccuracy in the process of learning and predicting data, although the prediction model is good, the predictions are incorrect.

Faced with this challenge, two solutions were possible: the resumption of operations to collect physico-chemical parameters with this time the need to take equitably from roosts with the presence of larvae and breeding sites without the presence of larvae on the one hand and on the other hand to balance the data from our existing database. The first option involves huge mission costs coupled with the time required for processing in order to have a suitable database, we opted for the second option which is to balance the database.

Therefore, we used the SMOTE algorithm to balance our data. Thanks to the over-sampling method applied to the data, we were able to obtain after execution of the logistic regression a correct confusion matrix to re-evaluate our data prediction system.

This reassessment was made possible thanks to the ROC curve. The results from the ROC curve indicate that the SMOTE algorithm significantly improved the accuracy of our prediction system. Furthermore, it confirmed that the learning and prediction system, based on the crucial parameters and logistic regression as previously reported in [4], is functioning correctly.

We plan conducting comprehensive field tests to further refine the system and effectively relaunch larval control efforts in order to reduce the malaria prevalence rate.

References

1. Despite continued impact of COVID-19, malaria cases and deaths remained stable in 2021. Accessed 28 Mar 2023. https://www.who.int/news/item/08-12-2022-despite-continued-imp act-of-covid-19--malaria-cases-and-deaths-remained-stable-in-2021
2. Fact sheet about malaria. Accessed 28 Mar 2023. https://www.who.int/news-room/fact-she ets/detail/malaria
3. Le paludisme au Sénégal en 2021 (document). Accessed 09 Apr 2023. https://infomed.sn/le-paludisme-au-senegal-en-2021-document/
4. Parkoo, K.M., Gueye, B., Sarr, C., Dia, I.: Data prediction system in malaria control based on physio-chemical parameters of anopheles breeding sites. EAI Endorsed Trans. Internet Things 8(4), e3–e3 (2022). https://doi.org/10.4108/eetiot.v8i4.2936
5. Chawla, N.V., Bowyer, K.W., Hall, L.O., Kegelmeyer, W.P.: SMOTE: synthetic minority over-sampling technique. J. Artif. Intell. Res. 16, 321–357 (2002). https://doi.org/10.1613/jai r.953
6. Sowjanya, A.M., Mrudula, O.: Effective treatment of imbalanced datasets in health care using modified SMOTE coupled with stacked deep learning algorithms. Appl. Nanosci. 13(3), 1829–1840 (2023). https://doi.org/10.1007/s13204-021-02063-4
7. Chawla, N.V., Lazarevic, A., Hall, L.O., Bowyer, K.W.: SMOTEBoost: improving prediction of the minority class in boosting. In: Lavrač, N., Gamberger, D., Todorovski, L., Blockeel, H. (eds.) PKDD 2003. LNCS (LNAI), vol. 2838, pp. 107–119. Springer, Heidelberg (2003). https://doi.org/10.1007/978-3-540-39804-2_12
8. Han, H., Wang, W.-Y., Mao, B.-H.: Borderline-SMOTE: a new over-sampling method in imbalanced data sets learning. In: Huang, D.-S., Zhang, X.-P., Huang, G.-B. (eds.) ICIC

2005. LNCS, vol. 3644, pp. 878–887. Springer, Heidelberg (2005). https://doi.org/10.1007/11538059_91

9. He, H., Bai, Y., Garcia, E., Li, S.: ADASYN: adaptive synthetic sampling approach for imbalanced learning. In: presented at the Proceedings of the International Joint Conference on Neural Networks, pp. 1322–1328 (2008). https://doi.org/10.1109/IJCNN.2008.4633969

10. Bunkhumpornpat, C., Sinapiromsaran, K., Lursinsap, C.: Safe-level-SMOTE: safe-level-synthetic minority over-sampling technique for handling the class imbalanced problem. In: Theeramunkong, T., Kijsirikul, B., Cercone, N., Ho, T.-B. (eds.) PAKDD 2009. LNCS (LNAI), vol. 5476, pp. 475–482. Springer, Heidelberg (2009). https://doi.org/10.1007/978-3-642-01307-2_43

11. Yi, X., Xu, Y., Hu, Q., Krishnamoorthy, S., Li, W., Tang, Z.: ASN-SMOTE: a synthetic minority oversampling method with adaptive qualified synthesizer selection. Complex Intell. Syst. **8**(3), 2247–2272 (2022). https://doi.org/10.1007/s40747-021-00638-w

12. Tremblay, C.: Imbalanced data et machine learning. Kobia. Accessed 10 Apr 2023. https://kobia.fr/imbalanced-data-et-machine-learning/

13. Alexandre. Managing Unbalanced Classification Problems - Part 1. Data Science Courses | DataScientest. Accessed 10 May 2023. https://datascientest.com/en/management-of-unbalanced-classification-problems-i

14. ROC Curve—Machine Learning—DATA SCIENCE. Accessed 20 July 2023. https://datascience.eu/machine-learning/understanding-auc-roc-curve/

Tactile Internet and Internet of Things

Performance Evaluation of LoRa in a Linear Deployment Scenario

Ass Diane, El Hadji Malick Ndoye[✉], and Ousmane Diallo

Laboratoire d'Informatique et d'Ingénieurie pour l'Innovation (LI3), Université
Assane Seck de Ziguinchor, Ziguinchor, Senegal
a.diane20150545@zig.univ.sn, {elm.ndoye,odiallo}@univ-zig.sn

Abstract. The Internet of Things (IoT) has become an essential daily
field. This is mainly because of the advances in digital technologies,
miniaturization, the reduced cost of devices, and wireless connectivity.
LPWAN (Low Power Wide Area Network) technologies such as LoRa
provide effective connectivity solutions for IoT applications deployed in
vast areas. Indeed, they offer a long transmission range and low energy
consumption. LoRa is ideal for monitoring pipelines, railway infrastructures, roads, borders, etc., which have linear topology.

This article aims to study the coverage and connectivity of a LoRa network in the context of a linear deployment to provide a basis for explor-
ing a border surveillance application in the Lower Casamance region of
southern Senegal in West Africa. A deployment method for LoRa nodes
is proposed to achieve complete coverage and connectivity. An analytical
study is accomplished based on the transmission success probability of a
given Lora node. Using Omnetpp, through Flora, we simulate different
values of the parameters on which the probability of success depends to
analyze their impact.

Keywords: Internet of Things · LPWAN · LoRa · LoRaWAN · linear
deployment

1 Introduction

The Internet of Things (IoT) is a very successful concept due to the significant
progress in computing, telecommunications, and electronic miniaturization [1].
It contributes to the development of several areas, including health with the connection of medical equipment and easy access to patient medical records, smart
cities with intelligent street lighting and a smart environment, agriculture and
livestock with the innovative irrigation system and "connected collar", industry with predictive maintenance. Some applications of the Internet of Things
require a long-range transmission and low energy consumption. Low Power Wide
Area Network (LPWAN) [2] technologies, such as LoRa, have emerged to meet
communication needs in IoT applications. Some applications, such as borders,
gas pipelines, oil pipelines, aqueducts, and roads, need linear topology for node

O. Habachi et al. (Eds.): UNet 2023, LNCS 14757, pp. 99–111, 2024.
https://doi.org/10.1007/978-3-031-62488-9_8

deployment. Border surveillance is a real challenge for governments since the world faces an ever-increasing crime rate. Globalization has made it possible to open borders between countries to facilitate the free movement of people. In Senegal, the Casamance region in the southern is the crossroads of three countries (Gambia to the north, Guinea-Bissau, and Guinea-Conakry to the south). The border areas of Casamance face several problems, including cattle theft and drug trafficking. Conventional monitoring methods have reached their limits, so it is necessary to turn to modern solutions based on the IoT. LoRa-based solution for border monitoring in the case of Casamance can help achieve area coverage and connectivity for data routing. Therefore, this paper proposes a method for placing nodes, and the probability of success is defined to estimate connectivity. The influence of the number of gateways, node density, and LoRa physical layer parameters on connectivity is analyzed by simulation using FLoRa [3] based on OMNeT++.

The rest of the paper is organized as follows. Section 2 presents an overview of LoRa technology, including the physical and MAC layers. Section 3 summarizes the leading work on the performance of LoRa networks in different environments, in various sectors, and with other metrics. System modeling, including linear node deployment and probability of success, is described in Sect. 4. Section 5 presents and discusses the results of simulations with different parameters. Finally, the paper is concluded in Sect 6 with further research directions for future work.

2   Fundamentals of LoRa Technology

A Lora network's architecture comprises four components: end devices, gateways, a network server, and an application server. The end devices have LoRa modules for sending and receiving radio signals and communicating with the gateways. These have an interface that allows them to have TCP/IP-based communication with the network server that allows the administration of the whole network. Indeed, it routes information from the end nodes to the corresponding application servers and removes redundant packets.

2.1   The LoRa Physical Layer

LoRa is based on spread spectrum modulation, which uses the Chirp technique (signal in which the frequency increases (up-chirp) or decreases (down-chirp) with time). Spread spectrum is a technique that allows an information signal to be transmitted over a bandwidth several times greater than the minimum Bandwidth required. The modulated signals have a constant amplitude with a variable frequency. Spread spectrum modulation reduces energy consumption and increases resistance to interference. In LoRa, signals are modulated in the ISM (Industrial, Scientific, and Medical) the frequency band without a license varies according to the region (e.g., 868 MHz in Europe, 915 MHz in North America) [4].

The performance of LoRa nodes depends mainly on the following parameters:

The **spreading factor** is a quantity defined by the ratio between chip rate and symbol rate. A chip represents pulses of a spread spectrum code, and a symbol represents several chips. A chirp contains 2^{SF} bits per symbol. In a LoRa network, the spreading factor is an integer between 7 and 12 [5]. This parameter allows the transmission range and rate to vary and send simultaneously on a given channel. A high spreading factor implies a long transmission range and a low data rate [1].

Bandwidth is the maximum and minimum frequency difference. High bandwidth values result in high data rates [5].

Code rate: LoRa uses the FEC (Forward error correction) technique to detect errors in transmitted frames and correct them too. Extra bits are added in the frame, more precisely at the payload level. In LoRa, these extra bits are controlled by the code rate (CR). The values that the code rate can take are 1, 2, 3, or 4.

2.2 The LoRaWAN Protocol

LoRaWAN (Long Range Wide Area Network) is an open protocol proposed by LoRa Alliance (Organization in charge of promoting LoRaWAN). It corresponds to the MAC layer (Medium Access Control) of the OSI (Open Systems. Interconnection) reference model. LoRaWAN is designed to connect objects equipped with LoRa modules and powered by battery energy to the Internet. A LoRaWAN network consists of LoRa nodes, gateways equipped with LoRa modules, an interface for connecting to the Internet, a network server, and an application server. LoRaWAN uses the channel access technique of the ALOHA type [6]. Each node in the network can transmit whenever it wishes. According to the LoRaWAN specification [7], Data transmission is performed on multiple channels. Indeed, each device has a maximum of 16 tracks that can be preconfigured before a terminal joins a LoRaWAN network. A LoRa frame consists of a preamble, a header, the payload, and an error control field. If the title contains information about the CRC (Cyclic Redundancy Check) and the CR (Code Rate), the frame is said to be explicit; otherwise, it is implicit.

The LoRaWAN specification defines three modes of operation for end nodes suitable for various IOT applications. Each method of operation is commonly referred to as a class (class A, class B, and class C).

3 Related Work

In recent years, research has focused more on LoRa technology. The performance of LoRa networks under different environments, in other sectors with different metrics, and using this technology in a linear deployment context have been the subject of several researches.

In [8], the authors set themselves the goal of developing a LoRa-based architecture for monitoring the formation of black powder in gas pipelines. To achieve this, they opted for a linear multi-hop topology and proposed a new protocol based on node synchronization with a low-duty cycle. Still within the framework of linear deployment, the authors of this article [9] have developed a new LoRa MAC protocol called pm-LoRa. This protocol can set up a multi-hop ad-hoc network for monitoring and control applications where linear sensor deployment is required. In wide-area monitoring, the authors of [10] support using LoRa technology with multi-hop communication. They proposed a reliable multi-hop communication protocol for a linear network, including the construction and data exploitation periods based on LoRa.

Papers [11] and [12] propose an empirical evaluation in an indoor and a mountain environment, respectively. The indoor climate considered is the University of Oulu in Finland. By performing the experiments with different spreading factors, bandwidth, and transmit power, the authors [11] concluded that with a spreading factor equal to 12 and a transmit power of 14 dBm, a single base station can cover the entire campus area (570 m North to South and over 320 m East to West) based on the successfully delivered packet rate. In [12], the effectiveness of LoRa technology is evaluated for mountain search and rescue operations. Experimental results are used to compare LoRa with other technologies such as Bluetooth, Wi-Fi, and ARVA in terms of range, robustness of communication links, and battery life. From this comparison, it appears that LoRa (76.6% overall score) is more adequate than Wi-Fi (42.5% overall score), Bluetooth (31.6% overall score), and ARVA (65.4% overall score).

The authors of [13,14], and [15] discussed the use of LoRa in different sectors such as agriculture, smart buildings, industry, etc. The authors of [13] studied the performance of LoRa in an open-field agricultural landscape using simulation. The data retrieval rate and energy consumption are measured depending on different parameters. The results showed that, obviously, the parameters of the PHY layer impact both metrics and similarly, the dimensions of the deployment area influence the retrieval rate and energy consumption. In [14], LoRa is used as an acquisition and communication tool in an intelligent building. LoRa nodes are distributed in a 16-storey building. The two performance indicators are the network transmission delay and the packet loss rate. The propagation of the LoRa signal inside the building is studied with different values of transmission power, payload length, and communication rate. A use case of LoRa in the flower industry is highlighted in [15]. Indeed, trolleys represent the network nodes and have to communicate with a server through a gateway. The measurements showed that a gateway can cover 34000 m2 of indoor area with a spreading factor of 7, but a gateway can relay messages from 6000 nodes. The conclusions are based on the RSSI and SNR values at different locations in the warehouse and the packet loss rate.

Despite numerous performance evaluations of LoRa under several scenarios, to our knowledge, only some studies target the use of LoRa in a linear deployment framework. This paper characterizes LoRa in a linear node layout scenario. In a simulation environment, we see the impact of several configurations of the LoRa physical layer on the network performance regarding packet delivery.

4   System Model

Monitoring specific infrastructures such as pipelines, railway, roads, etc., requires a linear placement of the network nodes. We consider a linear topolgy composed of LoRa nodes for border line surveillance purposes. It is assumed that the nodes are deployed deterministically and the distance between two adjacent nodes is constant. Indeed, the coverage and the connectivity are related to the nodes' placement. The long communication range and low energy consumption motivate the choice of LoRa technology, as described above. They are crucial for evaluating a LoRa surveillance network's reliability. The topology comprises a set of LoRa nodes. $(N_1, N_2, ..., N_n)$, several gateways $(G_1, G_2, ..., G_m)$ and a network server as illustrated in Fig. 1. The LoRa nodes use the LoRaWAN protocol to communicate with the gateways. The communication between the gateways and the network server is done via IP(Internet protocol).

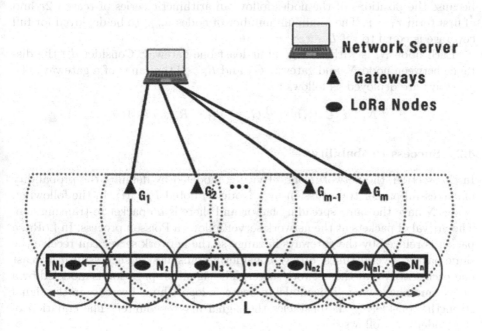

Fig. 1. Network topology.

4.1   Linear Placement of End-Nodes

We consider a linear monitoring area (in 1D) of length L and n LoRa nodes $\{N_1, N_2, ..., N_n\}$ stationary deployed in the area. We have opted for a deterministic deployment of LoRa nodes because the information related to the zone is always known in advance [16]. The location of each node N_i is given by x_i where $i = 1, 2, ..., n$. d_i is the distance between two adjacent nodes N_i and N_{i+1}. The nodes have the same sensing radius $r > 0$. The coverage of the deployment area can be partial or total, depending on the application's requirements. In the context of this work, full coverage will be ideal, e.g., detecting drug trafficking at the border, so we define full coverage by the following formula:

$$\forall x \in [0, L] \; ; \; \exists N_i \diagup |x - x_i| \leq r \, , \, i \in [1, n] \tag{1}$$

In the case of full coverage, a given point may be covered by more than one LoRa node. This does not optimize the cost of deployment and increases the density of nodes, affecting the network's performance. The advantage of full coverage lies in the fact that it increases the robustness of the network and the faults tolerance. So if we aim to optimize the cost by deploying fewer nodes (n_{min}) to achieve full coverage, we propose a central deployment ($d_i = 2r$), the position of a node i is given by :

$$x_i = x_1 + 2(i - 1)r \; with \; x_1 = r \tag{2}$$

because the positions of the nodes follow an arithmetic series of reason $2r$ and of first term $x_1 = r$. The minimum number of nodes n_{min} to be deployed for full coverage is equal to i if $L - x_i \leq r$.

Each node N_i is within range of at least one gateway. Consider d_{ij} the distance between node N_i and gateway G_j and $R_c > 0$ the range of a gateway. The gateways are deployed as follows :

$$\forall N_i \, , \, i \in [1, n] \; ; \; \exists G_j \diagup d_{ij} \leq R_c \, , \, j \in [1, m] \tag{3}$$

4.2   Success Probability

In this section, the network connectivity is modeled by defining the probability of successful packet transmission by a Node N_i noted $P_{succ}(i)$. In the following, Nodes N have the same spreading factor and there is no packet re-transmission. The arrival of packets at the network server follows a Poisson process. In LoRa, a packet is relayed by the gateways in range so the network server can receive the same packet several times. So, we consider a transmission successful if at least one packet arrives at the network server. The signal propagation is modeled by a LogNormalShadowing. This model indicates a logarithmic decrease in the signal strength, considering the obstacles the signal may encounter. The equation of the model is as follows:

$$PL_{dB}(d) = PL_0 + 10\gamma Log_{10}(\frac{d}{d_0}) + X_\sigma \tag{4}$$

where PL_{dB} is the path-loss by the signal during propagation, PL_0 represents the path loss over a reference distance d_0 which can be between 1 and 10 m for small areas or 1 km in larger areas [17]. γ is the path loss exponent with a value between 2 and 6. d is the distance between the LoRa end-device node and the gateway. X_σ is a random variable reflecting noise causing signal attenuation due to obstacles. The received power of signal k transmitted from a node N_i to a gateway G_j is expressed as:

$$PR_{ij}(k) = TP_i(k) - PL_{dB}(d) \tag{5}$$

where $TP_i(k)$ is the transmission power of packet k by node N_i. The successful transmission of a packet depends on the transmission time given by the formula $T(k)$ defined in [18] and the traffic intensity. A LoRa frame is lost if one of the following conditions occurs:

- The power difference between the first and the second frame, arriving at the same time on a gateway with different SF, is lower than the received signal-to-interference-plus-noise ratio (SINR) of the first frame (see Table 1)(Inter-SF collisions)
- The received power difference of two Lora frames, arriving at the same time on a gateway with the same SF and same bandwidth, is less than 6 dB(Intra-SF collisions). In this article, only intra-SF collisions are considered.

Table 1. Minimum sinr required to demodulate per spreading factor (SF) [21]

SF	Min SINR (dB)
7	−7
8	−9
9	−11.5
10	−14
11	−16.5
12	−19

The probability of a successful transmission from a N_i node in an Aloha protocol is given by the formula [19]:

$$P_{succ}(i) = e^{-2G} \tag{6}$$

where G is the number of packets transmitted at the time the N_i node transmits, it depends on the intensity of the traffic (λ) and the time required (T) to transmit a packet on the channel. Then, $G = \lambda \times T$. Assuming all nodes have the same SF, we can estimate the traffic intensity λ as the ratio between the number of nodes and the average time interval(T_{avg}) for each node to generate packets. Thus, $\lambda = \frac{n}{T_{avg}}$. T is a function of the packet's length (Len) and the number of bits that can be transmitted per unit of time (the bit rate). According to information provided by Semtech [20], the bit rate (R_b) is equal to:

$$R_b = SF \times \frac{CR}{\frac{2^{SF}}{BW}} bits/sec \tag{7}$$

The time required to transmit a packet is $T = \frac{Len}{R_b}$. The probability of a successful transmission is now written as :

$$P_{succ}(i) = e^{-2 \times \lambda \times T} = e^{-\frac{n \times 2^{SF+1} \times Len}{T_{avg} \times SF \times CR \times BW}} \tag{8}$$

5 Results and Discussion

The probability of success(P_{succ}) is simulated using omnnet++ and FLoRa (Framework For LoRa) [3]. The objective is to analyze the impact of LoRa physical layer parameters, the traffic intensity λ, and the number of gateways in the network (m). The simulation topology comprises LoRa nodes, gateways, and a network server, as shown in Fig. 2.

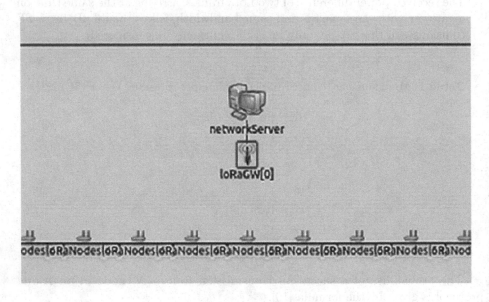

Fig. 2. simulation topology

We consider a 10km linear monitoring area where n LoRa and m gateways are deployed. Simulation parameters are represented in the Table 2. As defined above, the traffic intensity is a function of the network's number of nodes and the time that a node takes to generate a packet. With a constant T_{avg}, high traffic intensity reflects high node density n. Unsurprisingly, the higher the traffic intensity induces a lower probability of success (see Fig. 3). This is due to the increased interference caused by high node density.

To analyse the physical factors such as SF, CR and BW, the number of terminal nodes (n) is equal to 100 and the average time (T_{avg}) for a node to generate a packet is 50 s. The code rate has no significant impact on the probability of

Table 2. Main simulation parameters

Parameters	Values
L	10 km
λ	$2.02, 1.02, 0.68, 0.52, 0.42$
m	$\{1, 2\}$
Mac Protocol	LoRaWAN
Simulation time	1 day
Repeat simulation	3
Spreading factor	$\{7, 8, 9, 10, 11, 12\}$
Transmitting power (TP)	14 dBm
Code rate (CR)	$\{1, 2, 3, 4\}$
bandwith	$\{125, 250, 500\}\, KHz$
Spread model	LogNormalShadowing
d_0	1000 m
γ	2.08
X_σ	3.57

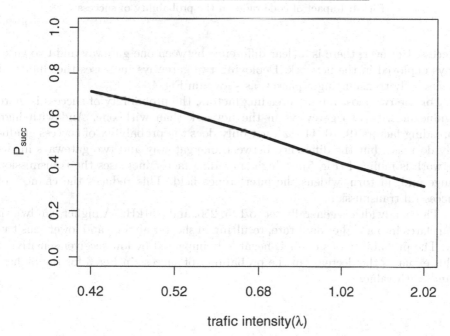

Fig. 3. Probability of success as a function of traffic intensity

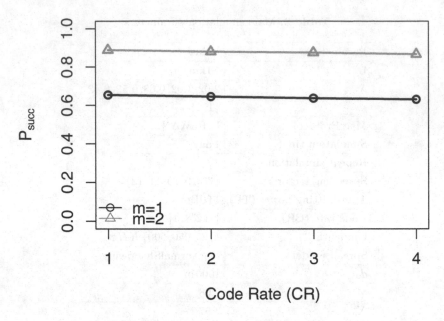

Fig. 4. Impact of code rade on the probability of success

success. However, there is a clear difference between one gateway and two gateways deployed in the network. Deploying two gateways increases the chance of successfully transmitting a packet, as shown in Fig. 4.

For the two most minor spreading factors, the probability of success is more significant with two gateways in the network than with one. And with high spreading factors (9, 10, 11, 12), not only does the probability of success gradually decrease, but the difference between one gateway and two gateways in the network is minimal (Fig. 5). A high spreading factor increases the transmission range and, in turn, widens the interference field. This reduces the chances of successful transmission.

The bandwidth is generally set to 125, 250, and 500 kHz. A higher bandwidth translates into a higher data rate, resulting in shorter airtime and lower sensitivity. The probability of success is negatively impacted by low receiver sensitivity. This explains the decrease in the probability of success in Fig. 6 for the highest bandwidth value.

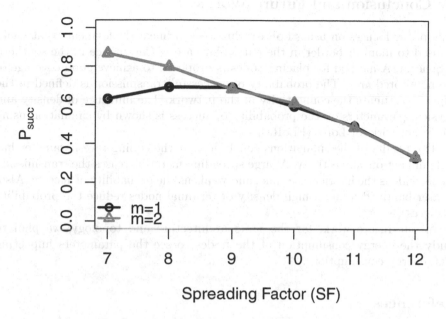

Fig. 5. The probability of success as a function of the spreading factor

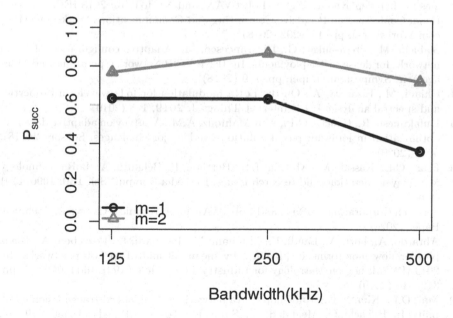

Fig. 6. influence of bandwidth on the probability of success

6   Conclusion and Future Works

This paper focuses on using LoRa technology in linear deployments that could be used to monitor border in the particular case of Casamance in the southern of Senegal. A method for placing nodes is proposed to achieve good coverage of the monitored area. The probability of successful transmission is defined in the paper to estimate the connectivity in the network. The influence of density and physical parameters on the probability of success is shown by simulation using the Framework for LoRa (FLoRa).

The results of the simulations conclude that the coding rate parameter has little impact on connectivity. A large spreading factor increases the transmission range, widens the interference zone, and weakens the probability of success. Also, greater bandwidth and a high density of terminal nodes reduce the probability of success.

In our future work, for the same architecture and topology, we plan to study the energy consumption of the nodes to see the parameters impacting this (energy consumption).

References

1. Mekki, K., Bajic, E., Chaxel, F., Meyer, F.: A comparative study of LPWAN technologies for large-scale IoT deployment. ICT Exp. **5**(1), 1–7 (2019)
2. Mekki, K., Bajic, E., Chaxel, F., Meyer, F.: Overview of cellular LPWAN technologies for IoT deployment: Sigfox, LoRaWAN, and NB-IoT. In: 2018 IEEE International Conference on Pervasive Computing and Communications Workshops (Percom Workshops), pp. 197–202 (2018)
3. Slabicki, M., Premsankar, G., Di Francesco, M.: Adaptive configuration of LoRa networks for dense IoT deployments. In: IEEE/IFIP Network Operations and Management Symposium, Taipei, pp. 1–9 (2018)
4. Chiani, M., Elzanaty, A.: On the LoRa modulation for IoT: waveform properties and spectral analysis. IEEE Internet Things J. **2019**, 1–8 (2019)
5. Kufakunesu, R., Hancke, G.P., Abu-Mahfouz, A.M.: A survey on adaptive data rate optimization in lorawan: recent solutions and major challenges. Sensors **20**(18), 5044 (2020)
6. Fehri, C.E., Kassab, M., Abdellatif, S., Berthou, P., Belghith, A.: LoRa technology MAC layer operations and research issues. Procedia Comput. Sci. **130**, 1096–1101 (2018)
7. Semtech Corporation. LoRa® and LoRaWAN®: A Technical Overview. Technical Paper (2020)
8. Abrardo, A., Fort, A., Landi, E., Mugnaini,M., Panzardi, E., Pozzebon, A.: Black powder flow monitoring in pipelines by means of multi-hop LoRa networks. In: 2019 II Workshop on Metrology for Industry 4.0 and IoT (MetroInd4. 0&IoT), pp. 312–316 (2019)
9. Mai, D.L., Kim, M.K.: Multi-hop LoRa network with pipelined transmission capability. In: Habachi, O., Meghdadi, V., Sabir, E., Cances, J.P. (eds.) UNet 2019, vol. 12293, pp. 125–135. Springer, Heidelberg (2020). https://doi.org/10.1007/978-3-030-58008-7_10

10. 16. Duong, C.T., Kim, M.K.: Reliable multi-hop linear network based on LoRa. Int. J. Control Autom. **11**, 143–154 (2018)
11. Petäjäjärvi, J., Mikhaylov, K., Hämäläinen, M., Iinatti, J.: Evaluation of LoRa LPWAN technology for remote health and wellbeing monitoring. In: 10th International Symposium on Medical Information and Communication Technology (ISMICT). Worcester, MA, USA, pp. 1–5 (2016). https://doi.org/10.1109/ISMICT.2016.7498898
12. Bianco, G.M., Mejia-Aguilar, A., Marrocco, G.: Performance evaluation of LoRa LPWAN technology for mountain Search and Rescue. In: 2020 5th International Conference on Smart and Sustainable Technologies (SpliTech), Split, Croatia, pp. 1–4 (2020). https://doi.org/10.23919/SpliTech49282.2020.9243817
13. Griva, A., Boursianis, A.D., Wan, S., Sarigiannidis, P., Karagiannidis, G., Goudos, S.K.: Performance evaluation of LoRa networks in an open field cultivation scenario. In: 2021 10th International Conference on Modern Circuits and Systems Technologies (MOCAST), Thessaloniki, Greece, pp. 1–5 (2021). https://doi.org/10.1109/MOCAST52088.2021.9493416
14. Liang, R., Zhao, L., Wang, P.: Performance evaluations of LoRa wireless communication in building environments. Sensors **20**(14), 3828 (2020). https://doi.org/10.3390/s20143828
15. . Haxhibeqiri, J., Karaagac, A., Van den Abeele, F., Joseph, W., Moerman, I., Hoebeke, J.: LoRa indoor coverage and performance in an industrial environment: case study. In: 2017 22nd IEEE International Conference on Emerging Technologies and Factory Automation (ETFA), Limassol, Cyprus, pp. 1–8 (2017). https://doi.org/10.1109/ETFA.2017.8247601
16. Abdulwahid, H.M., Mishra, A.: Deployment optimization algorithms in wireless sensor networks for smart cities: a systematic mapping study. Sensors **22**(14), 5094 (2022). https://doi.org/10.3390/s22145094
17. Ousmane, D., Congduc, P., Ousmane, T.: Comparing and adapting propagation models for LoRa networks. In: IEEE Conference Proceedings, vol. 2020, no. WiMob, pp. 1–7 (2020)
18. Zorbas, D., Papadopoulos, G.Z., Maillé, P., Montavont, N., Douligeris, C.: Improving LoRa network capacity using multiple spreading factor configurations. In: 2018 25th International Conference on Telecommunications (ICT), pp. 516–520 (2018)
19. Croce, D., Gucciardo, M., Mangione, S., Santaromita, G., Tinnirello, I.: LoRa technology demystified: from link behavior to cell-level performance. IEEE Trans. Wirel. Commun. **19**(2), 822–834 (2020). https://doi.org/10.1109/TWC.2019.2948872
20. AN1200.22 LoRa™ Modulation Basics. https://www.frugalprototype.com/wp-content/uploads/2016/08/an1200.22.pdf
21. Varsier, N., Schwoerer, J.: Capacity limits of lorawan technology for smart metering applications. In: 2017 IEEE International Conference on Communications (ICC), pp. 1–6 (2017)

Convergence of Blockchain Enabled Internet of Things (IoT) Framework: A Survey

Vatsala Upadhyay[1]([⊠]), Abhishek Vaish[1], and J. Kokila[2]

[1] Department of Information Technology, Indian Institute of Information Technology, Allahabad, UttarPradesh, Prayagraj 211015, India
`vatsau01@gmail.com`
[2] Department of Computer Science and Engineering, Indian Institute of Information Technology, Trichy, Tiruchirappalli, Tamil Nadu 620012, India

Abstract. Recent research and experiments in the field of Internet of Things (IoT) security have found that these devices are vulnerable to various attacks, ranging from cyber-attacks to physical attacks on devices. Internet of Things (IoTs) have certain features of resource optimization and small storage capacity that make them vulnerable to attacks, as the manufacturer pays less attention to the security and privacy part of the device in use. Considering the constraints of the Internet of Things (IoTs),*Blockchain* has been lately proposed as a possible solution for feasibility with the Internet of Things (IoTs). The popularity of Blockchain lies in its major features of **Security, Anonymity, Unanimous and Decentralization** and thus, made it synchronizable with the Internet of Things (IoTs). This paper shall present an overview of the Blockchain parameters used in the Internet of Things (IoT) along with the concept of "lightweight blockchain" being discussed as a new concept and considered by researchers and experimenters as a feasible model for the Internet of Things (IoT) devices.

Keywords: Attacks on Internet of Things (IoT) · Blockchain · Internet of Things (IoT) · Lightweight Blockchain · Research Directions

1 Introduction

1.1 Internet of Things (IoT) Devices

The usage of Internet of Things (IoT) devices is rapidly growing day by day. IoTs enable various devices to connect across a network for purposes like *Data sharing, Communication, security, connection with remote devices, sensing nearby objects, connection with the server for communication with the application interface*, and the list continues. IoT devices have intelligent sensing abilities and connectivity between 2 or more devices over Wi-Fi, Bluetooth, etc. Due to their small sizes, IoT devices deliver efficiency in terms of precision and performance. Figure 1 shows the widespread use of IoT, covering almost every aspect of our lives the agriculture sector, the food industry, automobile, home automation, healthcare, industrial Internet of things, the finance sector, etc.

© The Author(s), under exclusive license to Springer Nature Switzerland AG 2024
O. Habachi et al. (Eds.): UNet 2023, LNCS 14757, pp. 112–128, 2024.
https://doi.org/10.1007/978-3-031-62488-9_9

With the growing dependence on IoTs in health care applications, business management, industry, home automation, etc., a need arises to protect the entities associated with them, mainly data, things, and processes. Security in IoT addresses the following:

1. Tamper resistance.
2. Content Security
3. Secure storage of data
4. Secure network access
5. User authentication and identification

In these systems, the property of fulfilling the required functionality brings some loopholes. The manufacturers of these systems focus on the design aspect, as given below:

! **Compact designing**: Since a specific functionality has to be addressed, manufacturers of the systems opt for small device sizes (Table 1).

Table 1. List of acronyms used in the paper

Acronyms	Description
AI	Artificial Intelligence
DAG	Directed Acyclic Graph
DDoS	Distributed Denial of Service
ECC	Elliptic Curve Cryptography
HSM	Hardware Security Modules
IoT	Internet of Things
IC	Integrated Circuits
IIoT	Industrial Internet of Things
IoMT	Internet of Medical Things
IoTA	Internet of Things Applications
IPFS	Inter Planetary File Systems
ML	Machine Learning
PBFT	Practical Byzantine Fault Tolerance
PUF	Physical Unclonable Functions
PoW	Proof of Work
PoS	Proof of Stake
RSA	Rivest Shamir Adleman

! **Portability**: So that it is easy to carry around and is available to the user as and when needed; also it can adapt to any environment and operating system.
! **Low computing power**: Manufacturers look for cost-cutting by employing low power consumption.

! **Short memory capacity**: For efficient system usage, the Random Access Memory (RAM) and Read only Memory(ROM) of the devices usually have short storage capacities [38].

These properties make the devices vulnerable to attacks, which can occur directly on the device or by compromising the software of the device. The system's design is such that attackers can compromise the device's security.

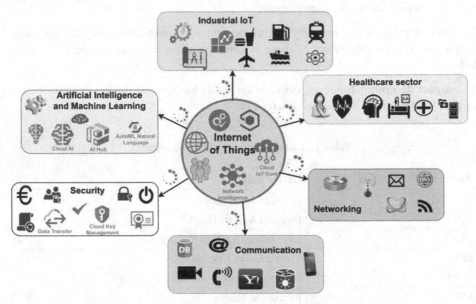

Fig. 1. The widespread use of Internet of Things in primary sectors

1.2 Attacks Occurring on Internet of Things (IoT) Devices

Internet of Things(IoT) security is crucial for the safety of the user's data – be it storage of the data, the communication taking place between 2 devices, etc. (Fig. 2).

Insecure default settings, outdated components, and insecure update mechanisms, among others, are some of the improper security measures that can lead to mismanagement and misconfiguration of the devices. At times, the efficiency of the device is preferred over the security of the manufacturers, thus making the devices vulnerable to malware, hardware attacks, etc.

Some of the attacks that directly affect the hardware of the system are:

– **Physical attacks**: Whenever an IoT device is attacked physically, it leads to a change in the normal working parameters of the device; also, it can cause physical harm to the device, called tampering. As a result, the device can stop working normally and get destroyed. The most prominent among the physical attacks are the Side-Channel attacks, where the attacker continuously monitors the incoming and outgoing signals

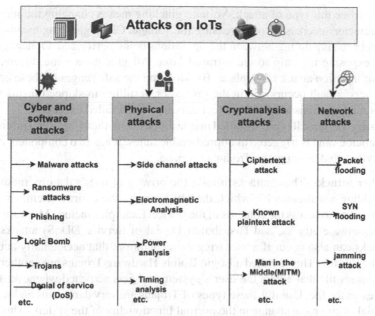

Fig. 2. Types of attacks occurring on IoT

to intercept the cryptographic keys exchanged, and the information sent between the sender and receiver. In this way, the attacker learns about the secret details of the system and thus tries to weaken the system by breaking its protection mechanism. Usually, these types of attacks occur at the time of manufacturing of the device, and when the Integrated Circuit(IC) of the system is being designed and fabricated. These types of attacks occur in the form of:

1. **Side channel attacks**: In this type of attack, the attacker extracts information by comprehending the cryptographic keys (a template attack). An attacker can access the device's data by intercepting the electromagnetic radiation from the hardware, such as the monitor or hard drive. Attackers look for a security exploit in the device and try to extract the secret key from the system's chip. The current flowing from the system's supply, the electromagnetic emissions coming out from the system, etc., contribute to this type of attack (also known as an"electromagnetic attack").

2. **Timing attacks**: Another way the data can be compromised is by analyzing the time the machine takes to respond to different inputs and execute the cryptographic algorithm. The device most affected by this attack is the cryptosystems. To attack using this technique, a hacker must have a deep knowledge of the system's architecture and gain physical access. Nowadays, the most commonly used device in every sector, smart cards, are more prone to this type of attack.

3. **Fault injection attack**: An attacker temporarily tampers with the processor's electrical inputs, disrupting the program counter, modifying the device's firmware, etc. Usually, this type of attack requires hardware modification of the target device. It is typically done to alter the intended behavior of the system. The term"glitch" is

used to define this type of attack. Voltage glitching means changing the initial voltage parameters-decreasing or increasing the voltage. Clock glitching means altering the synchronizing timing between the operations being performed. Optical glitching means exposing the chip to the infrared laser. All glitches are the different ways the fault injection attack takes place. By violating the safe ranges of these operating parameters, a fault occurs within the processor, resulting in skipped instructions or corrupt memory transactions, incorrect data fetch, and failed execution.

4. **Hardware Trojans**: It is pre-installed inside the device without the user's information. It is malicious and is triggered at unpredictable times. It has two components: trigger and payload to determine the Trojan's purpose.

   - **Cyber attacks**: These attacks invade the privacy of user's data by modifying it or adding a malicious file which thereby corrupts the entire system, or denying permission to access the contents of the device. Examples include Malware attacks, Ransomware attacks, and Distributed Denial of Service(DDoS) attacks. These attacks can also occur if a user triggers a condition, that accidentally activates a malicious file. This is called a Logic Bomb. Hardware Trojans are another type of malicious file that enters the user's system and gets activated whenever the user accesses the file. Usually, these types of Trojans are very dangerous and result in a partial or complete change in the normal functionality of the system. This usually occurs at the time of the manufacturing of the IC, whereby the attacker inserts a malicious code in the circuitry so that the system gets destroyed.
   - **Crypt-analysis attacks**: The attacks occur when a key exchange occurs between 2 devices or the data is encrypted for safe transmission. The attack can comprehend the keys by the Brute Force technique, or some known encryption algorithm, where the attacker finds the keys used in the encryption process. An attacker can be active within a network and listen to the secret transmission details between the sender and receiver, without their permission and information.
   - **Network Attacks**: These types of attacks occur on the transmission network between the connected devices. Examples of such attacks include Packet flooding, SYN flooding, etc., where the attacker compromises the server granting the requests, with a large number of packets and requests simultaneously, thereby increasing the load on the server and temporarily shutting it down.

The attacks described above partially occur in the physical presence of the device with the attacker, as well as the device getting hacked by Cyber attacks. A possible way of mitigating these attacks is to look out for electromagnetic radiation coming out from the device and employ robust cryptographic algorithm methods for the encryption and decryption of data.

1.3   Basic Concept of Blockchain

Blockchain can be termed as an abstract data structure, which consists of blocks connected via cryptographic hashes. These cryptographic hashes ensure security as well as the unique identification of a block in the network. Each block in the chain stores records, transactions, timestamps, headers, etc. in the form of **nodes** - which can be light or full nodes depending upon the contents of the block. Figure 3 above shows the basic structure of blocks in a Blockchain network.

Blockchain has become a popular technology owing to its unique characteristics. It is being widely used nowadays for various purposes: making safe and secure transactions, supply chain management, IoT device security, generating and investing in cryptocurrency, etc

The characteristics that make it popular are described below in brief:

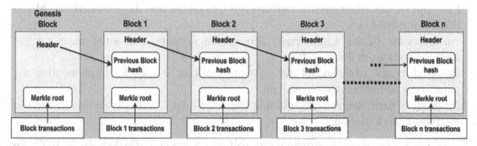

Fig. 3. Basic structure of a block in the Blockchain network

1. **Immutability**: The immutability property states that once a record is stored in the block, it cannot be changed or modified. This is achieved with the help of cryptographic hashes which cannot be reversed once generated.
2. **Transparency**: This feature implies that any changes made in the network of blocks are visible and known to every participant. In short, the transactions are traceable and unchangeable.
3. **Decentralization**: Instead of a central server or authority controlling the whole network, every node acts as an authority; this is achieved in a distributed ledger, where a copy of the transaction is known and shared with all accounts. Similarly, a copy of the transaction is available with every node in the chain.
4. **Security**: The most critical aspect of any application lies in its security, i.e. how resistant the application is towards malicious attacks, and how it guarantees the safety of data. In the blockchain, this is attained by employing *Asymmetric Key Cryptography*. The use of public key and private key for encryption-decryption of data ensures safe and secure transmission and information storage.
5. **Verifiable**: To verify the authenticity of the transaction and information stored, verification is done with the help of *digital signatures* and *public key cryptography*. Using the help of digital signatures, a virtual fingerprint is thus obtained for the transaction, which can prove useful in future. These digital signatures are granted by the **Certification Authority(CA)**, which binds the cryptographic hashes obtained with the digital certificates received for the transaction.
6. **Unanimous**: Using the help of consensus algorithms, all the nodes participating in the network arrive at a common agreement for various purposes: for adding a new block in the chain, executing a transaction, allocating resources to a block, allocation of a puzzle to a miner, solving the puzzle by the miner, etc. All these

are fulfilled using the help of **Consensus algorithms**. These algorithms consume energy and power for actions performed by the miner, measured in Watts(W). Some of the Consensus algorithms in practice are namely **Proof of Work(PoW), Proof of Stake(PoS), Delegated Proof of Stake(DPoS), Proof of Elapsed Time(PoET), Proof of Capacity(PoC), Proof of Authentication(PoA),** etc.

The main contributions of this paper have been listed below:

- Survey on the recent works done in Blockchain and IoT divided into 3 modules - PUF and ECC, Consensus mechanisms through tables, and the use of AI and ML in this convergence
- An overview of the Lightweight Blockchain concept and some ideas on the implementations in this direction.
- Proposal of new experiments and software that can be used for implementing the parameters of lightweight blockchain.
- Proposal of experiments by combining the 3 modules - PUF, Consensus, and AI in the Future work section.

The rest of the paper is structured as follows: Section 2 **Blockchain & IoT: An overview** discussing the convergence of Blockchain and IoT and the advantages and disadvantages of the conjunction; Section 3 on **Converging technologies of Blockchain and IoT security** discussing the use of Machine Learning, Hardware security primitives and other such modules being integrated with Blockchain; Section 4 on **A brief Literature Review of Lightweight Blockchain and IoT security** talking about the concept of lightweight blockchain gaining limelight in the past 3 years and a survey of the existing works done in this area. Section 5 discusses the future work and challenges that need to be investigated and worked upon in the integration of Blockchain and the Internet of Things, and finally, Section 6 presents the Conclusion of the whole work.

2   Blockchain and Internet of Things (IoT): an Overview

There are several advantages of integrating Blockchain Technology with the Internet of Things(IoT) for the latter's security and efficient performance, which have been briefly described in Table 2. This table shows how the *decentralized architecture* of Blockchain can fit well with the *centralized architecture* of the IoT.

Figure 4 shows a general representation of how authentication is established between the Blockchain nodes and IoT devices: As evident from the figure, the IoT devices are being *"authenticated"* using **Inter Planetary File System** (IPFS) nodes. Each IoT device is assigned a unique IPFS hash for identification. For registering a device on the blockchain, smart contracts are used - accounts are created for the transfer of ether between the accounts. The accounts created using smart contracts represent the individual IoT devices that are communicating and available on the network. The above model can be extended to produce a model for *"Lightweight security and privacy model for IoT devices"*.

Although there are many benefits of using blockchain in IoT, there are some limitations when Blockchain and IoT are integrated for the latter's security, which are:

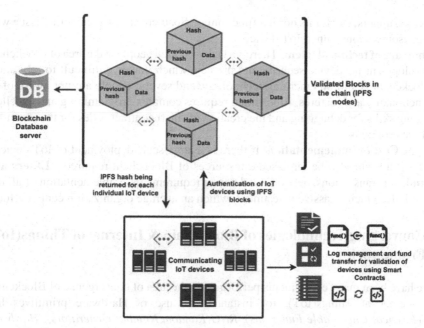

Fig. 4. A general representation of authenticating IoT devices using Blockchain

Table 2. Benefits of Blockchain with Internet of Things(IoT)

Blockchain Property	Feasibility with IoT	Description
Immutability	✓	Hash value of registered IoT can't be changed
Transparency	✓	Important data is traceable to all participating devices
Security	✓	Use of asymmetric key cryptography for encryption-decryption of data
Verifiability	✓	Digital signatures and Public-key cryptography
Consensus	✓	Modification in the network only using consensus algorithms
Efficiency	✓	Recording the time to authenticate using timestamps

1. **High Power consumption**: With the addition of new blocks and puzzle solving, there arises a concern for controlling the power consumption of the blockchain, which is not scalable with the low power requirement of the embedded device.
2. **Huge Resource requirement**: The IoT devices require less amount of resources for normal functioning as compared to the blockchain, which requires resources like new

blocks, miners, etc. for its normal functioning. So, there arises a scalability issue with the resource-constrained IoT device.

3. **Shortage of technical talent**: There's a lack of skilled people in the area of Blockchain development for device security and privacy, which makes it difficult to rely upon. Blockchain is still an emerging technology, and several people are not aware of its functionality and features. Blockchain requires complex programming and excellent coding skills for debugging and the creation of smart contract codes for the execution of the programs.

4. **Huge Cost in implementation**: If there is a large-scale deployment of IoT devices, then there will also be large-scale resources of Blockchain required - **Ethers and funds** for transactions, network, and power requirements. Implementation of all this will indeed incur massive investment, which an average organization cannot afford.

3   Converging Technologies of Blockchain & Internet of Things(IoT) Framework

There have been many experiments performed in the area of convergence of Blockchain and Internet of Things(IoT), for instance, the use of Hardware primitives like *PUF(Physical Unclonable Functions), RNG(Random Number Generators), Hardware security modules(HSM)*, use of Artificial Intelligence and application of machine learning and deep learning models like **neural networks** :

- **Hardware Security Modules (HSMs)**: As the name implies, HSMs are physical computing devices that manage the security of the secret keys shared between the devices to provide strong authentication. These have tampered-resistant hardware devices that can help secure the generation of secret keys, digital signatures, and certificates. It is an external device that can be attached to the system. These days, HSMs are widely used in Public Key Infrastructure (PKI) environments and financial sectors.

- **Physical Unclonable Functions (PUFs)**: PUFs have emerged as a hardware security technique that offers improved cryptography, anti-counterfeiting on Integrated Circuits (ICs), etc. It is a technique in hardware security that exploits inherent device variations to produce an unclonable, unique response for a given input. For a given"challenge"/input, a unique output is generated every time, which is unclonable. A response is generated in a PUF circuit when a challenge input is given. The unique identifier or key is not stored for a PUF. Instead, it is generated only when the response needs to be produced(based on CRPs-Challenge Response Pairs), giving it an edge over other security mechanisms.

- **Random number generators**: There are two types of random number generators:

i **Pseudo-random number generators(PRNG)**: are software-generated random numbers based on mathematical calculations and formulas. The number is generated in a short period and is also efficient.

These can be used in cipher algorithms for successful cryptographic key generation

ii **True random number generators(TRNG)**: It is a sort of device based on a phenomenon called"entropy source"; being unpredictable, it generates nondeterministic data and thus helps to seed security algorithms. These are being widely used nowadays in gaming, cryptography, key generation for various algorithms, chip manufacturing for devices, nonce generation, authentication of devices, and protection against physical attacks. This has emerged as a trustworthy option for security in embedded devices.

– **Machine Learning and Artificial Intelligence**: To analyze the patterns and train the model in order to alert the system/device against possible attacks, and to leverage the use of Blockchain by learning these patterns generated by the Machine Learning models and increasing the security and privacy of data. For example, the authors in [1] proposed a novel framework for detecting and classifying attacks on IIoT devices called **COSNN**-Convivial Sprinter Neural Networks, and a lightweight consensus protocol, called *LCPoW*, i.e. Lightweight Consensus Proof of work algorithm in order for preserving privacy in IIoT systems. Such models can help in the accurate classification of attacks, as well as reduce the time of execution of algorithms due to training on already available data.

Based on the above-discussed modules, Table 3 and Table 4 summarize the works done between the years **2019-2023** in these areas with the findings, the tables being divided into 2 parts: PUF and Blockchain in IoT devices and the Use of Consensus Algorithms in IoTs.

4   A Brief Review on Blockchain-Enabled IoT Framework

The increase in the number of users and transactions in the blockchain network requires intensive energy consumption, along with a high computation power, which the low power requirement & limited resource IoT devices cannot support. Lightweight blockchain has additional features of data reliability, low computation burden, low storage needs, high throughput, and high energy efficiency [2]. It also has features of low resource consumption, and low power consumption, which is scalable with the IoT device. The *lightweight blockchain* can accommodate approximately 1 million authentication processes each second, which is more than sufficient for a resource-constrained IoT network.

Broadly speaking, there are 5 main aspects of a lightweight blockchain framework along with the main parameters that have been depicted through Fig. 5 (Table 5).

Some experimenters have found out that the platforms that can be used for implementing a lightweight blockchain framework, as also stated in [2] are listed below:

1. Hyperledger fabric
2. Ethereum
3. IBM Blockchain
4. Hyperledger Sawtooth

For instance, the authors in [37] discuss and propose a Lightweight Blockchain framework that encompasses 3 aspects for which the findings and comparison have been depicted through the graphs in Fig. 6, Fig. 7. Named as **HLOChain**, the model proposes a new Consensus mechanism and provides optimized storage for resource-

Table 3. PUF and ECC in IoT security

Module used	Objective	Results
Arbiter PUF and IoMT [8]	Designing an embedded PUF module for IoMT (Internet of Medical Things) using Arbiter PUFs and private blockchain	From obtained 200 PUF keys, 75% are reliable; Hamming distance of the PUF module is 48%. The randomness of 47% is achieved from the PUF module
SRAM & Arbiter PUF for IIoT [9]	Use of Arbiter and SRAM PUF for IIoT (Industrial Internet of Things) device authentication, and developing smart contracts for implementing the above module on the devices	Hamming distance in the authentication phase of the PUF module is 57.7%. The accuracy of the PUF module comes out to be 99.9% by training the model using SVM on Windows 10 OS 1.61 GHz processor
PUF [10]	Unified authentication scheme for IoT device security based on PUF model and then storing the model parameters in each node of the blockchain network	Reliability of the data source, compact authentication scheme, tamper-proofing, etc. for the IoT device was achieved using the proposed scheme
PUF and NFTs [11]	NFTs (Non-Fungible Tokens) have been employed with PUF for the unique identification of IoT devices; and use of ESP-32 IoT devices with Ethereum blockchain	Verification of the devices using signatures was achieved in 165.6 ms (approx.), which is efficient for the application
Comparison of ECC & RSA [12]	A survey on ECC (Elliptic curve cryptography), RSA and its significance in blockchain for reduced key size for IoT device, decentralization, and security	A comparative analysis between RSA and ECC shows that ECC is more efficient than RSA when it comes to IoT device security

constrained IoT devices. The IoT devices have been divided into 3 levels *High, Medium, and low* according to their computing and storage capabilities, and correspondingly, the architecture has been proposed for layering based on the type of devices. The use of *Ethereum Blockchain,Merkle Patricia tree*, and *Full ledger and state ledger nodes* have been used for optimum storage; *Proof of Random* as the "lightweight consensus" algorithm, where any miner node is selected at random for mining purposes rather than drawing a comparison between the miner nodes based on the stake results in an efficient mining process.

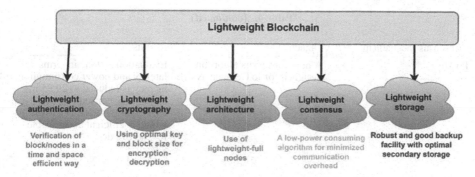

Fig. 5. Aspects of a lightweight blockchain framework

Table 4. Consensus Algorithms and IoT

Consensus mechanism	Objective	Results
CBCIoT [14]	A new consensus algorithm for blockchain-based IoT applications for improving the scalability of IoT devices	Throughput lies in the range of 250–1500 samples/sec for 1000–7000 samples, indicating a high throughput. The verification speed of the block is 5 s, better than the other algorithms
EIoT-PBFT	A multi-stage consensus algorithm, EIoT-PBFT, proposed for IoT edge computing on the basis of the PBFT algorithm	EIoT-PBFT takes 36.4% less time than PBFT for a single consensus, the average single consensus elapsed time is 406.818 ms for 2500 nodes, with a standard deviation of 5.135, which is stable and efficient for the system
Consensus for IoMT [16]	Review of blockchain technology & consensus algorithms for IoT healthcare devices	PoS(Proof of Stake), DPoS (Delegated Proof of Stake), and PBFT(Practical Byzantine fault Tolerance) are the consensus protocols suitable for IoT medical device efficiency because of high throughput, low computational overhead, and low latency
Hybrid Consensus algo. For Healthcare [18]	Blockchain based hybrid consensus algorithm for smart healthcare devices	CPU consumption is 2%, whereas memory consumption is 50% of the total memory, which is efficient for the system. Using the height of the Merkle tree, the security of the model is evaluated. Blocks are rewarded & punished according to malicious activity detected

(continued)

Table 4. (*continued*)

Consensus mechanism	Objective	Results
PoAh	A new consensus algorithm designed for IoT edge network	Evaluation is done in terms of latency and power consumption; latency is reduced to 29.35 ms, and energy consumption for each transaction is 44.31 mJ, which is efficient and feasible for the IoT de-vice

Table 5. Characteristics of a Lightweight Blockchain

S.no	Characteristic	Description
1	Type of Blockchain	Permission or Permission-less Blockchain
2	Structure of Blockchain architecture	Miner nodes or IoTA or DAG
3	Consensus Protocol	Custom-based or Generic Protocols like PoW, PoS, PBFT, etc
4	Type of Storage	Off-Blockchain/On-Blockchain/Cloud storage

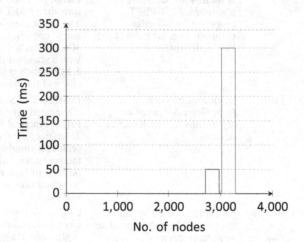

Fig. 6. Avg. time taken by algorithms to reach the consensus vs. PoR (in blue)[37]

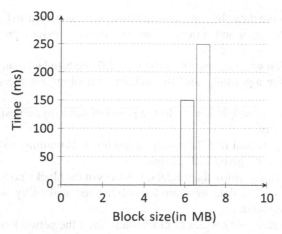

Fig. 7. Avg. time taken to attain transaction throughput by algorithms vs. PoR (in blue)[37]

5 Future Work and Challenges

The works done in the area of Blockchain and IoT suggest that although the convergence is beneficial from the view of IoT security, there are problems that can arise because of the ever-increasing number of nodes in the blockchain network that becomes a restriction for the IoT device's low resource requirement. To combat this difficulty, a "lightweight blockchain" has been introduced to overcome the existing obstacles in the Blockchain-IoT convergence. Although there have been many works done in this area, there have been some research directions proposed by the experimenters for a more stable and secure architecture and privacy model for the IoTs that have been listed below (Table 6):

Table 6. Proposed prototype for the 5 aspects of a lightweight blockchain

S.no	Parameter	Possible models for implementation
1	Lightweight consensus	PoS, PBFT, PoAh, optimized PoW or custom-based for time-efficient mining and less communication overhead
2	Lightweight Storage	Use of ledger nodes(full/state), Merkle Patricia tree, partial storage of transactions on blockchain as well as off-blockchain
3	Lightweight Cryptography	PUF and ECC for encryption-decryption and generation of keys
4	Lightweight architecture	Lightweight full nodes that mine efficiently and are space efficient, e.g. DAG, IoTA, Ethereum account
5	Lightweight Authentication	Ethereum Smart Contracts, IPFS(Inter-Planetary File Systems) nodes

1. A model for secure data sharing between resource-constrained IoT devices which is lightweight in terms of authentication, and can provide privacy preservation for the devices.
2. An authentication scheme, possibly PUFchain 2.0 needs to be created for integrating Machine learning algorithms and Blockchain technology for the smart healthcare industry.
3. An ECC-based lightweight key exchange protocol needs to be designed to enhance IoT device security.
4. To explore the potential of ML in order to optimize Hamming distance, Accuracy, and randomness for a given PUF module.
5. A model which can optimize the validation process of the blocks/nodes in the network.
6. The use of DAG as a data structure for solving the scalability issue of IoT with blockchain is required.
7. Addressing the scalability issues of blockchain given the network limitations.
8. A lightweight blockchain architecture for permission-less blockchain is demanded.
9. Lightweight cryptographic algorithms need to be designed for the security of IoT.

6 Conclusion

The article talks about the Convergence of Blockchain and IoT broadly, covering the advantages and disadvantages of the merger, the experiments done accompanying Blockchain and IoT with Hardware security modules (e.g. PUF), the use of Consensus Algorithms for IoT security, the application of AI for Blockchain and the concept of Lightweight Blockchain framework for IoT devices the summary for each has been depicted through tables. Based on the summarization of the main modules - *PUF, Consensus mechanisms, and Lightweight Blockchain*, some experiments have been proposed for further exploration in the Future Work and Challenges section.

References

1. Selvarajan, S., et al.: An artificial intelligence lightweight blockchain security model for security and privacy in IIoT systems. J. Cloud Comput. **12**(1), 1–17 (2023)
2. Stefanescu, D., et al.: A systematic literature review of lightweight blockchain for IoT. IEEE Access **10**, 123138–123159 (2022)
3. Mershad, K.: A taxonomy and review of lightweight blockchain solutions for internet of things networks. arXiv preprint arXiv:2212.06272 (2022)
4. Adebayo, N., et al.: Blockchain technology: a panacea for IoT security challenge. EAI Endor. Trans. Internet Things **8**, e3 (2022)
5. Malik, H.A.M., et al.: Resolving security issues in the IoT using blockchain. Electronics **11**(23), 3950 (2022)
6. Balogh, S., et al.: IoT security challenges: cloud and blockchain, postquantum cryptography, and evolutionary techniques. Electronics **10**(21), 2647 (2021)
7. Liu, Y., et al.: LightChain: a lightweight blockchain system for the industrial internet of things. IEEE Trans. Ind. Inf. **15**(6), 3571–3581 (2019)
8. Bathalapalli, V.K.V.V., et al.: PUFchain 2.0: hardware-assisted robust blockchain for sustainable simultaneous device and data security in smart healthcare. SN Comput. Sci. **3**(5), 344 (2022)

9. Li, D., et al.: Blockchain-based authentication for IIoT devices with PUF. J. Syst. Arch. **130**, 102638 (2022)
10. Li, D., et al.: Unified authentication scheme for IoT blockchain based on puf. In: 2021 IEEE International Conference on Parallel and Distributed Processing with Applications, Big Data and Cloud Computing, Sustainable Computing and Communications, Social Computing and Networking (ISPA/BDCloud/SocialCom/SustainCom). IEEE (2021)
11. Arcenegui, J., et al.: Secure combination of IoT and blockchain by physically binding IoT devices to smart non-fungible tokens using PUFs. Sensors **21**(9), 3119 (2021)
12. Yadav, A.K.: Significance of elliptic curve cryptography in blockchain IoT with comparative analysis of RSA algorithm. In: 2021 International Conference on Computing, Communication, and Intelligent Systems (ICCCIS). IEEE (2021)
13. Iqbal, U., et al.: ECC-based authenticated key exchange protocol for fog-based IoT networks. Secur. Commun. Netw. **2022**, 1–5 (2022)
14. Uddin, M., et al.: CBCIoT: a consensus algorithm for blockchain-based IoT applications. Appl. Sci. **11**(22), 11011 (2021)
15. Khan, M., den Hartog, F., Hu, J.: A survey and ontology of blockchain consensus algorithms for resource-constrained IoT systems. Sensors **22**(21), 8188 (2022)
16. Arul, P., Renuka, S.: Blockchain technology using consensus mechanism for IoT-based e-healthcare system. In: IOP Conference Series: Materials Science and Engineering, vol. 1055, no. 1. IOP Publishing (2021)
17. Gan, B., et al.: EIoT-PBFT: a multi-stage consensus algorithm for IoT edge computing based on PBFT. Microprocess. Microsyst. **95**, 104713 (2022)
18. Prabha, P., Chatterjee, K.: Design and implementation of hybrid consensus mechanism for IoT based healthcare system security. Int. J. Inf. Technol. **14**(3), 1381–1396 (2022)
19. Maitra, S., et al.: Proof-of-authentication consensus algorithm: blockchain-based IoT implementation. In: 2020 IEEE 6th World Forum on Internet of Things (WF-IoT). IEEE (2020)
20. Shafiq, M., et al.: The rise of "Internet of Things": review and open research issues related to detection and prevention of IoT-based security attacks. Wirel. Commun. Mob. Comput. **2022**, 1–12 (2022)
21. Bahaa, A., et al.: Monitoring real time security attacks for IoT systems using DevSecOps: a systematic literature review. Information **12**(4), 154 (2021)
22. Msgna, M.: Anatomy of attacks on IoT systems: review of attacks, impacts and countermeasures. J. Surv. Secur. Saf. **3**(4), 150–173 (2022)
23. Butun, I., Österberg, P., Song, H.: Security of the Internet of Things: vulnerabilities, attacks, and countermeasures. IEEE Commun. Surv. Tutor. **22**(1), 616–644 (2019)
24. Mohsin, A.A.: Internet of Things (IoT) a study on security attacks and countermeasures. Al-Mansour J. **32**(1), 83–99 (2019)
25. Vignesh, R., Samydurai, A.: Security on internet of things (IoT) with challenges and countermeasures. Int. J. Eng. Dev. Res. IJEDR **5**(1), 417–423 (2017)
26. Li, S., Xu, L.D.: Securing the internet of things. In: Syngress (2017)
27. Storage Needs for Blockchain Technology Point of View. IBM (2018)
28. Ahmed, A., Tayseer, M., et al.: Authentication-chains: blockchain-inspired lightweight authentication protocol for IoT networks. Electronics **12**(4), 867 (2023)
29. Bisiach, J., Elfving, V.: PUF-enabled blockchain for IoT security: a comparative study (2021)
30. Mahmoud, M.A., et al.: Review and development of a scalable lightweight blockchain integrated model (LightBlock) for IoT applications. Electronics **12**(4), 1025 (2023)
31. Cheikhrouhou, O., et al.: A lightweight blockchain and fog-enabled secure remote patient monitoring system. Internet Things **22**, 100691 (2023)
32. Williams, P., Dutta, I.K., Daoud, H., Bayoumi, M.: A survey on security in internet of things with a focus on the impact of emerging technologies. Internet Things **19**, 100564 (2022)

33. Aqeel, M., Ali, F., Iqbal, M.W., Rana, T.A., Arif, M., Auwul, R.: A review of security and privacy concerns in the Internet of Things (IoT). J. Sensors **2022**(1–20), 2022 (2022)
34. Lee, J.Y., Lee, J.: Current research trends in IoT security: a systematic mapping study. Mob. Inf. Syst. **2021**, 1–25 (2021)
35. Vasilevskaya, M.: Security in Embedded Systems: A Model-Based Approach with Risk Metrics (Doctoral dissertation, Link¨oping University Electronic Press) (2015)
36. Hanes, D., Salgueiro, G., Grossetete, P., Barton, R., Henry, J.: IoT fundamentals: networking technologies, protocols, and use cases for the internet of things. Cisco Press (2017)
37. Xie, Q., Dong, F., Feng, X.: HLOChain: a hierarchical blockchain framework with lightweight consensus and optimized storage for IoT". Security and Communication Networks **2023**, 1–14 (2023)
38. Ghasempour, A.: Internet of things in smart grid: Architecture, applications, services, key technologies, and challenges. Inventions **4**(1), 22 (2019)
39. Zahoor, A., et al.: An access control scheme in IoT-enabled Smart-Grid systems using blockchain and PUF. Internet Things **22**, 100708 (2023)
40. Gangwani, P., et al.: IoT device identity management and blockchain for security and data integrity. Int. J. Comput. Appl. **184**(42), 49–55 (2023)

Design of a Microstrip Triangular Patch Array at 5.8 GHz for Enhancing UAV Autonomy in IoT Applications

Ilham Salhane[✉] [iD], Mounir RIFI, Hanae Terchoune, and Soumaya Elmorabeti

Laboratory RITM/ESTC IGA Institute, Hassan II University Casablanca,
Casablanca, Morocco
`ilham.salhane@iga.ac.ma`

Abstract. Research progresses, the potential of IoT-driven drones grows, paving the way for intelligent, adaptive, and interconnected aerial systems. Integrating IoT with drones offers a transformative paradigm, enabling real-time data exchange and decision-making. Drones can collect environmental data, perform adaptive maneuvers, and collaborate with other devices. However, managing drone battery autonomy is a real challenge, requiring careful optimization to maximize flight time while maintaining safe and reliable flight performance. Our approach is to use wireless energy transmission as an efficient and sustainable means of powering drones and aerial vehicles. Our work consists in building a wireless energy harvesting antenna array for remote recharging. The antenna array presented in this paper consists of four microstrip triangular patch antennas fed by a microstrip line. It operates at a resonant frequency of 5.8 GHz. The measured peak gain is 7.32 dBi.

Keywords: Internet Of Thing (IoT) · Wireless Power Transmission · Near Field · Unmanned Aerial Vehicle (UAV)

1 Introduction

The emergence of new wireless transmission technologies and the growing number of applications using the principle of communicating objects have made the Internet of connected objects technology an indispensable solution in virtually every sector [1,2]. In industry, for e-health applications, or even for military missions, the list of connected objects is constantly growing. The IoT forms a vast network of mission-critical connected sensor devices. The use of drones is also ubiquitous in systems based on the Internet of Things, particularly for carrying out tasks that are costly, dangerous, or even impossible with human intervention [3–5]. On the other hand, massive use of the Internet of Things requires energy. Drones, for example, need new batteries. Indeed, battery life is limited. This wastes considerable time with each battery change, and has a serious impact on the application's operational efficiency, as can be the case with drones used in disaster zones. In these emergency situations, it is important to think about remote loading solutions to guarantee their operation. This line of research has aroused the interest of several researchers [6,7], with the aim of developing a remote recharging system to guarantee the best possible operation of the drone [8,9]. In this paper, we consider the problem of enhancing the directivity and gain of a triangular microstrip patch antenna array that is used as a receiver in a wireless power transmission system (WPT). The WPT concept involves the use of radio waves and microwaves. There are two mainsections: transmission and reception. On transmit, the RF source converts DC current to generate microwave energy. The transmitting antenna then radiates this energy uniformly across free space to the rectifying antenna (Rectenna). On reception, the latter receives the transmitted microwave energy and converts it into electrical energy (direct current) [21]. The study of the directivity of antennas in the transmitting part is very important because of its influence on the efficiency of the system, so transmitting techniques have been deployed to reinforce the transmitted energy [22]. The paper is organized as follows: Sect. 2 explains the design procedure of the triangular microstrip patch antenna array, and Sect. 3 is about the simulation results and discussion in addition to the analysis of a comparative performance between our triangular microstrip patch antenna array and another conventional patch in the literature for better understanding. Section 4 gives a conclusion and anticipates future works.

2 Proposed Patch Antenna for Wireless Power Transmission System

2.1 Single Element Triangle Patch

Our patch operates at a resonant frequency of 5.8 GHz. The parameters defining the patch dimensions were previously calculated using transmission line equations [20]. The Fig. 1 shows the structure of triangle patch antenna. The ground plane and radiating patch of the suggested patch antenna are composed of copper, and it is constructed on a FR4-lossy substrate with permittivity r = 4.4 and thickness (h) of 1.6 mm. In order to attain the greatest directivity, we must operate the antenna (fr) at 5.8 GHz. The list dimension of our triangle patch is given in the following Table 1.

Dual Element Triangle Patch. The following Fig. 2 is shown for dual element triangle patch microstrip antenna. We can note that, due to the electromagnetically linked effect, it is necessary to calculate the distance between the two patches in dual elements. Equation 1 may be used to determine the distance between two items.

$$d = c/(2fr) \tag{1}$$

– c is velocity of light (c = 3×108 ms^{-1})
– fr is resonant frequency 5.8 GHz.

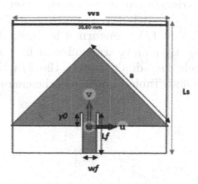

Fig. 1. Structure of single triangle patch antenna

Table 1. List of design parameters for triangle patch antenna

Antenna dimension	Value (mm)
a (length of triangle patch)	16.43
Ls (length of substrate)	24.29
Ws (width of substrate)	35
Wf (width of feeding)	3.055
Lf (length of feeding)	6.16
y0 (length of side length)	3.29
W0 (with of slot)	0.5
h (thickness of substrate)	1.6

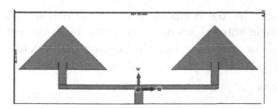

Fig. 2. Structure of dual triangle patch antenna

In our case, the calculated distance is d = 25.86 mm. The following Fig. 2 is shown for dual element triangle patch microstrip antenna. We can also notice that for dual element triangle patch, the T-Junction 70.7 is needed to divide the power for both patches [23]. A 1/λ transformer is required to maintain the input impedance of 50 (Fig. 3). By adding transmission line impedance Z0 between two transmission channels that don't match, the 1/4 transformer acts as an impedance matching method. Table 2 illustrates the characteristic parameters of the TJunction.

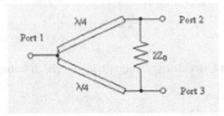

Fig. 3. T-Junction as power divider

Table 2. The characteristic parameters of the TJunction.

T-Junction dimension	Value (mm)
Wf1 (with for 50 Ω)	3.055
Lf1 (length of 50 Ω)	6.16
Wf2 (width of 70.71 Ω)	1.62
Lf2 (length of 70.71 Ω)	7.25

3   Results of Simulation

Table 3 below illustrates the comparison details of one triangle patch antenna and the 1×2 triangle antenna array. As a result, in a wireless energy recovery system, the use of our antenna array will increase the system's efficiency.

3.1   Return Loss

Table 3 illustrates result for return loss (S11) for single element and 1×2 element.For good result, the return loss (S11) should be less than −10 dB. it is clear that the simulation result after optimization for single element for S11 is −14.07 dB at resonance frequency 5.8 GHz.

Table 3. Comparison between single patch and array antennas

Number of patches	S11(dB)	Directivity (dBi)	Gain (dB)
1	−14.07	4.25	4.14
2	18.4	7.32	7.04

3.2 2D Diagram

The performance of a single triangle antenna in our array was illustrated in Fig. 4 with a directivity of 4.25 dBi. Our 1×2 antenna array achieved a higher directivity of 7.32 dBi at 5.8 GHz. The Fig. 6 and 7 show the 3D Radiation Pattern and polar Plot of Radiation Pattern of our new 1×2 triangle patch antenna array. We can clearly see that the proposed antenna array ensures directional behavior with half-power beamwidths (HPBW) of 34° and 56° for the E-plane and Hplane respectively, and provides excellent directivity of around 7 dB at 5.8 GHz. These many characteristics will make it possible to supply significant energy to ensure wireless power transfer for distant equipment (Fig. 5).

Fig. 4. 3D Radiation Pattern for a single element triangle patch

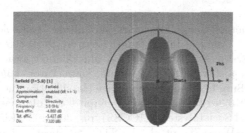

Fig. 5. Front view of the radiation pattern of a 1×2 triangular patch antenna array for the 5.8 GHz frequency

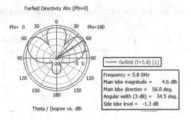

Fig. 6. Polar Plot of Radiation Pattern 1×2 triangle patch antenna array (PHI = 0)

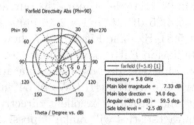

Fig. 7. Polar Plot of Radiation Pattern 1×2 triangle patch antenna array (PHI = 90)

4   Conclusion

In this article, a triangular microstrip patch antenna with one and two elements is designed and presented. Both proposed antennas are suitable for 5.8 GHz WLAN applications, for use in wireless power transmission, ensuring remote UAV charging. Both antennas have good performance and nearperfect impedance matching. The manufactured antenna has good performance and near-perfect impedance matching. We can We can conclude that the results are promising for ensuring the smooth operation of a wireless energy transfer system.

References

1. Ray, P.P.: Internet of things for smart agriculture: technologies, practices and future direction. J. Ambient Intell. Smart Environ. **9**(4), 395–420 (2017)
2. Perera, C., Zaslavsky, A., Christen, P., et al.: Context aware computing for the internet of things: a survey. IEEE Commun. Surv. Tutor. **16**(1), 414–454 (2013)
3. Sun, J., Cai, X., Sun, F., et al.: Scene image classification method based on Alex-Net model. In: 2016 3rd International Conference on Informative and Cybernetics for Computational Social Systems (ICCSS), pp. 363–367. IEEE (2016)
4. Bai, J., Zeng, Z., Wang, T., et al.: TANTO: an effective trust-based unmanned aerial vehicle computing system for the Internet of Things. IEEE Internet Things J. **10**(7), 5644–5661 (2022)
5. Liu, Q., Yin, J., Xiao, J., Shen, X.: Energy-efficient UAV deployment for wireless rechargeable sensor networks in IoT. IEEE Internet Things J. **4**(6), 2265–2276 (2017)

6. Singh, D., Chauhan, A.K., Kumar, N.: A survey on UAVs based applications in Internet of Things. In: 2017 International Conference on Information Technology (ICIT), pp. 162–167. IEEE (2017)
7. Liu, L., Lv, X., Chen, J., Lyu, S.: UAV-enhanced Internetof Things: framework and future directions. IEEE Internet Things J. 5(6), 4440–4452 (2018)
8. Qin, Y., Wen, C., Ma, Z., Xu, L., Tao, X.: Multi-UAV enabled wireless powered IoT: a reinforcement learning approach. IEEE Internet Things J. 6(1), 224–233 (2019)
9. Sun, H., Zhang, J., Xu, C., Zhang, L.: Cooperative control of UAVs for wireless power transfer in large-scale IoT networks. IEEE Internet Things J. 6(3), 4278–4289 (2019)
10. Ma, Z., Liu, X., Chen, C., Qin, Y.: Joint trajectory and power control for multi-UAV based wireless powered IoT networks. IEEE Trans. Ind. Inf. 16(6), 4176–4186 (2020)
11. Raza, U., Cosenza, B., Pelliccia, R.: UAV-enabled Internet of Things: a comprehensive survey. IEEE Access 8, 93797–93819 (2020)
12. Duan, L., Feng, Z., Li, Y., Wang, Y.: Multi-UAV assisted wireless powered IoT networks with trajectory optimization. IEEE Trans. Commun. 69(1), 173–188 (2021)
13. Kurs, A., Karalis, A., Moffatt, R., Joannopoulos, J.D., Fisher, P., Soljacic, M.: Wireless power transfer via strongly coupled magnetic resonances. Science 317(5834), 83–86 (2007)
14. Awan, A.A., Tan, C.S., Gurbuz, A.C.: Energy harvesting and wireless power transfer for UAVs: challenges and opportunities. IEEE Wirel. Commun. 23(4), 102–111 (2016)
15. Kim, J.H., Hagerty, J.: Design of a UAV wireless charging system for extended endurance. In: 2017 IEEE International Conference on Electro Information Technology (EIT), pp. 180–184. IEEE (2017)
16. Chen, K., Zeng, Y., Zhang, R., Zhang, L.: Joint trajectory and power allocation for multi-UAV enabled wireless power transfer. IEEE Trans. Wirel. Commun. 17(3), 2109–2121 (2018)
17. Han, Z., Yang, Y., Xu, K., Zhang, R.: Wireless power transfer for UAVs: challenges and opportunities. IEEE Commun. Mag. 57(1), 96–101 (2019)
18. Yan, S., Jiao, Y., Guan, H., Zeng, Y., Zhang, R.: UAV-enabled wireless power transfer: trajectory design and energy allocation. IEEE Trans. Wirel. Commun. 19(1), 276–288 (2020)
19. Yang, L., Li, H., Zhou, X., Guo, S.: Trajectory design and power allocation for multi-UAV enabled wireless power transfer in urban scenarios. IEEE Trans. Veh. Technol. 69(10), 10836–10850 (2020)
20. Sotyohadi, R.A., Hadi, D.R.: Design and bandwidth optimization on triangle patch microstrip antenna for WLAN 2.4 GHz. In: MATEC Web of Conferences, ICESTI 2017, vol. 164, p. 01042 (2018). https://doi.org/10.1051/matecconf/201816401042
21. Taybi, A., Tajmouati,A.: Design of a new 5.8 GHz RFDC rectifier structure for wireless power transmission. In: IEEE International Conference on Wireless Technologies, Embedded and Intelligent Systems (WITS), FEZ, Morocco (2017)
22. Jawad, A.M., Nordin, R., Gharghan, S.K., Jawad, H.M., Ismail, M.: Opportunities and challenges for near-field wireless power transfer: a review. Energies 10(7), 1022 (2017)
23. Pradipta, W.D., Setijdi, E., Hendrantoro, G.: Jurnal Teknik ITS 1, 1 (2012). http://ejurnal.its.ac.id/index.php/teknik/article/view/64

Ubiquitous Communication Technologies and Networking

Toward Best Performance of Node's Radio Module Setting for Use in IoT-Based Maritime Petroleum Waste Recovery Prototype System

Bilal Abdellaoui[✉], Abdelhadi Ennajih, Saâd Lissane Elhaq, Adnane Mounadel, and Mohammed Sadik

Laboratory of Engineering Research (LRI), National Higher School of Electricity and Mechanics (ENSEM), Hassan II University, 20100 Casablanca, Morocco
bilal.abdellaoui.doc20@ensem.ac.ma

Abstract. The IoT paradigm continues to expand as its potential helps businesses to prosper and be more competitive. Its structure is comprised of several units, the sensors being a mainstay. Among fundamental questions raised in the context of IoT design and implementation are: Which sensor to choose from among the existing options? How to configure it for optimal performance? To respond to these questions, this study compares two radio modules with different settings to select the best for IoT-based maritime petroleum waste recovery use case needs. This latter is a small-scale system to simulate the transmission of ship-generated oily waste tank levels. The experimentation is managed within a closed area. The requirement for the distance is up to 50 m, while the data packet size is 40 bytes. There was no notable preference for a radio module over the other, as the experimentation results showed proof of the superiority of one solution over the other depending on the current assessment criterion (i.e., distance or data packet size). Thus, the Analytical Hierarchy Process (AHP) tool has been applied to make an objective multi-criteria choice that considers the case constraints and the sensors' performance. The outcome of this paper will be integrated into a larger research project to develop an end-to-end prototype for the collection, transmission, processing and dashboard display of tank filling status of oily waste generated by ships and stored in ports. This system will provide the external reception and collection managers with real-time tracking and monitoring features to carry out efficient IoT-based collection operations and eventual recovery.

Keywords: Internet of Things · Sensor setting · Radio modules · Data transmission · Analytic Hierarchy Process

1 Introduction

The Internet of Things comprises a set of connected layers. The sensing layer is the one at the very front of this structure. It is the starting point and the interface across which all the functionality is powered up. Obviously, this layer is endowed with several distinctive characteristics to support the peculiarities of each application case. In this context, the

O. Habachi et al. (Eds.): UNet 2023, LNCS 14757, pp. 139–148, 2024.
https://doi.org/10.1007/978-3-031-62488-9_11

setting of sensing devices appears in its full significance. In fact, the adjustment of the radio frequency communication parameters has an essential role. When data is ready, these end devices create a packet, put the data inside and send it out.

Despite the diversity of their types (e.g., liquid level, temperature, humidity, distance), the joint role of sensors is to detect a property in the outside environment and communicate it through a medium in a readable format [9]. The input is in the form of an electrical signal in terms of variation in voltage, for example, described relative to signal amplitude and phase (i.e., energy converter). The sensing operation explores and applies physical principles (e.g., capacitance, magnetism, resistance). Radiofrequency, optical and infrared are common wireless communication schemes [3]. The related taxonomy is rich, and criteria vary, building on a myriad of possibilities (e.g., simple/complex, active/passive, digital/analogue). Its ability to interact with the real outside and to perform precise measures beyond human possibilities constitutes the foundations of its development.

In view of the composition of the sensor, it lists a micro-processing unit, storage capacity unit, power system, analog-to-digital converter and radio frequency interface [4]. The sensor devices are constrained and very limited concerning their capabilities (e.g., restricted storage space, weak processing performance, finite battery capacity). The serial adapter interface of this node (i.e., sensor) permits accessing, programming, debugging and charging it [2]. The sensor lifetime depends on the cumulative energy consumption of its individual components (i.e., working mode, current draw). The resource-restricted nature of these devices stresses the need for efficient management of packets using the least amount of available memory and processing.

Not only raw sensor data are stored, but more importantly, the meaningful metadata [13]. The sensor data is organized following small-size structured information. The values represented refer to quantitative and qualitative values. This information tends to be spatiotemporal and real-time [10]. Depending on the object type (i.e., fixed, mobile), they encompass a set of characteristics such as the sensor identifier, the measure, the position, the period of time, etc. How often the content is sent can be set to be periodic or depend on a trigger point. Data indexing later affects the system as it prepares the ground to start serving client requests and enabling data exploration and analysis.

This study aims to provide an appropriate level of detail on the problem of sensor configuration to perform a transmission task given the individual case conditions and circumstances. First, it introduces the characteristics and parameters of a transceiver module, taking the HC-12 as an example. The following sections describe a case study performed to highlight how the setting of a radio transceiver module can affect the transmission operation in the case of a prototype of an IoT-based maritime petroleum waste collection system.

2   Background

The background is provided based on the standard wireless transceiver module HC-12. The information comes from various versions of the original manual users [7, 8, 11, 12].

2.1 Characteristics and Specifications

In the beginning, the baud rate (i.e., the flow of bits per second) an HC-12 can transmit is 5000 bps. The travelling distance can reach 1 km in a free space. It is half-duplex and can work as a transmitter or receiver but not simultaneously. The transmitted signal working frequency (i.e., number of occurrences per unit of time) ranges from 433.4 to 473 MHz. A channel step is 400 kHz with a total of 100 channels. It is a shared medium.

The maximum power of transmission is 100 mW. The ratio of electrical power is of 20 dBm (i.e., decibel-milliwatts); that means each mW unit is amplified with a ratio of 20 dB. The sensitivity at the receiver is −117 dBm, approximately equivalent to 2.10^{-12} mW; that means the receiver can demodulate a signal at low power (i.e., above the sensitivity threshold). The maximum transmitted power is defined at the transmitter side and the sensitivity is defined at the receiver side, then the losses (e.g., distance, obstacles) determine if the signal will successfully attain its destination. The maximum link budget is of 137 dBm. Figure 1 summarizes the characteristics mentioned above.

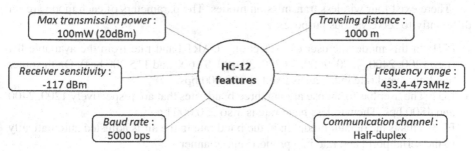

Fig. 1. HC-12 salient transmission features

The HC-12 module comprises a set of pins with a power supply input, ground, Universal Asynchronous Receiver Transmitter (UART) receiver and transmitter, SET pin and antennas.

The principle behind this is to replace physical wiring with wireless transmission modules to realize the same data exchange scheme (See Fig. 2). HC-12 modules are usually used in pairs. They communicate through radio waves, while the devices are linked to them by serial ports.

Fig. 2. Wireless transmission paradigm

2.2   Transmission Modes:

The transmission modes can be selected at will depending on the user requirements (i.e., FU1, FU2, FU3 and FU4). The operation of data transmission must occur between the same modes. There is a relation between the distance travelled and the baud rate set; the farthest is the distance, the lowest is the baud rate and vice-versa.

The default transmission mode is FU3. Its serial port baud rate controls the baud rate in the air (i.e., wireless transmission). For instance, if the serial port baud rate is 4800 or 9600 bps, the one in the air will be 15 000 bps. Therefore, the serial port baud rate should be kept to a minimum to achieve a maximum distance. Otherwise, the reasoning can be reversed if the goal is to transmit a high amount of data at a short range. Another relation exists between the baud rate and the receiving sensitivity in wireless communication. Indeed, each rise in the wireless baud rate causes a decrease in the receiving sensitivity. For example, if the baud rate goes from 5000bps to 15 000 bps, the sensitivity is reduced by 5 dBm. As a rule, a 6 dBm diminution in the receiver sensitivity is equivalent to a distance cut to half.

There exist four wireless transmission modes. The parameters of each mode are set differently to serve various purposes:

- FU1: In this mode, the user can select any UART baud rate from the available list (i.e., 1200, 2400, 4800, 9600, 19 200, 38 400, 57 600 and 115 200 bps). On the other hand, the baud rate in the air is fixed at 250 000 bps.
- FU2: The user has to choose among three baud rates that are respectively 1200, 2400 and 4800 bps. The wireless baud rate is also 250 000 bps.
- FU3: This is the default mode. In it, the baud rate in the air is adjusted automatically to the serial port baud rate in a proportional manner.
- FU4: It supports only the 1200 bps baud rate. The corresponding air baud rate is relatively small (500 bps). This setting is adapted to long-distance communication.

The modification of setting parameters is done using AT commands. The command instructions include: AT + Bxxxx (i.e., baud rate), AT + Cxxxx (i.e., channels), AT + FUx (i.e., modes), AT + Px (i.e., transmission power) and AT + Uxxx (i.e., data bits, check bit and stop bit).

3   Methodology and Materials

Now that the context of a radio transceiver module has been established, quantitative research could introduce greater clarity for better understanding; to that end, two modules were elected to carry out transmission tests. The first module is HC-12, and the second is nRF24L01 + with a Power Amplifier and Low Noise Amplifier (i.e., PA and LNA). For more information on this latter, the reader is referred to Nordic Semiconductor product specification [5].

Under the conditions of this experimentation, a transmitter is used to send a packet of 100 bytes over a shared channel to a receiver located at variable distances. The distance step is set at 10 m. The testing procedure takes place in a confined space instead of an open space to reflect conditions which are the most similar to the real operating circumstances. The maximum distance the working space is allowed is approximately 70 m. The height of the radio modules is kept at 1 m. The modules used are purchased from the electronic market in Morocco, and there is no guarantee of proving their originality. Thus, the results of this study are concerning these modules. Figure 3 shows the figuration of the experience progress.

Four operational modes were adopted for each device. The HC-12 disposes of pre-configured modes as presented above (See Sect. 2.2). They were programmed and tested consecutively to collect the results of each separate one. For analysis purposes, the collected data gives numerical information on the number of bytes transmitted successfully in relation to the distance between where the receiver is put and the current state of the transmitter location. The same applies to the nRF24L01 + device, except that the configurations are set and defined in detail as described in Table 1.

Table 1. Nrf24l01 + settings

Mode	Air data rate	Power amplifier control
1	2 Mbps	High
2	2 Mbps	Low
3	250 Kbps	High
4	250 Kbps	Low

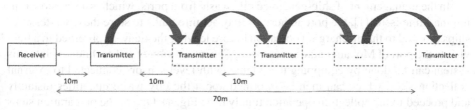

Fig. 3. The transmission experimentation progress

4   Results

Table 2 presents the measures corresponding to the number of bytes transmitted successfully in the different iterations, using different sending and receiving events settings. Overall, the configuration changes affect the metrics of the transmission. The distance can vary approximately between 20 m to 40 m. The data size goes from 17 bytes up to 60 bytes. The fourth mode showed better performance regarding distance achieved and data size transmitted. Nevertheless, the other modes can have other advantages. For example, the FU2 is the best economical choice with regard to power saving [12].

On the other hand, the nRF24L01 + with PA and LNA had the same execution, whatever the configuration (See Table 3). That means no difference exists in the performance metrics (i.e., transmission distance, amount of data) due to a change in the transmission parameters below a distance of approximately 70 m. Nevertheless, the data size achieved was at most 32 bytes; this remains relatively limited and restrictive.

Table 2. The HC-12 results of the transmission distance and the number of bytes received

Distance (m)	Modes				
	FU1	FU2	FU3	FU4	
10	60	60	17	60	The number of bytes received successfully upon
20	60	60	17	60	sending a packet of **100 bytes** over **channel 0**
30	X	60	17	60	
40	X	X	17	60	
50	X	X	X	X	
60	X	X	X	X	
70	X	X	X	X	

Note. The sign "X" means that the transmission was not successful (i.e., the packet did not reach the destination). The erroneous bytes were not accounted for in the reported results. The modes FU3 and FU4 showed steady performance, unlike the FU1 and FU2, which were unstable

5   Use Case and Discussion

This section is a use case description and evaluation of the choice of a radio module to perform the transmission of data for some local constraints.

In the management of ship-generated oily waste from ports, which is a very concerning maritime issue [1], the port authorities may acquire tanks to store these wastes after ships proceed to the discharging operation before leaving the quay, as observed in a field visit to the port of Mohammadia in Morocco. The integration of IoT technology into this system can be done by equipping these tanks with level sensors connected to external collection sites, which can then be informed about the oily waste quantities instantly and proceed to the collection operation timely (See Fig. 4). One of the preparation steps for the implementation of such a system is the conception of a prototype at a small scale. This paper intends to respond to the following question: Which radio module can efficiently perform the data transmission in the proposed system?

The results obtained in Sect. 4 should help decide which radio module is suitable for use and can offer better outcomes about the above-expected utilization. The conditions of the transmission in the prototype system are as follows:

- The simulation of the transmission of the tank level is required at a distance of no more than 50 m.
- The data packet size is fixed at 40 bytes (i.e., including an identifier and metric value).

To evaluate the available alternatives objectively, there is a need to have recourse to the multi-criteria decision-making methods. The AHP method (i.e., Analytic Hierarchy Process) is deemed suitable for this context [6]. The alternatives are the four modes of both modules, while the transmission distance and the data packet size represent the criteria. The latter criterion was given a little more importance than the former (i.e., more weight). The goal is to choose the best module and mode to perform the transmission task efficiently. An initial brief assessment has favoured the FU4 mode from the HC-12

Table 3. The nRF24L01 + results of the transmission distance and the number of bytes received

Distance (m)	Modes				
	Mode1	Mode2	Mode3	Mode4	
10	32	32	32	32	The number of bytes received successfully upon sending a packet of **100 bytes** over **channel 0**
20	32	32	32	32	
30	32	32	32	32	
40	32	32	32	32	
50	32	32	32	32	
60	32	32	32	32	
70	32	32	32	32	

Note. All modes demonstrated regular steadiness. The same behaviour was observed, whatever the mode used

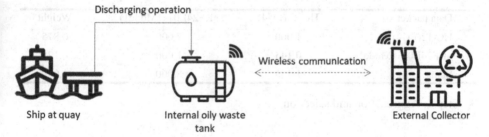

Fig. 4. IoT-based ship generated oily waste collection scheme

module and the four modes from nRF24L01 + (See Table 4). Besides, as the four modes of the nRF24 + L01 had equal behaviour, only Mode1 was selected for inclusion in the AHP procedure. For this, the Mode1 of the nRF24L01 + is deemed more important in terms of distance than the FU4 mode of the HC-12, while the data packet is much more important in this latter (See Table 5).

Table 4. Initial assessment based on eligibility criteria

Criteria	Modes							
	HC-12				nRF24L01 + (with PA and LNA)			
	FU1	FU2	FU3	FU4	Mode1	Mode2	Mode3	Mode4
Distance	✗	✗	✗	✗	✓	✓	✓	✓
Data packet size	✓	✓	✗	✓	✗	✗	✗	✗
Constancy	✗	✗	✓	✓	✓	✓	✓	✓
Total	1	1	1	2	2	2	2	2

Table 5. AHP process steps

- Step 1: Criteria weighting

Criteria	Distance	Data packet size	Weight
Distance	1,000	0,333	0,250
Data packet size	3,000	1,000	0,750
Sum	4,000	1,333	1,000

- Step 2: Alternative rating against criteria

Distance	HC-12(FU4)	nRF24L01+(Mode1)	Weight
HC-12(FU4)	1,000	0,200	0,167
nRF24L01+(Mode1)	5,000	1,000	0,833
Sum	6,000	1,200	1,000

Data packet size	HC-12(FU4)	nRF24L01+(Mode1)	Weight
HC-12(FU4)	1,000	7,000	0,875
nRF24L01+(Mode1)	0,143	1,000	0,125
Sum	1,143	8,000	1,000

- Step 3: Aggregation and selection

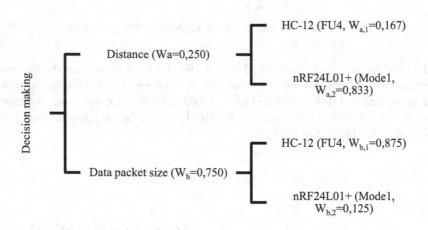

- Step 4: Final evaluation

Mode	HC-12(FU4)	nRF24L01+(Mode1)
Priority	0,698	0,302

Given the circumstances of the experimentation and the target set, the global score favours the FU4 mode of the HC-12 over the other modes. Above all, this can be attributed to the small extent of the transmission and the criticality of the data volume. In case of a need for a longer distance and fewer bytes, nRF24L01 + modes would be better placed.

6 Conclusions

This study intended to decide which radio module will respond better to the transmission conditions in the prototype's frame to reproduce and simulate the functioning pattern of a level sensor of a ship-generated oily waste tank in a closed environment. It has focused attention on the parameters of the transmission distance and the data size buffer. The experimentation has shown that each module had an advantage over the other based on the specific assessment criteria. As there was no agreement on the choice, the AHP method intervened to elicit a rational and objective rank by establishing weights, pairwise comparing and prioritizing,

In real-world applications, each situation's separate evaluation, in terms of the environment constraints and the objective of the implementation of the IoT system, would determine the needs and the associated correct amount of the sensor capabilities. In fact, the practical requirements of diversity impose that the transmission parameters should be tuned for optimal matching to derive the maximum potential benefit. However, more is needed, as several solutions could exist with different behaviours, requiring one to refer carefully to the product technical data sheet. The bottom line is that the best solution is combining better choosing and tuning.

The comparison based on experimentation results and objective criteria selected according to the nature of the case is a good preparation for an ulterior use and implementation, as well as a strong and decisive ground. The adopted methodology capitalises on the factual and quantitative outcome depending on the actual conditions of a particular experience in combination with theoretical aspects rather than simply focusing on these latter. It is then a specific usage-oriented study. The issue is pretty well decided based on the particular application needs. The more the results are tightly circumscribed within a near-real framework, the higher level of assurance that can be provided. Additionally, any change would have had an implication on the final result.

The limitations of this study include the case-oriented results that cannot be generalized. That means that more elaborate experimentation with no restrictions on the distance, and with consideration to an open space environment as well, could provide additional insights. The comparison methodology involved the subjective view of the authors. An objective assessment of the situation concerning other criteria would cover more aspects (e.g., battery lifespan) and refine the results. Prospects for improvement and extension include adopting radio modules with more robust capabilities (e.g., the transmission distance of several kilometres, proprietary modulation techniques). Another aspect is to move from prototyping conditions to a real-world implementation to unveil eventual constraints.

Acknowledgment. This research work was supported by the Ministry of National Education, Vocational Training, Higher Education and Scientific Research (MENFPESRS, Morocco), the

Digital Development Agency (ADD, Morocco) and National Centre for Scientific and Technical Research (CNRST, Morocco).

References

1. Arslan, O., Solmaz, M.S., Usluer, H.B.: Determination of the perception of ship management towards environmental pollution caused by routine operations of ships. Aquat. Res. **5**(1), 39–52 (2022). https://doi.org/10.3153/ar22005
2. Förster, A.: Anatomy of a sensor node. In Introduction to Wireless Sensor Networks, vol. 4, pp. 11–31 (2016). https://doi.org/10.1002/9781119345343.ch2
3. Iqbal, M. A., Hussain, S., Xing, H., Imran, M.: Sensing principles and wireless sensor network: fundamentals, design and applications. In Enabling the Internet of Things, pp. 49–74 (2021). https://doi.org/10.1002/9781119701460.ch3
4. Krishnamurthi, R., Kumar, A., Gopinathan, D., Nayyar, A., Qureshi, B.: An overview of iot sensor data processing, fusion, and analysis techniques. Sensors (Switzerland) **20**(21), 1–23 (2020). https://doi.org/10.3390/s20216076
5. Nordic Simicondutor. Preliminary Product Specification v1.0, pp. 1–75 (2008). https://www.sparkfun.com/datasheets/Components/SMD/nRF24L01Pluss_Preliminary_Product_Specification_v1_0.pdf
6. Piton, G., Philippe, F., Tacnet, J.-M., Gourhand, A.: Aide à la décision par l'application de la méthode AHP (Analytic Hierarchy Process) à l'analyse multicritère des stratégies d'aménagement du Grand Büech à la Faurie. Sciences Eaux & Territoires, Numéro **26**(2), 54–57 (2018). https://doi.org/10.3917/set.026.0054
7. Rozee, R.: HC-12 wireless serial port communication module- User Manual v1.18 (2012). https://www.elecrow.com
8. Rozee, R.: HC-12 wireless serial port communication module- User Manual v2.3A (2016). https://www.elecrow.com
9. Sehrawat, D., Gill, N.S.: Smart sensors: analysis of different types of IoT sensors. In: Proceedings of the International Conference on Trends in Electronics and Informatics, ICOEI 2019, pp. 523–528 (2019). https://doi.org/10.1109/ICOEI.2019.8862778
10. Servigne, S., et al.: Gestion de masses de données au sein de bases de données capteurs. Revue Internationale de Géomatique **19**(2), 133–150 (2009). https://doi.org/10.3166/geo.19.133-150
11. HC-12 Wireless RF UART Communication Module- User Manual v2.4 (2016). https://www.hc01.com
12. HC-12 Wireless RF UART Communication Module- Manual User v2.6 (2018). https://www.hc01.com
13. Zaslavsky, A., Perera, C., Georgakopoulos, D.: Sensing as a service and big data. Proceedings of the International Conference on Advances in Cloud Computing (ACC), pp. 21–29 (2013). http://arxiv.org/abs/1301.0159

Modeling of Noise due to a Plasma-Based Contactless Power Transmission System for Ultra-High-Speed Transportation

Bentolhoda Kazemzadeh[1]([✉]), Ryan Janzen[2], Hamid Meghdadi[3], Vahid Meghdadi[1], and Abbas Bradai[4]

[1] XLIM, UMR CNRS n7252, University of Limoges, Limoges, France
bentolhoda.kazemzadeh@etu.unilim.fr
[2] TransPod Inc., Toronto, Ontario, Canada
[3] TransPod France, Limoges, France
[4] XLIM, UMR CNRS n7252, University of Poitiers, Poitiers, France

Abstract. This paper studies plasma effects in the FluxJet, an ultra-high-speed vehicle being designed for transportation at aircraft-like speeds, running in a guideway between cities. The effects are studied relating two different systems: plasma-based power transmission used to power the vehicle at high speed, and RF (Radio Frequency) signals for vehicle communication and control. The effect of noise from the plasma power transmission is analyzed and modeled by a two-state Markov model. The noise is characterized, and by using a cost function, we observe that the noise states given by our model, are well matched with the measured signals.

Keywords: TransPod · FluxJet · plasma · impulsive noise · Markov model

1 Introduction

The *FluxJet* is a newly-proposed aerospace vehicle for ground transportation at over 1000 km/h [1,2]. A *TransPod line* is proposed to connect major cities and transportation hubs, with FluxJet vehicles for passengers and cargo [2]. The infrastructure is a guideway designed for multiple FluxJet vehicles to travel, using electrically-powered propulsion. This vehicle can be thought of somewhat like an aircraft without wings [2]. Technology in this system includes plasma power transmission [3], magnetic propulsion [4,6], and veillance flux [7–9]. The FluxJet vehicle is powered using a patented plasma-based high-speed power transmission system [1,3].

This paper analyzes the measured data, represents the plasma arc current, in the context of contactless power transmission system for a TransPod FluxJet line. This kind of energy transferring could become a source of impulsive noise. Impulsive noise has a significant impact in many communication settings, as

© The Author(s), under exclusive license to Springer Nature Switzerland AG 2024
O. Habachi et al. (Eds.): UNet 2023, LNCS 14757, pp. 149–159, 2024.
https://doi.org/10.1007/978-3-031-62488-9_12

recent literature points out: power-line communications [10]; digital subscriber loop [11]; wireless networks and OFDM (Orthogonal frequency-division multiplexing) [12]; wireless sensor networks [13]; acoustic communication [14] and different vehicular communications scenarios [15]. In this paper, we focus on two major areas of impulsive noise: noise detection and noise modeling.

The presented methodology can be used also for the railway systems, considering communication to/from a train in the presence of highly inductive electrical arcing from mechanical contact between a pantograph on the train and a catenary wire above the train, or between a pickup shoe on the bottom of the train and a power rail.

The paper is organized as follows: Sect. 2 presents the FluxJet transportation system for TransPod line. In Sect. 3, we discuss the plasma-based high-speed power transmission system employed in the FluxJet. Section 4 covers a brief review on impulsive noise models. A proposed noise model is presented in Sect. 5. The numerical results are provided in Sect. 6 and concluding remarks are drawn in Sect. 7.

2   FluxJet Transportation System

More precisely about the FluxJet transportation system, a *contactless EMV (Electric, Magnetic, Veillance) FluxJet vehicle* is defined by the use of (1) electric flux, (2) magnetic flux, and (3) veillance flux, to power, propel, and control the vehicle without any physical contact between the vehicle and its guideway [1]. Specifically: (1) plasma is used to carry electric current to the vehicle without contact. The plasma is generated and controlled by power pickup systems on the vehicle, in order to maintain this plasma current flow across a contactless gap, thus delivering power obtained from the grid to the vehicle [3]. Then, using that power, (2) the vehicle is levitated and propelled using magnetic fields. On the vehicle, linear motors and power inverters generate magnetic fields which move in a wave-like pattern, leading to propulsive force on the vehicle due to electromagnetic induction [1,4,6]. Finally, (3) the vehicle's flight control system is controlled to stabilize motion in 6 axes of motion, by varying the magnetic fields [4]. Sensors deliver information based on *veillance flux* [7–9] – a method of "sensing of sensing", in order to build up a spatial information map of known knowns, and unknown unknowns, in order to enhance safety at high-speed [1].

3   Plasma-Based Power Transmission System

We will focus on electrical discharge phonemena in the FluxJet, as a source of interference in the communication system. Since the power transmission system and communication system will exist in the same environment inside a steel guideway isolated from the outside world, it is important to make the communication system resilient to this interference, seen in Fig. 1.

Experimental data was obtained from previous measurements in [1] (with permission).

These previous experiments were set up to verify the high-speed operation of a plasma-based power transmission. These measurements replicated the conditions of (a) high altitude, low-pressure environment, (b) high-velocity motion, and (c) high electric field. The experiments were performed using a vacuum chamber and pressure control system, along with a custom-built high-voltage power system which was designed with a multiplexer circuit to control and maintain plasma [1]. The high-voltage power and monitoring signals were delivered into the vacuum environment using an epoxy-sealed penetration [1]. A robotic arm was installed to remotely manipulate an electrode, which carried plasma through to a motorized rotating disc, controlled by a 3-phase inverter and electronic speed controller [1]. High-voltage signals were measured and recorded. A sample of these signals is used in this paper, particularly demonstrating a highly unstable conduction mode as a worst-case scenario.

By analyzing the measured data, we observe that the instantaneous noise variance is correlated with the current, which is drawn in the plasma arc discharge. It means that a signal at the receiver can be contaminated by a kind of impulsive noise.

Fig. 1. Schematic of the TransPod system with the power transmission system and transmitter/receiver inside a steel tube.

4   Impulsive Noise Models

The impulsive noise degrades the received signal quality over a large frequency spectrum for short but repeated time intervals. The impulsive noise can be considered as a series of pulses with random interval between successive pulses and random duration. During the pulses, the added noise variance is very high which can potentially corrupt a received signal. Through this paper, we aim to produce a mathematical model for the impulsive noise due to the plasma source. Examples of commonly employed memoryless impulsive noise models are Middleton Class A [25] and Bernoulli Gaussian [26]. There are also with-memory models including Markov Middleton [23] and Markov-Gaussian [22]. Since we consider the plasma as the unique source of impulsive noise, a two-state Markov-Gaussian model is used in our modeling. An overview of this model is provided in the following section.

4.1   Two-State Markov-Gaussian Model

The two-state Markov-Gaussian model was introduced by Fertonani [22]. For this model, a set of real value noise samples is defined as $\{X_k, \ k = 1, 2, 3, .., K\}$

[16,17]. The statistical properties of the noise samples can be completely modeled by the states $s_k \in \{G, B\}$, where the state G corresponds to the "impulse off" condition when impulsive noise is absent, and the transmitted signal is impaired only by background Gaussian noise. The state B corresponds to the "impulse on" condition and the transmitted signal is additionally impaired by impulsive noise. Conditioned on s_k, the PDFs of X_k are represented by Gaussian distributions, expressed as [10]:

$$
\begin{aligned}
p\left(X_k \mid s_k = G\right) &= \frac{1}{\sqrt{2\pi\sigma_G^2}} \exp\left(-\frac{X_k^2}{2\sigma_G^2}\right) \\
p\left(X_k \mid s_k = B\right) &= \frac{1}{\sqrt{2\pi\sigma_B^2}} \exp\left(-\frac{X_k^2}{2\sigma_B^2}\right),
\end{aligned}
\tag{1}
$$

where σ_G^2 is the average noise power of the good channel, and σ_B^2 is the average noise power of the bad channel. The noise can be completely characterized by the state process $s^K = \{s_0, s_1, \ldots, s_{K-1}\}$ that can be expressed as a stationary first-order Markov process with

$$
p\left(s^{K+1}\right) = p\left(s_0\right) \prod_{k=0}^{K} p\left(s_{k+1} \mid s_k\right).
\tag{2}
$$

Therefore, the state process is described by the state transition probabilities $p_{s_k s_{k+1}} = p\left(s_{k+1} \mid s_k\right)$. From the state transition probabilities, the stationary probabilities of being in the state G and B, i.e., p_G and p_B are respectively obtained as [10]:

$$
\begin{aligned}
p_G &= p\left(s_k = G\right) = \frac{p_{BG}}{p_{GB} + p_{BG}} \\
p_B &= p\left(s_k = B\right) = \frac{p_{GB}}{p_{GB} + p_{BG}},
\end{aligned}
\tag{3}
$$

where p_{BG} denotes the transition probability from state B to state G and similarly, p_{GB} is the transition probability from G to B. Therefore, we can completely characterize the noise by the transition probabilities p_{GB} and p_{BG}. A two-state Markov process can be modelled by a Markov chain of two states as shown in Fig. 2 [16].

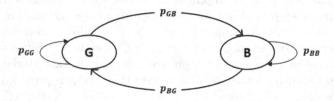

Fig. 2. Markov chain representation of the two-state Markov-gaussian noise model.

5   Noise Modeling

The recorded data are classified based on the distances between the vehicle electrodes and track electrodes [1]. The noisy signal in time domain can be characterized using statistical parameters like mean and variance. In this section we study how to analyze the measured data and model the noise.

5.1   Data Analysis

To analyze the measured data, the impulsive noise has to be modeled as a pulse train where the elapsed time between pulses, and pulse duration are considered as random variables. We define two variables *Pulse Distance*, P_D and *Pulse Width*, P_W describing the distance of two consecutive pulses, and it's duration, respectively.

The first step in the noisy signal interpretation is to detect the impulsive events and identify their time boundaries in the signal. For that, we compare the moving average of signal amplitude with an appropriate threshold [16]. A pulse is considered to have started when the noise moving average amplitude exceeds a specific threshold and ends when the noise level falls below that threshold. Once the pulse train has been created form the measured signal, the statistical parameters μ_{P_D} and $\sigma^2_{P_D}$ (μ_{P_W} and $\sigma^2_{P_W}$) can be computed as mean and variance of P_D (P_W).

5.2   Markov Chain Model

To characterize the Markov model, we need the initial probabilities of the states, and the conditional transition probabilities, which is presented by the matrix P as follows [29]:

$$P = \begin{bmatrix} p_{GG} & p_{GB} \\ p_{BG} & p_{BB} \end{bmatrix}. \tag{4}$$

The pulse distance (P_D) and pulse width (P_W) produced by the mdoel is denoted by ($\tilde{P}_D$) and ($\tilde{P}_W$). Based on the given probabilities, we generate a sequence of N noise samples. Then, we compute the statistical mean $\tilde{\mu}_{P_D}$ and variance $\tilde{\sigma}^2_{P_D}$ ($\tilde{\mu}_{P_W}$ and $\tilde{\sigma}^2_{P_W}$) of the random variables $\tilde{P}_D$ ($\tilde{P}_W$) of the noise series created by Markov chain model.

To adjust the created model with the measurements, we compare the mean and variance of the pulse distance and pulse width, which have been obtained from the measured data with the ones from the created Markov model. We define an appropriate metric to fit our model to the measured data. We are to minimize four cost functions given in (5)–(8) below, where the difference between the measured mean values and generated ones from the model, is to be minimized. Furthermore, we minimize the error of the variances between measured and modeled data.

$$J1_{P_D} = \min \| \tilde{\mu}_{P_D} - \mu_{P_D} \|^2, \tag{5}$$

$$J2_{P_D} = \min \|\tilde{\sigma}^2_{P_D} - \sigma^2_{P_D}\|^2, \tag{6}$$

$$J1_{P_W} = \min \|\tilde{\mu}_{P_W} - \mu_{P_W}\|^2, \tag{7}$$

$$J2_{P_W} = \min \|\tilde{\sigma}^2_{P_W} - \sigma^2_{P_W}\|^2. \tag{8}$$

This is known as multi-objective minimization. To solve the problem, we can minimize a single cost function which is the sum of four metrics (5)–(8). The cost function is defined as following:

$$J = J1_{P_D} + J1_{P_W} + J2_{P_D} + J2_{P_W}. \tag{9}$$

The coarse-to-fine search method has been applied to minimize the cost function. We create a grid, with coordinate axes p_{GB} and p_{BG}. The axes are in the range $[0, 1]$ with the step size of 0.1. We start with a coarser grid with a low grid resolution. We iterate over all (p_{GB}, p_{BG}) pairs on the created grid and compute the cost function in (9). For the minimum value of the cost function, a pair of (p_{GB}, p_{BG}) is obtained. The process repeats for the updated range of the axes around the obtained pair, i.e., we continue to search in a fine grid with a higher resolution. The process stops when the accuracy of the points on the axes is within 0.0001. The pseudo-code for the iterative minimization can be summarized in Algorithm 1.

Algorithm 1. Minimizing Algorithm

Input: $\mu_{P_D}, \sigma^2_{P_D}, \mu_{P_W}, \sigma^2_{P_W}$.
Output: p_{GB}, p_{BG}.

1: We initialize the p_{GB} and p_{BG} in the range $[0, 1]$.
2: Compute step size $\Delta_{p_{GB}} = \frac{p_{GB}[end] - p_{GB}[start]}{10}$ and $\Delta_{p_{BG}} = \frac{p_{BG}[end] - p_{BG}[start]}{10}$.
3: Create a grid with coordinate axes p_{GB} and p_{BG} with computed step size.
4: Compute the cost function (9) for each grid point.
5: Find the value $\hat{p}_{GB}, \hat{p}_{BG}$ which minimizes the cost function in (9).
6: Set the coordinates in the new ranges
$p_{GB} = \hat{p}_{GB} - \Delta_{p_{GB}}, \ldots, \hat{p}_{GB} + \Delta_{p_{GB}}$ and
$p_{BG} = \hat{p}_{BG} - \Delta_{p_{BG}}, \ldots, \hat{p}_{BG} + \Delta_{p_{BG}}$.
7: Stop if ($\hat{p}_{GB}$ and $\hat{p}_{BG}$) have the accuracy within 0.0001 or go to step 2 to refine grid over $\hat{p}_{GB}$ and $\hat{p}_{BG}$.

---

6   Numerical Results

The recorded data are presented in this section. The y coordinate of the plots are normalized between 0 and 1. For three different distances between the electrodes, the measured current signals corresponding to the plasma arc discharge are plotted. The blue line in Fig. 3 represents the measured arc current during a system transient at an electrode separation of 1mm, and the red line shows the state of the impulsive noise detected according to Sect. 5.1.

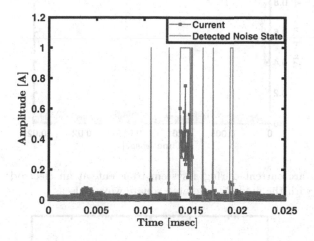

Fig. 3. Plasma arc current during a system transient, at an electrode separation of 1mm, overlaid with the model's generated square wave pulses.

Figures 4 and 5 illustrate the same results for the electrodes distance equal to 3 mm and 6 mm, respectively.

Figure 6 illustrates the noise samples produced by the model. Table 1 represents the mean and variance values of P_D and P_W are given for three different electrodes distances, as well as the mean and variance values extracted from the

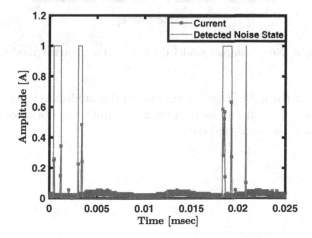

Fig. 4. Plasma arc current during a system transient, at an electrode separation of 3mm, overlaid with the model's generated square wave pulses.

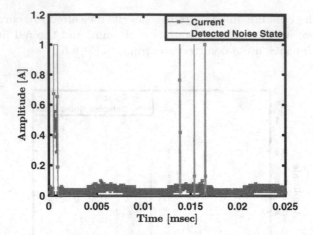

Fig. 5. Plasma arc current during a system transient, at an electrode separation of 6mm, overlaid with the model's generated square wave pulses.

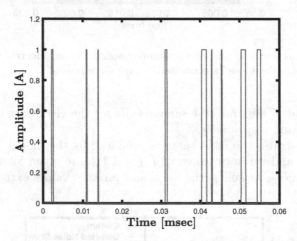

Fig. 6. Noise samples modeled by Two-state Markov model.

Markov model of the noise, that correspond to the minimum values of the given cost function in (9). As it can be seen from the table, the optimized models can well approximate the measured data.

Table 1. Comparison between the statistical parameters from the measured data and the model (E.D stands for the distance between electrodes).

Parameters	$\mu(P_D)$	$\sigma^2(P_D)$	$\mu(P_W)$	$\sigma^2(P_W)$
Measured	0.0036	1.5717e-5	4.5e-4	7.0083e-7
Model	0.0036	2.2108e-5	4.1632e-4	5.9847e-7
(E.D = 1mm)				
Measured	0.0056	2.0066e-5	6.3182e-4	2.3764e-7
Model	0.0056	3.1069e-05	6.3089e-4	3.1102e-7
(E.D = 3mm)				
Measured	0.007	4.3069e-5	3.9375e-4	2.4103e-7
Model	0.007	5.0821e-5	3.9102e-4	2.9932e-7
(E.D = 6mm)				

7   Conclusion

This paper reports the measured noise in the context of the contactless power transmission system, employed in the FluxJet vehicle designed to operate on the fully-electric TransPod line. We have analyzed a set of sample worst-case recorded current corresponding to the plasma arc discharge. We observed that the measurements are correlated with the instantaneous noise variance at the receiver of the communication system. Two-state Markov-Gaussian model was used to model the measured noise. We have shown that the model fits the measurements, and the differences between the observed values from the measurements and the predicted values from the model are small.

References

1. Janzen, R.: The FluxJet: a high-speed vehicle for transportation, based on electric flux, magnetic flux, and veillance flux (2022). (arXiv preprint; unpublished)
2. Janzen, R.: The FluxJet: unveiling of a novel vehicle concept, (product unveiling presentation (July 2022). TransPod Inc.; unpublished)
3. Janzen, R.: Transpod Inc, 2019. Plasma-based high-speed power transmission system. U.S. Patent, international WIPO app. no. 56186372-2PCT, filed 2017 Sept. 8 (2019)
4. Janzen, R.: Transpod Inc, 2022. Vehicle for travelling along a linear route guideway. U.S. Patent, international WIPO app. no. 56186372-1PCT, filed 2017 Sept. 8. "original provisional title: Predictive Suspension and Cascaded Multi-Actuator Traction System" (2022)
5. Nanevicz, J.E., Vance, E.F., Hamm, J.M.: Observation of lightning in the frequency and time domains. In: Lightning Electromagnetics, (pp. 191–210) Routledge (2017)
6. Boldea, I.: Linear Electric Machines, Drives, and MAGLEVs Handbook. CRC Press (2017)

7. Janzen, R., Mann, S.: Veillance flux, vixels, veillons: an information-bearing extramissive formulation of sensing, to measure surveillance and sousveillance. In: 2014 IEEE 27th Canadian Conference on Electrical and Computer Engineering (CCECE), (pp. 1–10). IEEE (May 2014)
8. Ryan, J. Mann, S.: The physical-fourier-amplitude domain, and application to sensing sensors. In 2016 IEEE International Symposium on Multimedia (ISM), (pp. 317–320). IEEE (Dec 2016)
9. Yang, S.: Veillametrics: an extramissive approach to analyze and visualize audio and visual sensory flux (Doctoral dissertation, University of Toronto (Canada)) (2018)
10. Xu, Z., Yang, C., Tan, Z., Sheng, Z.: Raptor code-enabled reliable data transmission for in-vehicle power line communication systems with impulsive noise. IEEE Commun. Lett. **21**(10), 2154–2157 (2017)
11. Bai, T., Zhang, H., Zhang, R., Yang, L.L., Al Rawi, A.F., Zhang, J., Hanzo, L.: Discrete multi-tone digital subscriber loop performance in the face of impulsive noise. IEEE Access **5**, 10478–10495 (2017)
12. Epple, U., Schnell, M.: Advanced blanking nonlinearity for mitigating impulsive interference in OFDM systems. IEEE Trans. Veh. Technol. **66**(1), 146–158 (2016)
13. Sarr, N.B., Yazbek, A.K., Boeglen, H., Cances, J.P., Vauzelle, R., Gagnon, F.: An impulsive noise resistant physical layer for smart grid communications. In: 2017 IEEE International Conference on Communications (ICC), (pp. 1–7). IEEE (May 2017)
14. Chen, P., Rong, Y., Nordholm, S., He, Z., Duncan, A.J.: Joint channel estimation and impulsive noise mitigation in underwater acoustic OFDM communication systems. IEEE Trans. Wireless Commun. **16**(9), 6165–6178 (2017)
15. Mahmood, A., Chitre, M.: Ambient noise in warm shallow waters: a communications perspective. IEEE Commun. Mag. **55**(6), 198–204 (2017)
16. Vaseghi, S.V.: Impulsive noise. In Advanced Signal Processing and Digital Noise Reduction (pp. 294–313). Vieweg+ Teubner Verlag (1996)
17. Middleton, D.: Statistical-physical models of electromagnetic interference. IEEE Trans. Electromagn. Compat. **3**, 106–127 (1977)
18. Blum, R., Zhang, Y., Sadler, B.M., Kozick, R.J.: On the approximation of correlated non-Gaussian noise PDFs using Gaussian mixture models. In Conference on the Applications of Heavy Tailed Distributions in Economics, Engineering and Statistics. Washington, DC, USA: American University (June 1999)
19. Andreadou, N., Pavlidou, F.N.: Modeling the noise on the OFDM power-line communications system. IEEE Trans. Power Delivery **25**(1), 150–157 (2009)
20. Laguna-Sanchez, G., Lopez-Guerrero, M.: On the use of alpha-stable distributions in noise modeling for PLC. IEEE Trans. Power Delivery **30**(4), 1863–1870 (2015)
21. Huang, S.Y., Chang, C.S., Tan, T.H.: Markov model parameters optimization for asynchronous impulsive noise over power line communication network. In: 2006 IEEE International Conference on Systems, Man and Cybernetics (Vol. 2, pp. 1570–1574). IEEE (Oct 2006)
22. Fertonani, D., Colavolpe, G.: On reliable communications over channels impaired by bursty impulse noise. IEEE Trans. Commun. **57**(7), 2024–2030 (2009)
23. Ndo, G., Labeau, F., Kassouf, M.: A Markov-Middleton model for bursty impulsive noise: modeling and receiver design. IEEE Trans. Power Delivery **28**(4), 2317–2325 (2013)
24. Alam, M.S., Selim, B., Kaddoum, G., Agba, B.L.: Mitigation techniques for impulsive noise with memory modeled by a two state Markov-Gaussian process. IEEE Syst. J. **14**(3), 4079–4088 (2020)

25. Middleton, D.: Institute of Electrical and Electronics Engineers, 1960. An introduction to statistical communication theory (Vol. 960). New York: McGraw-Hill
26. Ghosh, M.: Analysis of the effect of impulse noise on multicarrier and single carrier QAM systems. IEEE Trans. Commun. **44**(2), 145–147 (1996)
27. Awino, S.O., Afullo, T.J., Mosalaosi, M., Akuon, P.O.: Measurements and Statistical Modelling for Time Behaviour of Power Line Communication Impulsive Noise. Int. J. Commun. Antenna Propagation **9**(4), 236–246 (2019)
28. Theodoridis, S.: Machine learning: a Bayesian and optimization perspective. Academic press (2015)
29. Kijima, M.: Markov Processes for Stochastic Modeling. Chapman and Hall, London (1997)
30. Mirbadin, A., Vannucci, A., Colavolpe, G., Pecori, R., Veltri, L.: Iterative receiver design for the estimation of gaussian samples in impulsive noise. Appl. Sci. **11**(2), 557 (2021)

A Literature Review on Smart Greenhouse and AI: Paradigms, Opportunities and Open Issues

Wiam El ouaham, Youssef Mouzouna, and Mohamed Sadik[✉]

Department of Electrical Engineering, Networking Embedded Systems and Telecommunications (NEST) Research Group, Engineering Research Laboratory (LRI), National Higher School of Electricity and Mechanics (ENSEM), Hassan II University of Casablanca, Casablanca, Morocco
wiam.elouaham-etu@etu.univh2c.ma, m.sadik@ensem.ac.ma

Abstract. Controlled crop cultivation within smart greenhouses has become integral to smart agriculture. This system has been made more efficient, productive, and sustainable by applying various algorithms of machine learning that facilitate decision-making by farmers, this paper provides a short literature review of using machine learning applications in smart greenhouses, focusing on three important aspects: disease detection, climate control inside the greenhouse and robotic harvesting, to highlight the latest advances, challenges, and opportunities in this growing field.

Keywords: machine learning · greenhouse · disease detection · control micro-climate · robotic harvesting

1 Introduction

Over the next twenty years, the world population is expected to increase by up to 20% [1], requiring a 70% increase in food production [3]. Greenhouses have become an important solution in agriculture, with controlled environments [9], that increase crop yields [8], thereby reducing resource use, and minimizing the need for pesticides. To maximize productivity with minimal energy consumption, advanced technologies such as IoT and machine learning are integrated into greenhouse agriculture, enabling real-time monitoring, disease prevention, pest control, and accurately estimating crop yields.

Several notable advances have taken place in the agricultural sector, including robotic harvesting, disease and pest detection, and climate control in greenhouses. Using machine learning, the advanced computing power will analyze IoT data including various parameters such as plant images and environmental conditions to optimize crop growth and reduce energy consumption. Although technological advances have improved the efficiency of greenhouses, many challenges remain.

O. Habachi et al. (Eds.): UNet 2023, LNCS 14757, pp. 160–173, 2024.
https://doi.org/10.1007/978-3-031-62488-9_13

Throughout this review, we will consider both the oldest and newest research on greenhouse technology. Research will focus on applying machine learning to detect diseases, predict microclimate, and use robots in the harvesting process. The remainder of this review is organized into three parts. An overview of greenhouse studies using machine learning is followed by an analysis of the results, including machine learning models in greenhouses. In the final section, we will discuss the challenges and limitations of using machine learning algorithms in the greenhouse as well as future prospects.

2 Literature Review

Numerous research studies are conducted annually, utilizing machine-learning algorithms to enhance precision accuracy and reduce errors. In this review, we will examine a selection of these studies for three aspects of greenhouses.

2.1 Climate Control and Prediction

The agricultural industry has been revolutionized by smart greenhouses that allow vegetables to be produced year-round in a controlled environment. They excel at maintaining optimal conditions for plant growth. However, achieving this goal requires effective management of various parameters within the greenhouse while also taking into consideration the significant energy consumption [42]. Several important factors determine microclimates, such as temperature, humidity, and CO_2 concentration. These factors correlate with temperature affecting humidity and CO_2 levels, and vice versa. Any inadequate control of temperature can disrupt plant growth, leading to heat stress in cases of high temperatures or cold damage in cases of low temperatures [2]. On the other hand, high relative humidity can cause fungal diseases, leaf issues, and calcium deficiencies, while low humidity makes plants close their stomata, slowing photosynthesis and reducing yields in greenhouses. The concentration of CO_2 also plays a major role in biomass production; a higher CO_2 level increases the yield and quality of fruits [41]. Efficiently managing these factors remains a complex challenge for farmers. They must consider that internal factors like greenhouse dimensions and the efficiency of heating, cooling, and ventilation systems, along with external factors such as meteorological conditions (wind speed, solar radiation, temperature, and humidity), also profoundly affect the microclimate [5].

Machine learning approaches, time series analysis, and hybrid approaches that combine machine learning with time series or mathematical algorithms techniques have gained popularity in predicting greenhouse microclimates.

The Radial Basis Function (RBF) model has demonstrated promising results in predicting inside environment variables and energy loss. In [43], authors compared the performance of RBF, multilayer perceptron (MLP), and support vector machine (SVM) to predict inside air, soil, and plant temperatures. Results showed that the performance of the RBF model outperformed the other models based on the small Root Mean Square Error (RMSE) value ranging from 0.07°C to 0.12°C. In another study [47], the RBF neural network was fine-tuned by implementing the Levenberg-Marquardt (LM) algorithm to optimize the structural parameters and weights of the model for predicting temperature and humidity. Impressively, their model achieved a maximum relative error of less than 0.5% and an RMSE of 9.99e-006. In [17], a similar study was conducted, but this time, the dataset exclusively pertained to the external factors of the greenhouse. The study confirmed that the RBF model with the LM learning algorithm outperformed the SVM and the Gaussian Process Regression (GPR), in predicting indoor air temperature in terms of accuracy and reliability. The RBF model achieved an RMSE of 0.82°C and a MAPE of 1.21

Support Vector Machines (SVMs) models have also shown promising results; they effectively handle non-linear relationships. For predicting inside temperatures within the greenhouse. A study in [46] utilized the least squares support vector machine (LSSVM) model with parameters optimized by an improved particle swarm optimization (IPSO) technique. The resulting model offers temperature forecasts within a 6-hour time interval and achieves remarkable accuracy within just 4 h. In another study [15], a comparison was made between linear regression (LR) and Support Vector Regression (SVR). The data was divided into seasons for better analysis and modeling of the internal temperature. The results showed that SVR models were able to adapt to temperature outliers and presented the highest forecast accuracy among the proposed algorithms, with coefficient of determination (R^2) values ranging from 0.9808 to 0.9999 and RMSE values from 0.0549 to 1.7431. Authors in [11], combined fuzzy logic and multiclass SVM techniques to develop a model that adequately sets and monitors greenhouse farm parameters, such as temperature, humidity, and soil moisture. The fuzzy rules were able to enhance the performance in decision-making.

A study in [7] underscored the potential for enhanced accuracy by introducing time series data into classical machine learning models. **Time series data analysis**, owing to its consideration of trends, seasonality, and temporal correlations among closely spaced samples, has gained prominence in monitoring and controlling greenhouse environments. Among the traditional methods used for time series analysis, autoregressive models have gained prominence. In a related experiment, researchers compared Autoregressive models with external input (ARX) and Autoregressive moving average models with external input (ARMAX) models for modeling greenhouse temperature [13]. In another study [7], it was demonstrated that Autoregressive moving average models (ARIMA) combined with the RBF neural network showed higher prediction accuracy and improved stability compared to using the single models alone.

Artificial Neural networks ANN are widely used in greenhouses for predicting microclimatic parameters, producing remarkably precise results. They excel at handling complex relationships and solving nonlinearity problems [34]. In [37], an MLP-NN was trained using both external and internal data to predict internal temperature and relative humidity. The model was optimized using the LM backpropagation algorithm, with logistic sigmoid and linear functions as activations for the hidden and output layers, respectively. The following metrics were calculated: Mean Absolute Error (MAE), the RMSE, and the R^2. The results were as follows: 0.218 K, 0.271 K, and 0.999 for temperature, 0.339%, 0.481%, and 0.999 for relative humidity. In [33], further tests were conducted using ANNs to estimate crop transpiration rates based on environmental and growth factors. The study demonstrated that ANNs outperformed traditional estimation methods, achieving a small RMSE transpiration rate.

Deep Learning is a powerful subset of machine learning utilizing complex models and parallel processing that excels at solving intricate problems quickly and can outperform ANNs in certain scenarios [10]. In the agricultural sector, various techniques, including recurrent neural networks (RNNs) and long short-term memory (LSTM) have been applied to address complex system challenges and predictive tasks. Specifically, LSTM models are extensively employed for time series prediction, such as forecasting greenhouse environmental conditions. For instance, in [25], the authors developed the GCP-LSTM model, which utilizes an LSTM network to capture non-linear relationships among historical environmental factors. This model provides 5-minute forecasts of greenhouse temperatures, demonstrating the effectiveness of deep learning methods in handling time series data. Furthermore, in another study [20], Deep Neural Network Regression (DNNR) was compared with the LSTM and convolutional neural network-long short-term memory (CNN-LSTM) models to predict the solar greenhouse and crop water demand accurately. The DNNR models exhibited excellent prediction accuracy compared to the other models. Specifically, the error distribution of temperature and humidity at the 24-hour forecast fell within the range of [-7, 7] °C and [-19, 26]% respectively. One of the main challenges in the agriculture sector is the availability of large amounts of high-quality data to train and validate the models. Authors in [30], addressed this challenge by using generative adversarial networks (GANs) to generate synthetic temperature data. The study results show that the incorporation of synthetic data significantly improved the accuracy of AI/ML models compared to using only ground truth data. Notably, the GAN model proved capable of generating synthetic time series data of equal or higher quality than the original data.

Light Gradient Boosting Machine (LGBM) is an ensemble learning algorithm based on decision trees, which was released by Microsoft in late 2017. it's gaining popularity in the field of machine learning due to the key advantages involving low memory usage and high convergence speed. A comparative study conducted in [6] involved five different models: a Gradient Boost Decision Tree (GBDT) model based on the newly developed LGBM, a Back-Propagation (BP) Neural Network model, a Recurrent Neural Network (RNN) model, and two other GBDT algorithms, Extreme Gradient Boosting (XGBoost) and Stochastic Gradient Boosting (SGB). These models were trained and validated Using as inputs: climate variables, control variables, and five-year temporal information, These models were trained and validated to predict greenhouse internal temperatures; the results show that LGBM exhibited the best fitting ability for the temperature curves, with an RMSE value of 0.645°C. Furthermore, LGBM demonstrated the fastest training speed among all the algorithms, being 60 times faster than the other two neural network algorithms.

In recent years **Attention mechanisms** have been successfully applied in a wide variety of deep learning application domains. Originally implemented in Natural Language Processing (NLP). In a study [21], two models were proposed with the Luong attention-based sequence-to-sequence (seq2seq) architecture, using GRU and LSTM as encoder and decoder layers. For forecasting indoor condition variables in the Solar Dryer Dome (SDD) and optimizing energy consumption. The implementation of Luong attention in the seq2seq LSTM model reduced the test RMSE by 0.00962 on average for predicting indoor temperature, as well as decreased the RMSE by 0.095535 for predicting indoor humidity. The application of Luong's attention also improved the accuracy of the seq2seq GRU model by reducing the error by 0.021996 in RMSE for indoor humidity.

2.2   Diseases Detection

Plant diseases are one of the most severe obstacles to a productive agricultural sector, severely impacting crop yield, especially when not detected early, leading to widespread outbreaks. According to related studies, approximately 10% of global food production is lost due to plant diseases [32]. The most common method of disease control involves the uniform application of pesticides across the agricultural area, which is effective but comes with substantial financial costs and potential health concerns for humans. Therefore, it is crucial to identify and prevent plant diseases early to minimize crop damage and reduce the need for excessive pesticide use. While farmers may sometimes identify plant diseases, their methods are often unreliable and prone to errors. On the other hand, pathologists are experts capable of accurately diagnosing plant diseases. However, their diagnostic methods are often laborious and time-consuming, which can result in delays in treatment.

Researchers have turned to machine learning techniques to address complex challenges, given its prominence in various fields. **Classical machine learning algorithms** typically follow three key steps: image segmentation, feature extraction, and pattern recognition. In most cases, object features are extracted using manually designed feature extractors, such as the Histogram of Gradient (HOG), Scale-Invariant Feature Transform (SIFT), and Haar-like features. These features are then used as input for the machine learning algorithms [14]. One notable study, proposed in [16], focused on plant leaf disease detection using a color and texture-based approach, leveraging the K-nearest neighbor (KNN) classifier. This approach achieved an impressive detection and recognition accuracy of 96.76%. Another study, outlined in [19], introduced an approach based on a multiclass SVM classifier, which attained an accuracy rate of 95% in classifying diseases affecting potato plants.

In recent years, **deep learning methods** have made significant breakthroughs in computer vision, with applications extending to agriculture. CNN-based models, particularly those capable of automatically extracting features directly from input images, have gained popularity for their remarkable accuracy in object detection, eliminating the need for complex preprocessing. This makes them particularly effective in crop disease detection. CNN-based object detection models fall into two categories: two-stage and one-stage detectors. One well-known two-stage detector is the Region Convolution Neural Network (RCNN), which includes Fast/Faster-RCNN and Mask-RCNN. In a comparative study conducted in [14], researchers aimed to identify nine distinct types of pests and diseases affecting tomato crops. Their dataset consisted of various backgrounds, varying illumination conditions, and diverse object sizes. The experiments involved evaluating three different detection algorithms: Fast-RCNN, Single Shot MultiBox Detector (SSD), and Region-based Fully Convolutional Network (R-FCN). These detectors were combined with various feature extraction networks. By employing data augmentation techniques, a notable enhancement in the Average Precision metric was achieved. Remarkably, Faster R-CNN with VGG-16 achieved an impressive 85.98% accuracy in detecting plant diseases and pests.

In the realm of one-stage detectors, we have the SSD and the You Only Look Once (YOLO) algorithm. The YOLO algorithm has achieved a significant improvement in detection speed thanks to unifying the two tasks of target classification and localization in object detection into a regression problem. YOLO eliminates the need for Region Proposal Networks (RPN) and can perform direct regression to detect targets in the image. To support of the application of one-stage detectors, as detailed in [44], a dense connection module was introduced into the YOLOv3 architecture to effectively enhance network inference speed. Furthermore, the authors applied the K-means algorithm for anchor box clustering and implemented a multiscale training strategy. The YOLO-Dense model demonstrated superior performance when compared to alternative models, including SSD, Faster R-CNN, and the original YOLOv3 network. Impressively, the YOLO-Dense model achieved a remarkable mean Average Precision (mAP) and single-image detection time, with a notable score of 96.41%.

In the area of small data, applying transfer learning has proven to be a valuable strategy. In a notable example presented in [35], an EfficientNet model, specifically EfficientNet-B4, took center stage in the creation of a classification model encompassing four distinct classes. What sets this study apart is the integration of the Ranger optimizer into an improved variant of EfficiencyNet-B4. Capitalizing on this improved model architecture, a two-classification model was subsequently devised, aimed at distinguishing between two closely related cucumber diseases. The EfficientNet-B4 model outperformed a range of established networks, including AlexNet, VGG16, VGG19, Inception V4, ResNet50, ResNet101, SqueezeNet, and DenseNet, achieving superior accuracy while boasting fewer parameters and reduced computation time. Impressively, it achieved a commendable model accuracy of 97% across the four distinct classes, which include powdery mildew, downy mildew, healthy leaves, and the combined presence of powdery mildew and downy mildew. Additionally, the enhanced EfficientNet, leveraging the Ranger optimizer, attained an accuracy rate of 96% in the context of the two-classification model focused on cucumber-similar diseases.

Hyperspectral imaging methods have developed significantly over the past two decades [4] and are used to identify crop stress [28]. In [36], an extensive study explored the application of hyperspectral imaging and machine learning-based classification methods to detect powdery mildew on wild rocket leaves. The authors trained a Random Forest model with the four most contributory wavelengths falling in the range 403–446 nm to accurately discriminate between healthy and diseased wild rocket leaves. This study provides a non-destructive and effective disease detection method, which can contribute to the development of remote sensing techniques for crop disease detection. The method used for feature extraction in this paper is the Recursive Feature Elimination (RFE) algorithm.

Recent research has shown the remarkable effectiveness of attention-based techniques in improving deep learning networks, highlighting their versatility in various computer vision applications, including object detection. In [38], an innovative approach leveraged mobile phones to photograph tomato diseases in a greenhouse environment. To obtain important information and improve the accuracy of disease identification, the YOLOv5m network model was optimized by taking inspiration from the human visual attention mechanism. This optimization is accomplished by combining it with the squeeze-and-excitation (SE) module. This strategic restructuring of the model backbone has facilitated the efficient exploitation of essential features relevant to the detection target. Impressively, the upgraded SE-YOLOv5 shows a 1.78% increase in mAP@0.5 compared to the base YOLOv5 model.

2.3   Robotic Harvesting

In modern agriculture, greenhouses play a pivotal role in maximizing crop yields. However, the process of harvesting, though essential, often proves to be highly labour-intensive, placing substantial demands on the workforce. The gains in crop yield, while significant, can sometimes outstrip the available labour resources. This challenge becomes particularly pronounced during peak harvesting seasons, often resulting in operational bottlenecks and reduced efficiency for farm organizations. The recurrent issue of labour shortages compounds this problem, driven by both inter-sector labour competition and the demographic shift toward an aging or dwindling workforce [18]. Within this context, labour costs have emerged as a substantial component of overall agricultural production expenses, accounting for a staggering 50% of customary costs [29]. The viability of contemporary production systems is thus contingent on the integration of innovative technologies and cost-effective solutions that directly address labour scarcity. One such solution gaining traction is the deployment of harvesting robots, a concept initially proposed by Schertz and Brown [40]. These robotic systems typically comprise a mobile platform or vehicle, a robotic manipulator designed for fruit or vegetable collection, and a vision system equipped for crop scanning and precise target identification. To enhance the performance of these robots, machine-learning approaches have been employed in several tasks, including fruit localization, ripeness determination, obstacle localization, task planning, and motion planning.

Various approaches have been explored for automating crop harvesting tasks, particularly for fruits like tomatoes and sweet peppers. These methods encompass color-based techniques such as HOG descriptors paired with SVM classifiers [24], and Haar-like features with AdaBoost classifier and color analysis [48]. Additionally, older methods, such as the segmentation of mature tomatoes using color spaces like HIS and Lab space [12] have found applications in tomato harvesting. In a study conducted by [23], a sophisticated automated tomato harvesting system was developed, featuring two robotic arms for picking and detaching ripe tomatoes. A stereo camera captured images that were analyzed by a computer to identify ripe tomatoes and create a 3D map of the environment. Haar-like features and an AdaBoost classifier were used for tomato detection, along with color analysis. The system achieved a 96.5% recognition rate, and the robot harvested 87.5% of ripe tomatoes in real-time and the average time taken to harvest each tomato was approximately 29 s. In another notable study [22], introduced 'Harvey,' a robotic sweet pepper harvester designed for protected cropping environments. 'Harvey' utilized an RGB-D camera and focused on color-based fruit detection. It incorporated a novel peduncle segmentation system based on deep convolutional neural networks and a 3D post-filtering approach. 'Harvey' achieved a 76.5% success rate for fruit detection in a modified crop and a 47% success rate in an unmodified crop, with a cycle time of 36.9 s.

Among the various deep neural network (DNN) structures, CNNs are noteworthy as they excel in image-based learning. Regarding target detection, deep convolutional neural networks can be categorized into two main groups, as previously mentioned. In recent studies [39], researchers have devised an efficient method for harvesting cherry tomatoes. Their approach involves several key steps: firstly, the YOLOv4-Tiny detector is employed to locate clusters of cherry tomatoes and define a cutting point for their peduncles. Next, the YOLACT++ Network is utilized to segment the peduncle mask. This segmented mask is then fitted to a curve using the least squares method, resulting in the identification of three critical points on the curve. Finally, a geometric model is established to estimate the pose of the cherry tomatoes. This innovative tomato bunch detection method achieves an impressive precision rate of 92.7%, with a swift processing time of 0.0091 s per frame when using the YOLOv4-Tiny detector. In [31], the researchers developed a model based on the Faster-RCNN with Resnet-101 to autonomously detect intact green tomatoes on plants, even in the presence of occlusions or varying fruit growth stages. The model was trained using the Common Objects in Context (COCO) dataset. Detected boxes were consolidated into a unified image to create a tomato location map and estimate their sizes along a single row in the greenhouse. The results yielded an average accuracy of 87.83%. Notably, this accuracy was achieved under the realistic conditions of tomatoes growing in their natural environment, which can be more challenging than controlled conditions. In [27], the authors evaluated the performance of five deep-learning models for detecting green and reddish tomatoes cultivated in greenhouses. These models were rigorously trained and assessed using an annotated visual dataset of tomatoes. The two architectural contenders for the robotic platform specifications were the SSD and the YOLO. Their findings demonstrated that the system was proficient at detecting both green and reddish tomatoes, including those partially obscured by leaves. Among the models tested, SSD MobileNet v2 outperformed the others, achieving an F1-score of 66.15%, an mAP of 51.46%, and an inference time of 16.44 ms. Lastly, the authors in [26], use a Mask R-CNN in conjunction with the ResNet-101 and Feature Pyramid Network (FPN) architecture employed to detect green sweet peppers and their peduncles within greenhouse environments. This model generated mask images, providing binary masks through instance segmentation, thereby enhancing the localization process in 3D space for autonomous sweet pepper harvesting. Impressively, the model attained a precision rate of 84.53% for fruit detection, 71.78% for peduncle detection, and an overall mean average precision rate of 72.64% for model-wide instance segmentation. Additionally, the average detection time for sweet pepper fruit and peduncle, when employing high-resolution images, was a mere 1.18 s, aligning with the real-time requirements of autonomous harvesting.

3 Discussion

There are different approaches to modeling the environment in greenhouses, in order to grow crops in controlled environments. Traditional models for time series such as autoregressive models are simple but have low data utilization efficiency and cannot handle complex relationships between environmental parameters. Traditional machine learning models like decision trees, random forests, and SVMs can handle complex relationships with high data utilization efficiency but may require more feature engineering and tuning. Advanced machine learning models like DNNs can automatically extract relevant features from the data, fit complex relationships, and capture spatiotemporal correlations, making them the most promising approach for modeling the facility agriculture environment. The latest research direction in DNNs is the Attention mechanism, which can further improve accuracy by capturing complete spatiotemporal correlations.

For disease detection, several works show different algorithms for different tasks: image classification, object detection, or Image segmentation by using classical machine learning, which is needed in the first step of feature extraction based on tools for feature extraction. The results are used as input for training the models. However, they perform well, but the feature extraction task needs time. It can take features that are not useful or ignore useful features. However, the unavoidable noises are largely in disease images captured under natural conditions, such as field background, uneven illumination, and the shelter effect of the leaf. This problem can seriously affect the quality of feature extraction and the accuracy of disease recognition. With the development of fully connected algorithms, the results show promising results, specifically in object detection; we do not need to do manual feature extraction tasks; the algorithms have this ability in their owner. The research works in disease detection are almost tested on tomatoes in primary rank, followed by wheat, potato, and other vegetables or fruits. In all scenarios, the deep learning approach exceeds classical machine learning models in terms of robustness, dealing with high-dimensional data and complex tasks. However, they need a large amount of data.

Moving to robotic harvesting, one of the most critical challenges is the accurate detection and localization of fruits. Developing robotic harvest technologies requires identifying crops that may overlap with one another or be subject to varying lighting conditions. Also, in robotic harvesting, deep learning exceeds classical machine learning regarding robustness and time. While deep learning algorithms have shown significant improvements over traditional machine learning in many scenarios, they may not always be the best option. Recent developments in computer vision, such as transformational architectures and attention mechanisms, are promising for object detection and localization in robotic harvesting systems.

4   Challenges and Limitations

It is worth noting that, while the reviewed works have several advantages, there are still many problems that need to be addressed in this research field. Some studies have noted issues related to the availability of enough datasets [7], which can occasionally result in class imbalance, affecting a model's ability to generalize effectively for practical applications [14]. In some cases, addressing this data scarcity necessitates an increase in the number of training epochs, which in turn escalates the demand for computational resources and time [44]. Moreover, the use of datasets that lack the complexity of real-world environments, such as PlantVillage, primarily composed of leaf images against simple backgrounds, may lead to reduced accuracy when identifying tomato diseases in real-world scenarios [45]. Additionally, in terms of feasibility, algorithms must strike a balance between prediction performance and low computational and architectural complexity. Unfortunately, this aspect remains unaddressed in many articles. For instance, LightGBM, requiring numerous iterations to converge, poses the challenge of necessitating high-performance processors, which may be incompatible with commonly used embedded Linux controllers in greenhouse settings [6]. Furthermore, real-world testing of algorithms is essential to gain a true understanding of their performance. Many algorithms may exhibit high accuracy during testing but experience a decline in accuracy when deployed in practical, real-life agricultural settings. This decline is often attributed to the influence of environmental factors, especially in the original crop conditions [22]. For instance, the common challenge of leaf occlusion significantly impacts the effectiveness of tomato detection in multiple instances [23,39]. These issues hinder the generalizability and robustness of these methods when they fail to account for scenarios involving leaf or element obstruction, thus limiting their real-world applicability [39]. Likewise, machine-learning models must parade rigidity across different surroundings and crop types, emphasizing the need for robust, generalized models that can handle data variations. In general, there is a demand for high-quality as well as large quantities of data. More algorithms that can make comprehensive decisions while adhering to appropriate computational and architectural limitations also need to be developed. For the actual deployment models in real-world situations, these factors include model sizes, real-world scenario complexity, and technology limitations, these factors are essential for the practical deployment of models in real-world settings. To ascertain the actual correctness of algorithms, it is imperative to apply them to real-world situations.

5   Conclusion and Perspective

This review has analyzed several studies on the application of machine learning in greenhouses over the past few years. These studies have explored micro-climate prediction, disease detection, and robotic harvesting, among other areas. The results show that deep learning models outperform traditional machine learning models. Further research will focus on developing intelligent deep neural network models that leverage attention mechanisms, and transformers to improve accuracy and generalization in prediction tasks. Additionally, there is a need to explore other areas of agriculture, such as pest detection, robotic applications in general, yield estimation, and growth management. We can unlock new possibilities for sustainable and efficient agriculture by continuing to advance research in these areas.

References

1. World Health Organization. The State of Food Security and Nutrition in the World 2018: Building Climate Resilience for Food Security and Nutrition; Food and Agriculture Organization
2. Ahamed, M.S., Guo, H., Taylor, L., Tanino, K.: Heating demand and economic feasibility analysis for year-round vegetable production in Canadian prairies greenhouses. Inform. Process. Agricult. 6(1), 81–90 (2019)
3. Avtar, R., Tripathi, S., Aggarwal, A.K., Kumar, P.: Population-urbanization-energy nexus: a review. Resources 8(3), 136 (2019)
4. Bioucas-Dias, J.M., Plaza, A., Camps-Valls, G., Scheunders, P., Nasrabadi, N., Chanussot, J.: Hyperspectral remote sensing data analysis and future challenges. IEEE Geosci. Remote Sens. Mag. 1(2), 6–36 (2013)
5. Bot, G.P.A.: Physical modeling of greenhouse climate. IFAC Proc. 24(11), 7–12 (1991). https://doi.org/10.1016/b978-0-08-041273-3.50006-9
6. Cai, W., Wei, R., Xu, L., Ding, X.: A method for modelling greenhouse temperature using gradient boost decision tree. Inform. Process. Agricult. 9(3), 343–354 (2022). https://doi.org/10.1016/j.inpa.2021.08.004

7. Cao, Q., Wu, Y., Yang, J., Yin, J.: Greenhouse temperature prediction based on time-series features and lightgbm. Appl. Sci. (Basel, Switzerland) **13**(3), 1610 (2023)
8. Choab, N., Allouhi, A., El Maakoul, A., Kousksou, T., Saadeddine, S., Jamil, A.: Review on greenhouse microclimate and application: design parameters, thermal modeling and simulation, climate controlling technologies. Solar energy (Phoenix, Ariz.) **191**, 109–137 (2019). https://doi.org/10.1016/j.solener.2019.08.042
9. Choab, N., Allouhi, A., Maakoul, A.E., Kousksou, T., Saadeddine, S., Jamil, A.: Effect of greenhouse design parameters on the heating and cooling requirement of greenhouses in moroccan climatic conditions. IEEE Access: Practical Innov., Open Solutions **9**, 2986–3003 (2021). https://doi.org/10.1109/access.2020.3047851
10. Codeluppi, G., Davoli, L., Ferrari, G.: Forecasting air temperature on edge devices with embedded ai. Sensors (Basel, Switzerland) **21**(12), 3973 (2021). https://doi.org/10.3390/s21123973
11. Devi Thangavel, K., Seerengasamy, U., Palaniappan, S., Sekar, R.: Prediction of factors for controlling of green house farming with fuzzy based multiclass support vector machine. Alex. Eng. J. **62**, 279–289 (2023)
12. Eng, Q., Cheng, W., Zhou, J., Wang, X.: Design of structured-light vision system for tomato harvesting robot. Int. J. Agric. Biol. Eng. **7**, 19–26 (2014)
13. Frausto, H.U., Pieters, J.G., Deltour, J.M.: Modelling greenhouse temperature by means of auto regressive models. Biosys. Eng. **84**(2), 147–157 (2003)
14. Fuentes, A., Yoon, S., Kim, S., Park, D.: A robust deep-learning-based detector for real-time tomato plant diseases and pests recognition. Sensors (Basel, Switzerland) **17**(9), 2022 (2017). https://doi.org/10.3390/s17092022
15. García-Vázquez, F., et al.: Prediction of internal temperature in greenhouses using the supervised learning techniques: Linear and support vector regressions. Applied sciences (Basel, Switzerland) **13**(14), 8531 (2023)
16. Hossain, E., Hossain, M.F., Rahaman, M.A.: A color and texture based approach for the detection and classification of plant leaf disease using knn classifier. In: 2019 International Conference on Electrical, Computer and Communication Engineering (ECCE). IEEE (2019)
17. Hosseini Monjezi, P., Taki, M., Abdanan Mehdizadeh, S., Rohani, A., Ahamed, M.S.: Prediction of greenhouse indoor air temperature using artificial intelligence (ai) combined with sensitivity analysis. Horticulturae **9**(8) (2023)
18. Iida, M., et al.: Advanced harvesting system by using a combine robot. IFAC Proc. Vol. **46**(4), 40–44 (2013). https://doi.org/10.3182/20130327-3-jp-3017.00012
19. Islam, M., Dinh, A., Wahid, K., Bhowmik, P.: Detection of potato diseases using image segmentation and multiclass support vector machine. In: 2017 IEEE 30th Canadian Conference on Electrical and Computer Engineering (CCECE). IEEE (2017)
20. Jia, W., Wei, Z.: Short term prediction model of environmental parameters in typical solar greenhouse based on deep learning neural network. Appl. Sci. (Basel, Switzerland) **12**(24), 12529 (2022)
21. Setiawan, K.E., Elwirehardja, G.N., Pardamean, B.: Indoor climate prediction using attention-based sequence-tosequence neural network. Civil Eng. J. **9** (2023). https://doi.org/10.28991/CEJ-2023-09-05-06
22. Lehnert, C., McCool, C., Sa, I., Perez, T.: Performance improvements of a sweet pepper harvesting robot in protected cropping environments. J. Field Robot. (rob.21973) (2020). https://doi.org/10.1002/rob.21973

23. Ling, X., Zhao, Y., Gong, L., Liu, C., Wang, T.: Dual-arm cooperation and implementing for robotic harvesting tomato using binocular vision. Robot. Auton. Syst. **114**, 134–143 (2019)
24. Liu, G., Mao, S., Kim, J.H.: A mature-tomato detection algorithm using machine learning and color analysis. Sensors (Basel, Switzerland) **19**, 2023 (2019)
25. Liu, Y., et al.: A long short-term memory-based model for greenhouse climate prediction. Int. J. Intell. Syst. **37**(1), 135–151 (2022)
26. López-Barrios, J.D., Escobedo Cabello, J.A., Gómez-Espinosa, A., Montoya-Cavero, L.E.: Green Sweet Pepper Fruit and Peduncle Detection Using Mask R-CNN in Greenhouses. Appl, Sci (2023)
27. Magalhães, S.A., et al.: Evaluating the single-shot multibox detector and yolo deep learning models for the detection of tomatoes in a greenhouse. Sensors (Basel, Switzerland) **21**(10), 3569 (2021)
28. Mananze, S., Pôças, I., Cunha, M.: Retrieval of maize leaf area index using hyperspectral and multispectral data. Remote Sens. **10**(12), 1942 (2018)
29. Manzano-Agugliaro, F., García-Cruz, A.: Time study techniques applied to labor management in greenhouse tomato (solanum lycopersicum l.) cultivation. Agrociencia **43**, 267–277 (2009)
30. Morales-García, J., Bueno-Crespo, A., Terroso-Sáenz, F., Arcas-Túnez, F., Martínez-España, R., Cecilia, J.M.: Evaluation of synthetic data generation for intelligent climate control in greenhouses. Applied Intelligence (2023)
31. Mu, Y., Chen, T.S., Ninomiya, S., Guo, W.: Intact detection of highly occluded immature tomatoes on plants using deep learning techniques. Sensors (Basel, Switzerland) **20**(10), 2984 (2020). https://doi.org/10.3390/s20102984
32. Mutka, A.M., Bart, R.S.: Image-based phenotyping of plant disease symptoms. Front. Plant Sci. **5**, 734 (2014). https://doi.org/10.3389/fpls.2014.00734
33. Nam, D.S., Moon, T., Lee, J.W., Son, J.E.: Estimating transpiration rates of hydroponically-grown paprika via an artificial neural network using aerial and root-zone environments and growth factors in greenhouses. Horticult., Environ. Biotechnol. **60**(6), 913–923 (2019). https://doi.org/10.1007/s13580-019-00183-z
34. Of A Greenhouse Elanchezhian, A., et al.: Evaluating different models used for predicting the indoor microclimatic parameters of a greenhouse. Source: Appl. Ecol. Environ. Res. **18**, 2141–2161 (2020)
35. Pan, Z., Yang, L., Li, D.: Efficientnet-b4-ranger: a novel method for greenhouse cucumber disease recognition under natural complex environment. Comput. Electron. Agric. **176**, 105652 (2020)
36. Pane, C., Manganiello, G., Nicastro, N., Cardi, T., Carotenuto, F.: Powdery mildew caused by erysiphe cruciferarum on wild rocket (diplotaxis tenuifolia): hyperspectral imaging and machine learning modeling for non-destructive disease detection. Agriculture **11**(4), 337 (2021). https://doi.org/10.3390/agriculture11040337
37. Petrakis, T., Kavga, A., Thomopoulos, V., Argiriou, A.A.: Neural network model for greenhouse microclimate predictions. Agriculture **12**(6), 780 (2022)
38. Qi, J., et al.: An improved yolov5 model based on visual attention mechanism: application to recognition of tomato virus disease. Comput. Electron. Agric. **194**(106780), 106780 (2022)
39. Rong, J., Dai, G., Wang, P.: A peduncle detection method of tomato for autonomous harvesting. Complex Intell. Syst. **8**(4), 2955–2969 (2022)
40. Schertz, C.E., Brown, G.K.: Basic considerations in mechanizing citrus harvest. Trans. ASAE **11**, 343–0346 (1968)

41. Shamshiri, R.R., Jones, J.W., Thorp, K.R., Ahmad, D., Man, H.C., Taheri, S.: Review of optimum temperature, humidity, and vapour pressure deficit for microclimate evaluation and control in greenhouse cultivation of tomato: a review. Int. Agrophys.**32**(2), 287–302 (2018). https://doi.org/10.1515/intag-2017-0005
42. Shen, Y., Wei, R., Xu, L.: Energy consumption prediction of a greenhouse and optimization of daily average temperature energies **11** (2018)
43. Taki, M., Abdanan Mehdizadeh, S., Rohani, A., Rahnama, M., Rahmati-Joneidabad, M.: Applied machine learning in greenhouse simulation; new application and analysis. Inform. Process. Agricult. 5(2), 253–268 (2018)
44. Wang, X., Liu, J.: Tomato anomalies detection in greenhouse scenarios based on yolo-dense. Front. Plant Sci. **12**, 634103 (2021)
45. Wspanialy, P., Moussa, M.: A detection and severity estimation system for generic diseases of tomato greenhouse plants. Comput. Electron. Agric. **178**(105701), 105701 (2020)
46. Yu, H., Chen, Y., Hassan, S.G., Li, D.: Prediction of the temperature in a Chinese solar greenhouse based on LSSVM optimized by improved PSO. Comput. Electron. Agric. **122**, 94–102 (2016)
47. Yue, Y., Quan, J., Zhao, H., Wang, H.: The prediction of greenhouse temperature and humidity based on LM-RBF network. In: 2018 IEEE International Conference on Mechatronics and Automation (ICMA). IEEE (2018)
48. Zhao, Y., Gong, L., Zhou, B., Huang, Y., Liu, C.: Detecting tomatoes in greenhouse scenes by combining Adaboost classifier and colour analysis. Biosystems engineering **148**, 127–137 (2016). https://doi.org/10.1016/j.biosystemseng.2016.05.001

Q-Learning-Augmented Grant-Free NOMA for URLLC

Ibtissem Oueslati[1]([✉]), Oussama Habachi[2], Jean Pierre Cances[1], Vahid Meghdadi[1], and Essaid Sabir[3]

[1] Xlim, 123 Av. Albert Thomas, 87000 Limoges, France
ibtissem.oueslati@unilim.fr
[2] UCA, 49 Bd François Mitterrand, 63000 Clermont-Ferrand, France
[3] Department of Science and Technology, TÉLUQ, H2S3L4 Montreal, Canada

Abstract. Grant-Free (GF) Non-Orthogonal Multiple Access (GF-NOMA) has emerged as a promising technology for 5G networks requiring Ultra-Reliable Low Latency Communications (URLLC). However, the grant-free nature of these transmissions can introduce significant interference, thereby, negatively affecting URLLC system performance. To address this challenge, this paper introduces a novel, distributed GF-NOMA-based Q-learning framework that aims to minimize network latency based on a developed Mean Opinion Score (MOS) of packet age, while also maintaining high transmission success rates. Real-time feedback from the gNodeB (gNB) is employed to assist Machine-Type Devices (MTDs) in making adaptive decisions of joint power control and sub-carrier selection. Simulation results validate the effectiveness of our approach in minimizing delay and optimizing overall system performance.

Keywords: NOMA · URLLC · Q-Learning · Grant-Free Access · Low Latency

1 Introduction

Two critical applications of fifth-generation and beyond wireless networks (5GBN) are delivering Ultra-Reliable Low Latency Communications (URLLC) with strict demands for reliability and latency [1], and guaranteeing a massive number of devices over limited spetrum. To tackle these challenges, Non-Orthogonal Multiple Access (NOMA) has emerged as an effective technique [2] that enables the overlaying of signals from multiple User Equipments (UEs) on the same Resource Block(RB). This is achieved through multiplexing in either the power domain [3] or the code domain [4] at the transmitting side. At the receiving end, Successive Interference Cancellation (SIC) is employed to separate signals [5].

A recent technique within the realm of NOMA is Grant-Free NOMA (GF-NOMA) [6] where Machine Type Devices (MTDs) communicate on a shared

© The Author(s), under exclusive license to Springer Nature Switzerland AG 2024
O. Habachi et al. (Eds.): UNet 2023, LNCS 14757, pp. 174–184, 2024.
https://doi.org/10.1007/978-3-031-62488-9_14

time-frequency resource block with the gNB bypassing the need for demand-assigned access and thus, not only improving the efficiency of spectrum use but also minimizing the system's latency [7]. However, the stochastic nature of GF-NOMA in a massive acess is resulting in significant interference challenges affecting overall performance. This demands a smart approach to resource allocation in GF-NOMA networks for optimizing overall performance.

Recently, Machine learning (ML), was recognized as a groundbreaking technology for future wireless systems [8]. Reinforcement Learning (RL) algorithms, particularly Q-learning, have been progressively employed to adress those chanllenges by learning from the observed surrounding environment in order to make optimal decisions [9]. Specifically Di Wu and al. present in their recent paper [10] a distributed Q-learning algorithm in order to maximize successful access probability to prioritize emergency devices. Paper [11] presents a Multi-Agent Deep Reinforcement Learning (MADRL) to maximize the network Energy efficiency while fulfilling the URLLC requirements. The work by Tran et al. [12] focuses on optimizing access efficiency in GF-NOMA systems for URLLC applications using Q-Learning algorithms. Unlike the aforementioned works on GF-NOMA systems, we present a distributed, multi-agent framework to address the challenges of uplink communication in a GF-NOMA system, with a particular focus on meeting the stringent latency and reliability requirements set by the 3rd Generation Partnership Project (3GPP) for Ultra-URLLC (main problem is to achieve 1ms latency in real deployment scenario) [13]. To this end, our solution employs a Q-learning-based adaptive behavior for MTDs in a decentralized manner while receiving feedback from the gNB. Distinctively, we adapt the Mean Opinion Score (MOS) methodology, traditionally utilized in telephony for quality assessment, to establish a novel metric for packet age. This metric is specifically designed to align with URLLC's 1ms latency requirement. The paper's key contributions to the field are detailed below

- Our system employs a distributed multi-agent Q-learning approach at the MTDs side rather than the gNB. This eliminates the need for complex resource allocation procedures at the base station, thereby reducing computational overhead and enhancing system scalability.
- Our method is consistent with the standards established by the 3GPP. The standards highlight the significance of simplicity and the need to facilitate uplink GF and contention-oriented transmissions in the New Radio (NR) protocol. (For a comprehensive understanding, consult the specified references [14] and [13]).
- We introduce a novel Q-Learning approach with an innovative objective function in order minimizing the delay. MOS is primarily used for quality assessment in telephony, we introduce an MOS-based system for packet age, tailored to meet the 1ms latency requirement for URLLC as stipulated by the 3GPP
- Our focus is on minimizing end-to-end delay, a critical performance metric in URLLC. This is achieved by leveraging global feedback from the gNB for updating Q-tables in MTDs.

The paper follows the following structure. Section 2 introduces the system model. Section 3 formulates the proposed framework. The performance of the proposed technique is evaluated through simulation results in Sect. 4. The paper is concluded in Sect. 5, summarizing the key findings and contributions of the study.

2   System Model

We consider an uplink GF-NOMA system where a gNB is located at the central position of the cell, and a group of M MTDs are uniformly deployed throughout the coverage area as shown in Fig. 1. To model the positions of the MTDs, we employ a homogeneous Poisson point process (PPP) denoted as Φ_M, with a density of λ_M. It is important to emphasize that the selection of the PPP model is based on the inherent randomness in the distribution of MTDs throughout the network, where each MTD generates traffic independently according to its position, without any specific human intervention. Let us define $h_{m,k} = \frac{g_{m,k}}{l_m}$ as the channel coefficient between the gNB and the m-th MTD over the k-th sub-carrier, where $g_{m,k}$ and l_m respectively represent the Rayleigh fading and the path loss. The available spectrum is divided into K sub-carriers. We adopt the Free-Space path loss model to determine the path loss, which is expressed as $l_m = \left(\frac{\lambda\sqrt{G_l}}{4\pi d_m}\right)$. Here, G_l denotes the product of the transmit and receive antennas' field radiation patterns in the Line-Of-Sight (LOS) direction, λ represents the signal wavelength, and d_m is the distance between MTD m and the gNB [15]. The received signal at the gNB over the k-th sub-carrier can be represented as:

$$y_k = \sum_{m=1}^{M} h_{m,k}\sqrt{p_{m,k}}s_{m,k} + b_k, \tag{1}$$

where $s_{m,k}$ and $p_{m,k}$ indicate the transmit symbol and power allocation coefficient of MTD m for the sub-carrier k, respectively. The additive noise at the sub-carrier k with a variance of σ^2 is denoted by b_k. The transmit power of MTD m is limited by the maximum transmit power P_m^{max}.

Fig. 1. System Model.

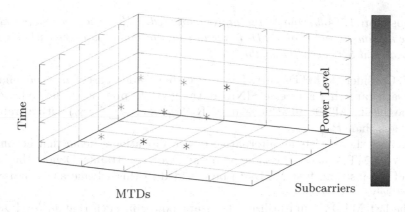

Fig. 2. 3D visualization of our NOMA system model.

As illustrated in Fig. 2, the x-axis represents the MTDs, the y-axis denotes the subcarriers, and the z-axis signifies time. Each point in this 3D space corresponds to a resource block allocated to an MTD. Clusters of MTDs sharing the same subcarrier are evident along the y-axis. The color bar indicates the power levels, with each asterisk marking the specific power allocation for an MTD on a particular sub-carrier at a given time.

3   Problem Formulation

In this section, we discuss the problem of minimizing delay in GF-NOMA URLLC network. We will outline the power control strategy, introduce the objective function for delay minimization, and finally discuss the Q-learning framework employed to meet these objectives.

3.1   Power Level Selection

In the presented framework, we address a power control strategy for MTDs to facilitate efficient SIC at the gNB. The iterative decoding process at the gNB necessitates that the MTD, whose signal is decoded last, must aim for a minimum receive Signal-to-Noise Ratio (SNR) threshold, denoted as γ_{th} in order to ensure successful decoding.

For an MTD whose signal is the penultimate one to be decoded, the transmit power should be set in a way that its SNR at the gNB surpasses $\gamma_{th}(\gamma_{th} + 1)$. MTD i targets an SNR γ_i at the gNB, calculated as:

$$\gamma_i = \gamma_{th} \times \left(1 + \sum_{j<i} \gamma_j\right) \tag{2}$$

where the summation runs over MTDs j decoded after MTD i.

Proposition 1. *Adhering to the aforementioned SNR targeting scheme allows for the maximal number of MTDs to operate on the same sub-carrier while ensuring successful SIC decoding at the gNB.*

Proof. Consider N MTDs sorted in descending order based on their channel gain, each targeting a receive SINR at the gNB as previously defined. Let us assume that no MTD can achieve an SNR of $\gamma_{th} \times (1 + \sum_{j=1}^{N} \gamma_j)$ with a transmit power less than P_{max}.

Suppose there exists an alternative power allocation scheme that accommodates $N+1$ MTDs under the same power and QoS constraints. Denote the target SNR of the last and first MTDs to be decoded in this scheme as $\bar{\gamma}_1$ and $\bar{\gamma}_{N+1}$ respectively.

The last MTD should utilize a transmit power $\bar{p}_1$ such that $\bar{p}_1 |h_{1,k}|^2 / \sigma^2 \geq \gamma_{th}$. For the penultimate MTD, it should target an SNR higher than $\gamma_{th}(1 + \bar{p}_1 |h_{1,k}|^2 / \sigma^2)$.

Following this logic, the first MTD should aim for an SNR greater than $\gamma_{th} \times (1 + \sum_{j=1}^{N} \gamma_j)$, leading to a contradiction.

3.2   Objective Function

In traditional telecommunication systems, the MOS is a well-established metric used to evaluate the quality of voice, video, or data services. However, MOS has not been traditionally mapped to packet age, especially not in the context of URLLC. In this work, we introduce a novel approach where we develop a new MOS metric denoted as MOS_{pktage}, tailored to measure packet age, thereby providing a nuanced assessment of system performance in meeting stringent URLLC requirements. Our 5G system operates with a time slot duration of 0.25 ms. According to URLLC specifications, a maximum latency of 1 ms is permissible, translating to precisely 4 time slots ($\frac{1\,ms}{0.25\,ms/slot} = 4\,slots$). The strategy we employ to map packet age to the MOS scale is as follows:

$$\text{MOS}_{pktage} = \begin{cases} 5, & \text{Excellent } (\leq 0.25\,ms) \\ 4, & \text{Good } (0.5\,ms \leq age \leq 0.75\,ms) \\ 3, & \text{Fair } (\leq 1\,ms, \text{URLLC}) \\ 2, & \text{Poor } (1.25\,ms \leq age \leq 2\,ms) \\ 1, & \text{Bad } (> 2\,ms) \end{cases} \tag{3}$$

The overarching objective of this study is to guide the Q-learning algorithm towards optimizing the MOS for all MTDs ,thereby minimizing the transmission delay across the network.

3.3   Learning-Based Access Mecanism

QL algorithm enables an agent to interact with its surrounding environment and learn from prior interactions. The agent's learning evolves over a time-ordered

$\{1, 2, \ldots, t, \ldots, T\}$. During each individual time step t, the agent moves from its present state $s_t \in \mathcal{S}$ to a next state s_{t+1} by selecting an action $a_t \in \mathcal{A}$. Concurrently, the agent acquires a corresponding reward r_{t+1}. The agent utilizes a state-action value function to update its interactions with the environment. Following each action a_t, the Q-function is updated as [16]

$$Q_{t+1}(s_t, a_t) = (1 - \alpha)Q_t(s_t, a_t) + \alpha \left(r_{t+1} + \gamma \max_{a \in \mathcal{A}} Q_t(s_{t+1}, a) \right) \quad (4)$$

where $0 \leq \alpha \leq 1$, is the learning rate, $0 \leq \gamma \leq 1$ is the discount facto, and r_{t+1} is the received reward.

To integrate the QL algorithm into our proposed framework, we envision a multi-agent system where each MTD is a learning agent. In this context, $Q_t(s_{m,t}, a_{m,t})$ represents the Q-value for MTD m at time-step t, given action $a_{m,t}$ and state $s_{m,t}$. The state corresponds to the packet age for the current MTD, and the action space encompasses combinations of subcarrier and power level selections. We consider K subcarriers and L fixed power levels, as described in the power level selection in Sect. 3.1.

Initially, MTDs utilize the ϵ-Decreasing strategy in Q-learning to intelligently select a sub-carrier and a target SNR level for uplink transmission approach. Subsequently, the gNB performs SIC to identify successful and unsuccessful users' packets. The gNB then sends a global ACK feedback on every subcarrier. For users who have chosen to transmit on subcarrier k at power level p, the feedback is given by:

$$X_{\text{ACK}} = p_1 \times x_s + p_2 \times x_s + \ldots + p_N \times x_f \quad (5)$$

The gNB uses two distinct sequences:

- The sequence x_s, which carries the binary value 11, indicates successfully decoded packets.
- The sequence x_f, represented by the binary value 00, signifies undecoded packets.

Upon receiving this ACK, the MTDs compute their respective rewards based on the current state and action. The reward calculation for each MTD is performed in two stages:

- **Stage 1: Immediate ACK-based Reward**
  Upon receiving an ACK symbol x_f for failed decoding, the MTD incurs a reward of -1 and enters a backoff phase. Conversely, an ACK symbol x_s yields a reward of +1, encouraging the MTD to continue its current strategy.
- **Stage 2: MOS-Based Reward Adjustment**
  The immediate reward is further adjusted based on the packet's age, assessed through the MOS framework as described in Sect. 3.2.

Finally, the reward encapsulates both the immediate reward and the MOS associated with the packet age:

$$\text{Reward} = (1 - \phi) \times \text{Immediate}_r(s, a) + \phi \times \text{MOS}_{\text{Pktage}}(s, a) \qquad (6)$$

where ϕ is a tuning parameter that lies within the range of $[0, 1]$. This parameter serves as a balancing factor between the immediate transmission success, represented by $\text{Immediate}_r(s, a)$, and the latency quality, denoted as $\text{MOS}_{\text{Pktage}}(s, a)$. A high value of ϕ prioritizes the minimization of latency, while a low value places emphasis on successful transmissions. Consequently, this reward metric steers the decision-making activities of MTDs. Figure 3 illustrates this interaction between the gNB and MTDs, along with their respective Q-tables. The proposed mechanism is summarized in Algorithm 1.

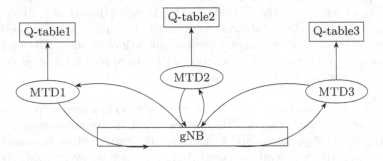

Fig. 3. Interaction between the gNB and MTDs through Q-learning

---

Algorithm 1. Q Learning-Based Mechanism for MTDs

Data: $M, K, \Gamma, \alpha, \gamma$, Maximum Iterations I
Result: Updated Q-tables for all MTDs

1 Initialize $Q(s, a)$ tables for all MTDs to zeros $i \leftarrow 1$
2 **while** $i \leq I$ **do**
3   **for** $m = 1$ *to* M **do**
4   MTDs select actions $a_{m,t}$ (sub-carrier and power level) using ϵ-Decreasing strategy
5   gNB performs SIC gNB sends global ACK feedback X_{ACK}
6   **for** $m = 1$ *to* M **do**
7   MTDs compute reward $r_{m,t+1}$ according to (6) and Update Q-table for MTD m using

$$Q_{t+1}(s_{m,t}, a_{m,t}) = (1 - \alpha)Q_t(s_{m,t}, a_{m,t}) + \alpha \left(r_{m,t+1} + \gamma \max_{a \in \mathcal{A}} Q_t(s_{m,t+1}, a) \right)$$

8      $i \leftarrow i + 1$

---

4   Simulation Results and Discussions

In this section, comprehensive simulations are conducted using MATLAB to assess the performance of our proposed Q-learning-based technique in a NOMA environment. We consider $M = 5000$ MTDs independently distributed based on a homogeneous PPP with a density of $\lambda_N = 0.1$ and $K = 15$ sub-carriers. The Q-learning parameters are set as follows: the learning rate $\alpha = 0.1$, the discount factor $\gamma = 0.9$, and the initial exploration parameter $\epsilon = 0.9$, which is multiplied by a decay factor of 0.99 as learning progresses. Our framework is compared against two other techniques. The first is a NOMA-Aloha scheme [17] that uses a simple random access (RA) method. The second is our prior algorithm [18] that utilizes power level control and makes adjustments based on acknowledgments from the gNB. The iterative adaptation process in this previous framework uses either the same or randomly selected new power levels depending on the success of the transmission. The key difference is that our proposed technique incorporates Q-learning to optimize decision-making. In Fig. 4, we examine the convergence behavior of our proposed Q-Learning algorithm through the variation of the global reward accrued by all MTDs over successive iterations. The results clearly indicate that an increase in the number of sub-carriers leads to more available resource blocks for the devices, thereby reducing the incidence of collisions and enhancing overall system performance. Importantly, we observe that the global reward initially increases over time, before stabilizing.

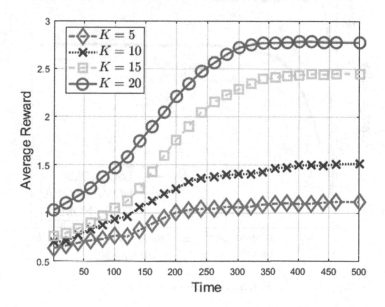

Fig. 4. Average Reward

In Fig. 5, we plot the transmission delay as a function of MTDs for a fixed set of 15 sub-carriers. As evident from the plot, our proposed Q-Learning algorithm QLGF-NOMA effectively reduce transmission delay up to a threshold of 3500 MTDs, outperforming both benchmark techniques. This efficiency is largely attributable to the reward structure and our objective function, which aids MDs in making informed decisions that maximize their MOS packet age and then minimize transmission delay. However, it is worth noting that beyond 3500 MTDs, our previous approach LoCoNOMA surpasses the current one in terms of minimizing transmission delay. This suggests that while our algorithm have good results in a massive access scenario, it may require further refinements in the state-action space to adapt to a larger user base. Additionally, the NOMA-Aloha benchmark technique, which relies only on RA without any adaptive mechanism, consistently exhibits the worst performance. Figure 6 presents the packet success rate versus the number of MTDs when having 15 sub-carriers. Our proposed Q-learning algorithm QLGF-NOMA demonstrates a superior packet success rate, maintaining acceptable value more than 0.3 even when scaling up to 4000 MTD. This success can be attributed to our Q-learning objective function which optimizes both success rate and delay. While our previous approach LoCoNOMA also yields good results, the gains achieved by our Q-learning algorithm stem from the integration of RL. In contrast, the NOMA-Aloha approach consistently performs the worst in terms of packet success rate.

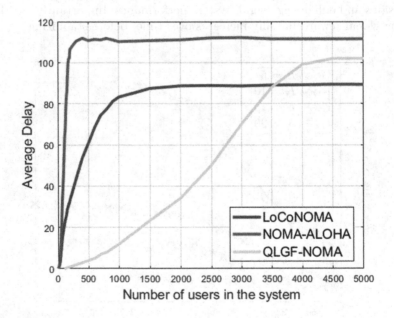

Fig. 5. Transmission Delay

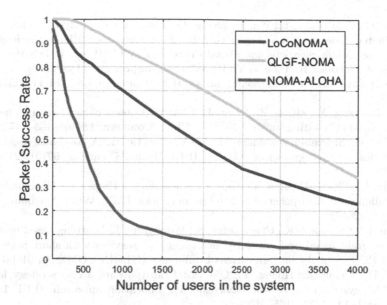

Fig. 6. Packet Success Rate

5   Conclusion

In this paper, we propose a novel Q-Learning-based framework designed to optimize our previous Grant-Free NOMA system, with a focus on URLLC.The objective function is designed to achieve successful transmissions while simultaneously minimizing end-to-end delay. Using this objective function as a guide, MTDs can autonomously adjust their power levels and sub-carrier selections based on real-time feedback from the gNB. This decentralized approach significantly reduces end-to-end delays and boosts throughput, thus outperforming traditional RA mechanisms. The effectiveness of our methodology is confirmed through extensive simulations, illustrating its superiority in achieving lower latency and enhanced system performance. To further minimize delay at very dense scenarios, we aim to refine the state and action spaces in future works.

References

1. Ji, H., Park, S., Yeo, J., Kim, Y., Lee, J., Shim, B.: Ultra-reliable and low-latency communications in 5G downlink: physical layer aspects. IEEE Wirel. Commun. **25**(3), 124–130 (2018)
2. Cirik, A.C., Balasubramanya, N.M., Lampe, L., Vos, G., Bennett, S.: Toward the standardization of grant-free operation and the associated noma strategies in 3g pp. IEEE Commun. Stand. Maga. **3**(4), 60–66 (2019)
3. Islam, O.A.D.S.M.R., Avazov, N., Kwak, K.S.: Power domain non-orthogonal multiple access (noma) in 5G systems: potentials and challenges. IEEE Commun. Surveys Tuts **19**(2), 721–742 (2017)

4. Gan, M., Jiao, J., Li, L., Wu, S., Zhang, Q.: Performance analysis of uplink unco-ordinated code-domain noma for sins. In: 2018 10th International Conference on Wireless Communications and Signal Processing (WCSP), pp. 1–6 (2018)
5. Ding, Z., Schober, R., Poor, H.V.: Unveiling the importance of sic in noma systems-part 1: state of the art and recent findings. IEEE Commun. Lett. **24**(11), 2373–2377 (2020)
6. Wu, L., Tang, X., Zhang, Z., Dang, J.: Enhanced power choice barring scheme for massive MTCS with grant-free NOMA. China Commun. **18**(10), 135–147 (2021)
7. Abbas, R., Shirvanimoghaddam, M., Li, Y., Vucetic, B.: A novel analytical frame-work for massive grant-free NOMA. IEEE Trans. Commun. **67**(3), 2436–2449 (2019)
8. Jiang, C., Zhang, H., Ren, Y., Han, Z., Chen, K.-C., Hanzo, L.: Machine learning paradigms for next-generation wireless networks. IEEE Wirel. Commun. **24**(2), 98–105 (2017)
9. Tran, D., Sharma, S.K., Chatzinotas, S., Woungang, I.: Learning-based multiplex-ing of grant-based and grant-free heterogeneous services with short packets. In: 2021 IEEE Global Communications Conference (GLOBECOM), pp. 01–06 (2021)
10. Wu, D., Zhang, Z., Huang, Y., Qin, X.: Priority-aware access strategy for GF-NOMA system in IIoT: the device-specific allocation approach. IEEE Internet Things J. **11**, 2152–2165 (2023)
11. Tran, D.-D., Sharma, S.K., Ha, V.N., Chatzinotas, S., Woungang, I.: Multi-agent DRL approach for energy-efficient resource allocation in URLLC-enabled grant-free NOMA systems. IEEE Open J. Commun. Soc. **4**, 1470–1486 (2023)
12. Tran, D.D., Ha, V.N., Chatzinotas, S.: Novel reinforcement learning based power control and subchannel selection mechanism for grant-free NOMA URLLC-enabled systems. In: 2022 IEEE 95th Vehicular Technology Conference: (VTC2022-Spring), pp. 1–5 (2022)
13. Technical Specification Group Radio Access Network; Study on Non-Orthogonal Multiple Access (NOMA) for NR (Release 16), 3GPP, v16.0.0 (2022)
14. Technical Specification Group Radio Access Network; Study on Non-Orthogonal Multiple Access (NOMA) for NR (Release 15). 3GPP, v0.0.0 (2018)
15. Goldsmith, A.: Wireless Communications. Cambridge University Press, New York (2005)
16. Li, R., et al.: Intelligent 5G: when cellular networks meet artificial intelligence. IEEE Wirel. Commun. **24**(5), 175–183 (2017)
17. Choi, J.: Noma-based random access with multichannel aloha. IEEE JSAC **35**(12), 2736–2743 (2017)
18. Oueslati, I., Habachi, O., Cances, J.P., Meghdadi, V.: Grant-free access for massive mtc: a low-complexity noma-based framework (loconoma). In: WCNC 2024 (2024)

Author Index

O. Habachi et al. (Eds.): UNet 2023, LNCS 14757, pp. 185–186, 2024.
https://doi.org/10.1007/978-3-031-62488-9

Printed in the United States
by Baker & Taylor Publisher Services